RENAISSANCE AND MODERN ESSAYS

Vivian de Sola Pinto

RENAISSANCE AND MODERN ESSAYS

Presented to Vivian de Sola Pinto
in celebration of his seventieth birthday

EDITED BY G. R. HIBBARD
with the assistance of
George A. Panichas and Allan Rodway

NEW YORK
BARNES & NOBLE, INC.

*First published
in the United States of America
1966*

© *Routledge & Kegan Paul Ltd 1966*

Printed in Great Britain

The Editorial Board expresses its thanks to the University of Nottingham for having provided the generous subsidy that has made the publication of this volume possible.

Contents

CONTENTS

Introduction

VIVIAN de Sola Pinto, the recipient of these essays, is also in a sense their only begetter, though not responsible for any imperfections they may have. They owe their origin to his gift for teaching and to his capacity for friendship. The initial impetus that led to their collection came from old students of his who wished to mark their gratitude for the stimulus and the sheer pleasure he had given them during their undergraduate and postgraduate years. They were soon joined by colleagues of his at Nottingham and by old friends, from the trenches of the First World War as well as from the quieter 'groves of Academe'.

It is right and fitting that the volume should have had these beginnings, for Pinto was—and still is—first and foremost a teacher, so devoted to the work that he was born to do and in which he finds such satisfaction, that, after four years in retirement, he is now in harness once more, redressing the balance of the New World by helping to keep the values and traditions of the Old alive on the shores of the Pacific at the University of California. Always a scholar, but never a pedant, he treats the study of literature as a gay science, not a laborious kind of verbal technology, and has never been afraid of voicing his own enthusiasms. Regarding his chosen subject as a continuous process of discovery and adventure, he has kept the zest and liveliness of youth in all that he has spoken and written about it. Catholic in his tastes, liberal by temperament and a humanist in outlook, he has a special fondness for the great tradition of nonconformity in English Letters. The neglected and the misunderstood have always engaged his sympathy and support. He made his name as a student of the Restoration and, above all, as the biographer and critic of Rochester. But, while his devotion to the poet and his age has never slackened, he abhors the specialization that narrows and constricts. E. M. Forster's injunction, 'only connect', has been at the very centre of his writing and teaching, leading him to see affinities between Rochester and Byron, or between Blake and D. H. Lawrence.

Coming to the Chair of English in the University College, as it then was, of Nottingham in 1938, he recognized the achievement of full university status some ten years later as the great opportunity of his life, a chance to put into practice ideas about the function and purpose of a School of English that had been maturing for many years. Convinced that English Literature ought to be the real centre of humanist studies in the twentieth century and that it could, if properly taught, be an adequate discipline in itself without any support from the uncongenial stiffeners that the Age of Whalebone had thought so essential, he instituted a series of radical reforms in the syllabus and in examinations. The main ends he had in view were three: to increase and deepen the student's personal apprehension of literature; to allow him as much liberty as possible to develop his own bent; and to make him aware of the necessary connections between great writing and the life and traditions in which it is rooted and by which it is fed. The effect on both students and staff was electrifying. A sense of common purpose, of shared experiment and endeavour, animated the entire department. Like Wordsworth at the beginning of the French Revolution, we all had the feeling that it was bliss to be alive, but we did not suffer the disillusion that came to him, for the new freedom brought no new tyranny in its wake. Under Pinto's genial guidance, the way to fresh experiment always remained open. Nor was his vision limited to the study of English; the introduction of American Studies into the University was largely his doing, and so was the creation of a Department of Fine Art.

When the Editorial Board first began to work on the preparation of this volume, they looked for some field or topic that might give it unity. It soon became clear that the search was a mistaken one. The interests that Pinto had aroused and nourished were too numerous and too diversified to be fitted into any preconceived strait jacket. They demanded precisely that freedom which he has always valued so much. Coming from several different countries, these essays are intended as an affectionate tribute to one who is still essentially the same man that Siegfried Sassoon met in 1918, and of whom he wrote:

> Velmore was a tall, dark, young man who had been up at Oxford for an academic year when the outbreak of war interrupted his studies. More scholastic than soldier-like in appearance (mainly because he wore spectacles) he had the look of one who might some day occupy a professorial chair. His previous experience at the front gave him a solid basis of usefulness, and to this was added a temperament in which kindliness, humour, and intelligence divided the honours equally, with gentleness and modesty in readiness to assert themselves by the power of non-assertion.
>
> With these valuable qualities he combined—to my astonishment and delight—what in conventional military circles might have been described as 'an almost rabid love of literature'. To hear poetry talked about in our company mess was indeed a new experience for me.

G. R. HIBBARD

Polygamy among the Reformers

GEOFFREY BULLOUGH

MY occasional reading has of late brought me into contact with writings and incidents in the sixteenth and seventeenth centuries oddly connected since they all were concerned with matrimonial problems and especially with the question of polygamy. Three monarchs were involved, and three great leaders of the Protestant Reformation, John Milton, a Bishop of the Church of England and a republican wit.

Modern students have occasionally been surprised that Milton devoted so much space in his *De Doctrina Christiana* to the problem of polygamy. Divorce, naturally, for that had long been one of his pet subjects, but why polygamy, which might seem a contradiction of all that he wrote about marriage in *Paradise Lost*, Bk. IV? Chapter *x* of the *De Doctrina*, 'Of the Special Government of Man before the Fall, including the Institutions of the Sabbath and of Mariage', makes his doctrinal position clear.[1]

> Marriage [declares Milton] was instituted, if not commanded, at the Creation, and . . . it consisted in the mutual love, help and comfort of the husband and wife, though with a reservation of superior rights to the husband. (Reference is made to Gen. ii. 18; 1 Cor. xi. 7–9; Gen. iii. 16, etc.)

[1] I use the translation by Bishop C. R. Sumner (1825) as cited in *John Milton, Complete Poems and Major Prose*, ed. M. Y. Hughes, N.Y., 1957.

In the definition which I have given, I have not said, in compliance with the common opinion, *of one man with one woman*, lest I should by implication charge the holy patriarchs and pillars of our faith, Abraham and the others who had more than one wife at the same time with habitual fornication and adultery; and lest I should be forced to exclude from the sanctuary of God as spurious, the holy offspring which sprang from them, yea, the whole of the sons of Israel, for whom the sanctuary itself was made. . . .

So far from the question respecting the lawfulness of polygamy being trivial, it is of the highest importance that it should be decided.

To us today this last assertion may seem strange, but the more one reads of post-medieval controversies about the Bible and Divine Law, and about the queer shifts of conscience among the great, the more one appreciates Milton's position. For centuries the polygynous lives of many Old Testament worthies had been a stumbling-block to theologians and had called in question the Church's teaching on monogamy. Lamech was the first man to have two wives (Gen. v. 19). Next Abram's childless wife Sara sent Hagar her Egyptian maid into him so that they might have children by her (Gen. xvi). Hagar bore Ishmael and then Sara had Isaac, and though Hagar was sent away God promised that both sons should father nations (Gen. xxi). After Sara's death Abram married again and had children by his concubines (Gen. xxv). Esau had more than one wife (Gen. xxviii), and Jacob had Leah and Rachel (Gen. xxix). When these two wives could not bear, they gave Jacob other women, so Jacob had two wives and two maidservants (Gen. xxxii). Esau had three wives (Gen. xxxvi).

Exodus has humane laws about the treatment of handmaids used as concubines should the master take another wife (xxi. 7–11). Lev. xviii. 7–8, prohibiting sex-relations with 'thy father's wife' as well as with 'thy mother', shows that polygyny was recognized. The same chapter forbade the Jacob bigamy, the marrying of two sisters. Chapter xx forbade a man to marry a girl and her mother. From Deuteronomy onwards there are frequent references to the domestic strife caused by bigamy. Moses seems to have had more than one wife. Elkanah in 1 Sam. i had two wives and the bigamy brought disputes. David was a polygamist and Solomon, who 'loved many strange women', had 'seven hundred wives, princesses, and three hundred concubines; and his wives turned away his heart' (1 Kings xi. 3). Rehoboam in 2 Chron. xi. 21 'took eighteen wives and three score concubines'.

One can trace the waning of polygyny as the normal way of marriage, and a rise of disapproval against it, but it was not forbidden even after Old Testament times. 'The wise men have given good advice, that a man should not marry more than four wives', says the Talmud;[2] but Maimonides was supposed to have declared that 'A man may have as many wives as he likes, even a hundred, whether together or one after another'.[3]

The New Testament did not expressly condemn polygyny, and the words of Christ were open to various interpretations. But the Fathers of the Church, many of whom disliked the remarriage of widows and widowers (digamy), were against it. Thus Tertullian, who regarded any marriage as a kind of fornication, wrote a treatise urging his own wife not to remarry after his death, and attacked polygyny. 'Plurality of marriage began with an accursed man (Lamech)', he asserted,[4] and explained the Old Testament practice by which 'the blessed patriarchs made mingled alliances not only with more wives than one but also with concubines', as allowed in order to fulfil God's command 'Increase and multiply!' But now God 'has checked the command which he issued and recalled the indulgence which he had granted'. Henceforth a distinction between the old dispensation and the new was often made.

Polygamy was not unknown among the later Roman emperors, and in the Middle Ages it was allowed to kings and sometimes to others (e.g. in Scandinavia). 'Charlemagne had two wives and many concubines; and one of his laws seems to imply that polygyny was not unknown even among priests.'[5] The Church had, however, from the first denied it to priests. Polygamy must not be confused with free love. By various antinomian movements marriage was condemned and free unions praised, to liberate the flesh or prove its spirituality—as among the Adamites of the second, twelfth and fifteenth centuries. The 'Brothers of the Free Spirit' (thirteenth to fifteenth centuries) believed that to a man made perfect all things were permissible, and he might assuage the inferior desires of the flesh as he wished. The movement had some underground influence on the Anabaptists of the Reformation, but when at Münster, during Jan Beuckelssen's shortlived 'Kingdom of Zion', polygamy went along with community of goods

---

[2] Cf. Westermarck, *Short History of Marriage*, 1926, Ch. IX.
[3] M. Siricius, *Uxor Una ex Jure Natura et divino*, 1669, p. 19.
[4] *The Writings of Tertullianus* (Ante-Nicene Christian Library, xvii) Vol. III, pp. 9–10, 39–40.
[5] Westermarck, op. cit., p. 236.

(1534–5), the later marriages were as sacred and binding as the first.[6]

On the whole the principal Reformers, like their Roman Catholic predecessors, were strongly against polygamy. Thus Henry Bullinger argued that, although our fathers 'usurped choice of many wives without blame', this 'may not stabilize polygamy for a law among us at these days', for 'Messias now is come into the world' and his is a new law (Dec. 2, Serm. x). Latimer also stated that 'although the Kings among the Jews had liberty to take more wives than one, we may not therefore attempt to walk inordinately. . . . Christ limiteth unto us one wife only, and it is a great thing for a man to rule one wife rightly and ordinately'.[7]

In an age, however, which set up the Bible as the absolute, unchanging Word of God, the examples of Abraham and other Hebrew leaders could crop up inconveniently from time to time to warrant departures from the norm of Christian monogamy; the more easily since many Reformers did not regard marriage as a Sacrament of the same holiness as the Lord's Supper.[8]

For Luther marriage was an external contract publicly made between two consenting parties; he did not like secret engagements or clandestine ceremonies; but he hated divorce. In his second great reforming pamphlet, The Prelude to the Babylonian Captivity of the Church (1520) he proposed that a woman married to an impotent man should be allowed, under certain conditions, to cohabit with another. And he stated, 'I so detest divorce that I prefer bigamy, but whether divorce is ever allowable or not I dare not say'. Eleven years later he had to return to these difficult problems when his former enemy Henry VIII of England (who had been awarded the title of Defender of the Faith by the Pope for his Assertion of the Seven Sacraments (1521) against Luther's pamphlet) applied to both Catholic and Lutheran theologians for support when the Pope refused to let him divorce Catherine of Aragon because she was his brother's widow. Not even to win an important convert would Luther allow divorce:

> I do not now question what a papal dispensation in such matters is worth, but I say that even if the King sinned in marrying his brother's widow it would be a much greater sin cruelly to put her away now. Rather let him take another queen, following the example of the patriarchs,

[6] Belfort Bax, Rise and Fall of the Anabaptists, 1903, pp. 249–51.

[7] H. Latimer, Sermons Parker Society, 1844, p. 94.

[8] 'Marriage,' wrote Thomas Rogers, 'or the wedded state, was never commanded by God to be taken for a Sacrament' (The Catholic Doctrine of the Church of England 1579–85), Parker Society, 1854. On Art. xxv, p. 260.

who had many wives even before the law of Moses sanctioned the practice, but let him not thrust his present wife from her royal position. I pray with all my heart that Christ may prevent this divorce. [To R. Baynes, 3 September 1531].[9]

Later embassies from England could not make Luther change his mind. It is said that the Pope also urged Henry to commit bigamy rather than divorce his Queen.

Eight years later Luther (with Martin Bucer) was involved in a similar matrimonial problem when Philip, Landgrave of Hesse, an evangelical prince but a man of dissolute life, syphilitic and at odds with his wife, repented of his frequent adulteries, and sought to avoid future temptation by marrying another, more attractive woman, namely Margaret von der Sale, lady-in-waiting to his sister the Duchess of Rochlitz. Recalling the Old Testament precedents he persuaded Margaret and her mother to agree to the union if the theologians would sanction it. This was not the first time that Philip had thought of bigamy as a solution for his spiritual troubles; in 1526 Luther had advised him 'that a Christian can have no more than one wife'— except in the most extraordinary circumstances. Martin Bucer now reluctantly considered the circumstances sufficiently extraordinary to justify bigamy as the Landgrave's only safeguard against sin, and on 9 December 1539, came to Wittenberg with a letter from Philip asking for the consent of Luther and Melanchthon to his marrying just one more wife, since he did not like his first one,[10] and could not control his passions. He reminded Luther not only of the historical precedents but also of his advice to Henry VIII; and he declared that, with the greatest reluctance, if the Protestants would not let him remarry, he would have to try the Pope and the (Catholic) Emperor. He hoped that the theologians would publish some tract justifying the marriage.

'Deeply horrified at this tale and at the offence which must follow, we begged his Grace not to do as he proposed'; the final stroke was his threat to apply to Rome. Luther and Melanchthon agreed to the marriage provided that it were kept secret. 'This he promised to do, and we accordingly agreed to help him before God and cover it up as much as possible with such examples as that of Abraham' (Luther to the Elector of Saxony, 10 June 1540). Unfortunately the girl's mother

[9] P. Smith, *The Life and Letters of Martin Luther*, 1911, pp. 195–8; J. Mackinnon, *Luther and the Reformation*, 1930, Vol. IV, pp. 265ff.

[10] She had borne him seven children. See J. Mackinnon, op. cit., pp. 265ff., and P. Smith, op. cit., Ch. xxxiv.

demanded an almost public wedding, which took place on 4 March 1540, with Bucer and Melanchthon present. The resulting scandal made Melanchthon fall ill. 'But why does the good man torment himself with this matter?' (wrote Luther). 'He cannot remedy it by worrying about it . . . I have grown callous; I am a peasant and a devilish hard Saxon'. He reproved the Landgrave, ordering him not to publish the marriage, so was furious when Philip got someone calling himself 'Neobolus' to write a pamphlet defending the bigamy (1541): 'If anyone shall follow the advice of that wretch and take more than one wife, the devil will prepare him a bath in the abyss of hell.' He had no intention of advocating polygyny as a normal practice. Poor Bucer was disturbed to find the *Dialogus Neobuli* attributed to him. Altogether the affair was one of the most difficult and disturbing experiences that the early Reformers had to endure.

Some eighteen years later Bernardo Ochino, a vicar-general of the Capuchins who turned Protestant and was for a time in England[11] wrote a *Dialogue of Polygamy* (1558) which became a *locus classicus* during two centuries of discussion. Answered by Theodore Beza (1568) and others, it was translated anonymously into English nearly a century afterwards, and became a link between two phases of controversy.

Ochino's work was lively and entertaining; a brief illustration from the first English version must suffice.[12] The debate is between Ochino himself (pretending to support monogamy) and Telypoligamus, who, having a sick, barren wife, wants another for child-bearing and pleasure. When Ochino tells him that God gave Adam only one wife, Telypoligamus retorts that since Abram, David and many others had more than one wife it is clear that the Old Testament (source of the Law) did not forbid it. Nor is polygamy contrary to natural reason, since it is practised in many countries. Although some animals are monogamous, cocks and bulls are not, so why should men be so? Ochino argues that the Patriarchs sinned when they took more wives than one, and that the Old Testament proves the domestic inconveniences that resulted. Telypoligamus blames the women for that, not polygyny— or the husbands.

[11] Ochino was in England from 1548 to 1552 as prebend at Canterbury and preacher to the Italian Church in London. His drama, composed of nine anti-Catholic colloquies, *Tragedie or Dialogue of the unjust usurped Primacie of the Bishop of Rome*, was translated by John Ponet (1549). His was a clever, erratic personality.

[12] *A Dialogue of Polygamy rendered into English by a Person of Quality*, 1657. Another version, with the interlocutors styled A and B, was published in 1732.

When a man by marriage gave the use of his Body to his wife, he did not so totally give the same, as to bereave himself of all power to give it to other wives also.

Ochino asserts that a husband cannot marry a second wife without detriment to the first. 'It is not, therefore credible that wives did, in their hearts consent, that their husbands should marry others.'

Telypoligamus now puts his position crudely:

Tel. It is possible my wife may prove barren; in which case it is her duty to consent that I should take another; and of her own consent to exhort me thereunto as *Sarah* did of old. And if she would not approve thereof, this will of hers were unjust, and so it were lawful for her husband to marry another, contrary to her unjust mind. Also when a woman is with Child, and sometime after she is brought to bed, seeing she is then unfit for procreation, as also when she is old and sick, her husband may without injury to her, have to do with another wife; yea, though a man's wife were sound, and fit for generation, yet she ought to take it in good part, if enjoying the company of her husband at some certain times, as it is with other living Creatures, she leave it free for him to enjoy the carnal acquaintance of his other wives.

Och. Do you think it lawful for one wife to have many husbands?

Tel. No.

Och. And yet there are sick Men, as well as sick women.

Ochino is afraid of overpopulation through polygamy; but his opponent declares that God will provide—and the English translator in 1657 mentions 'the New-found World . . . many large Tracts of ground in Hungaria, And other parts of Europe unpeopled'. 'God ordained that the number of Women should be greater than the number of Men' so that polygamy should be practised. 'The life of one Man equals that of two Women.'

Telypoligamus cites a letter of Gregory III to Boniface to prove that the Popes did not condemn bigamy:

If any Man have a Wife which by reason of some bodily infirmity, cannot afford her Husband due benevolence, he shall do well to abstain from her. But if he cannot contain (for that is a gift of God not given to all) it is better, that he should marry another Wife, then burn; provided he allow his first Wife all necessary maintenance. [The Landgrave of Hesse's case, exactly.]

Och. All that you can say, though you talk till Doomsday, will never make me think it fit, and lawful for a Man to have more than one Wife.

Tel. Suppose there are more Women than Men, what shall the poor Women do in this case?

Och. They must do, just as the Men should do, in case there were more Men than Women, *viz.* pray to God to give them the gift of continence.

The upsurge of Puritanism brought numerous antinomian sects, and it is not surprising that the orthodox accused separatists and frequenters of 'conventicles', who used 'Enthusiasm' in their religious exercises, of promiscuity and polygamous practices—as witness many literary references in Jacobean plays and in popular satire before the Civil War. The same suspicions had been felt towards the early Christians in Rome.

From all this it is obvious that 'the question respecting the lawfulness of polygamy' was anything but trivial when Milton wrote *De Doctrina Christiana.* He knew the Bible, Jewish history, the main events of the Reformation and the discussions about marriage in the chief authorities, both ancient and modern. Bucer was for Milton 'the pastor . . . of the nations', and he translated Bucer's *Justification* of divorce as a document supporting his own *Tractate.* He probably also knew the works of Ochino, whose book *The Labyrinth,*[13] on the multiplicity of views about free will, prescience and predestination he may have recalled when writing the lines in *Paradise Lost,* Bk. II, ll. 558–61, about the theological casuistries of those devils in Hell who sat apart

> and reasond high
> Of Providence, Foreknowledge, Will, and Fate,
> Fixed Fate, free Will, Foreknowledge absolute,
> And found no end, in wandring mazes lost.

He may well have read the *Dialogue of Polygamy,* and it is possible that the appearance of the English translation in 1657 led him to expatiate on the subject more solemnly than the lively ex-Capuchin had done.

Milton's argument is first directed to upsetting the three or four main passages of Scripture—Gen. ii. 24, with Matt. xix. 5; Lev. xviii. 18, and Deut. xvii. 17—usually cited by enemies of polygamy. 'These twain were one flesh' could be said truthfully of Abram 'with regard to Sarah and Hagar respectively'; and he finds passages, e.g. Exod. xxi. 10 which 'clearly admit the lawfulness of polygamy'. In 2 Sam. xii. 8 God Himself said 'I gave thee thy master's wives into thy bosom,' etc., and polygamy is 'alluded to by the holy prophets in their inspired hymns as a thing lawful and honourable' (Ps. xlv. 9, 14; Cantic. vi. 8–10), and commended for Joash in 2 Chron. xxiv. 2–3. In the New

---

[13] *Prediche nominate Laberinti del Libero over servo arbitrio,* Basle, 1561.

Testament, 1 Tim. iii. 2 and Titus. i. 6 forbid polygamy 'to the ministers of the church alone'.

Such passages establish 'that polygamy is allowed by the law of God'.[14] Milton adds examples of holy men 'who are among the lights of our faith'—Abraham, Jacob, Moses ('if I mistake not'), Gideon, and Elkanah (who 'took with him his two wives every year to the sacrifices and animal worship, into the immediate presence of God'), Caleb and David. 'I say nothing of Solomon . . . because he seems to have exceeded due bounds.' Milton concludes that 'the rule received among theologians [should] have the same weight here as in other cases'. 'The practice of the saints is the best interpretation of the Commandments.' And so he leaves the subject, and is soon re-stating the arguments for divorce which he had discussed in the *Tractates*, on the basis that 'conjugal affection is of more importance and higher excellence than the nuptial bed itself, and more worthy to be considered as the prime end and form of the institution'.

The handling of polygamy is drier and less passionately felt than that of divorce; but one recalls that among Milton's early titles for possible tragedies was one 'Salomon Gynæcocratumenos' ('Solomon ruled by women'); and, according to Edward Phillips, at one stage of Milton's separation from his first wife Mary Powell he was seriously considering taking another mate, a Miss Davis, 'a very Handsome and witty Gentlewoman' but (not surprisingly) 'averse to this Motion';[15] so perhaps the poet's private life and general theories were just as intricately bound up with one another in this respect as in others.

The problem of polygamy became a practical issue at the court of Charles II towards the end of the 'sixties when, owing to the failure of his Portuguese Queen to produce any children, it was suggested that the King should marry again in order to get a legitimate heir and prevent the accession of his Roman Catholic brother James, Duke of York. According to Gilbert Burnet some advisers thought that the marriage should be annulled:

> Others talked of polygamy; and officious persons were ready to thrust themselves into anything that could contribute to their advancement, Lord Lauderdale and Sir Robert Murray asked my opinion of these things. I said I knew speculative people could say a great deal in the way of

[14] Sir Philip Sidney would not agree. In *Arcadia* 1590, Lib. 2, Antiphilus is slain for 'having made a lawe of *Polygamie*' (ed. Feuillerat, p. 335). On the other hand Sir Thomas Browne, as yet a bachelor, was glad not to have been married, 'not that I disallow of second marriages: as neither, in all cases, of Polygamy'. *Religio Medici*.

[15] See H. Darbishire, *The Early Lives of Milton*, 1932, p. 66.

argument for polygamy and divorce: yet these things are so decried, that they were rejected by all Christian societies: so that all such propositions could throw us into great convulsions; and entail war upon us, if any issue came from a marriage so grounded.[16]

That Burnet was well acquainted with the case of Henry VIII and the theoretic arguments occasioned by it is proved by the long account in his *History of the Reformation of the Church of England* (Vol. I, 1679) of the views of Catholic and Protestant theologians in the fifteen thirties.[17] How exercised his mind was appears in the papers which he is said to have written about two relevant questions:

1. Is a Woman's Barrenness a just Ground for a Divorce, or for Polygamy?
2. Question the Second. Is Polygamy in any Case lawful under the Gospel?[18]

Burnet's first answer avoided a decision about polygyny, declaring, 'that if a Woman can only *receive* a Man, that makes her fit only for *Venery*, which is a secondary End of Marriage, that follows the Fall and Corruption of Mankind'. Being incapable of procreation, she 'must be *incapable* of *Marriage*', so the union should normally be annulled.

The resolution of the second question is based on the idea 'that *Marriage* is a *Contract* founded upon the *Laws of Nature*', and that the church rite 'is only a supervenient Benediction, or solemnizing of it'.

Before the Fall a single marriage was envisaged, and even afterwards 'a single Marriage was the perfecter, as being nearer to the Original'. Yet polygyny was often practised, and Moses's Law enacted that 'when any died without Issue, his Brother, or nearest Kinsman, was to marry his Wife, for raising up *Seed* to him'.

The paper concludes that 'Polygamy is not contrary to the *Law* and *Nature of Marriage*'. But Burnet does not like it, for:

> Polygamy falls short of the Intendment of *Marriage* in Innocency, to which State we that are under the *Gospel*, must return as near as is possible.

'Polygamy was much condemned by the Ancients', yet:

> I see nothing so strong *against* Polygamy, as to balance the great and visible imminent Hazards, that hang over so many Thousands, if it be not allowed.

[16] *Bishop Burnet's History of his own Time*, 1723, 1823 edn., Vol. I, pp. 453–4.
[17] Cf. 1829 edn., Vol. I, pp. 171–90.
[18] First printed in an Appendix to *Memoirs of the Secret Services of John Macky, Esq.*, ed. Spring Macky, 1733.

Obviously in deciding so reluctantly against the general tenour of his religion, Burnet had the current national dilemma in mind. His mind wavered, until thought of foreign and domestic political repercussions made him decide against advocating the King's remarriage.[19]

In *Some Passages of the Life and Death of the Earl of Rochester* (1680), Burnet gave more humane reasons against polygyny, in recounting how he met Rochester's arguments in its favour:

> For Polygamy, it is but reasonable, since Women are equally concern'd in the Laws of Marriage, that they should be considered as well as Men: But in a state of Polygamy they are under great misery and jealousie and are indeed barbarously used.

Like Milton Burnet believed that:

> Friendship and Converse were among the primitive Intendments of Marriage, in which as far as the man may exceed the Wife in greatness of Mind and height of Knowledge, the Wife some way makes that up with her affection and tender Love. . . . But all this is gone in a State of Polygamy, which occasions perpetual Jarrings and Jealousies. (pp. 110–15)

This sympathetic attitude recurred in other writers of that time. It is perhaps rather surprising to find such consideration for women expressed in the Restoration period, generally regarded as an age of cynicism, license and promiscuity. But it was also an age of 'Platonic' theories about love, of idealistic sentiment, as the Heroic Drama demonstrates. Burnet expresses a middle view, Scottish in its practicality and warmth.

On the whole the imaginative literature of the Restoration contained little discussion of polygamy as a legalized way of marriage. Dryden began *Absalom and Achitophel* with a jesting reference to Charles II's habits:

> In pious times, ere priesthood did begin,
> Before polygamy was made a sin;
> When man on many multiplied his kind,
> Ere one to one was cursedly confined;
> When nature prompted, and no law denied,
> Promiscuous use of concubine and bride,

such was the custom when David 'Scatter'd his Maker's image through the land', and such was the present monarch's way.

---

[19] Macky believed that the passage in *The History* had been falsified by an editor before publication.

Rochester in his 'History of Insipids' showed a better appreciation of the difference between licentiousness and polygyny when he contrasted his monarch with Henry VIII, who:

> Espoused half a dozen Wives.
> C/harls/ only one resolv'd to marry,
> And other Mens he never /swives/,
> Yet hath he Sons and Daughters more,
> Than e're had *Harry* by threescore.

The dramatists do not seem to have defended bigamy, although in Shadwell's *The Humourists* (1670) Lady Loveyouth marries again after being wrongly informed that her first husband is dead. In Aphra Behn's *The Forced Marriage* (1670) the husband in an unconsummated marriage surrenders his wife to her lover; and in Dryden's best comedy, *Marriage à la Mode* (1672), where two couples play naughtily with wicked ideas, Palamede says (V, i),

> What dost think of a blessed community between us four, for the solace of the women, and relief of the men? Methinks it would be a pleasant kind of life: Wife for the standing dish, and mistress and gallant for the dessert.

His friend Rhodophil however points out the probability of disagreements and concludes:

> Then I think, Palamede, we had as good make a firm league, not to invade each other's property.[20]

The interchange of partners is not polygamy. Nor is the frequent change of husbands allowed in the 'Amazon' plays of the period.[21]

The 'Amazon' notion probably owes something to Henry Neville's *The Parliament of Women* (1647) a prose parody in which the ladies, during their husbands' frequent absences in the Civil War, allow themselves other partners. This same Henry Neville was responsible after the Restoration for one of the most original short pieces of prose narrative of the period; *The Isle of Pines* (1668), which is very relevant to our present discussion.

Neville (1620–93), grandson of the Elizabethan courtier and diplomat Sir Henry Neville (friend of Shakespeare's Southampton), was a somewhat ambiguous figure. At Oxford he did not graduate, then toured the Continent, and on returning to England in 1645 took the Parliament

---

[20] For these and other references I am indebted to my colleague Mr Paul Vernon.
[21] E.g. J. Weston, *The Amazon Queen*, pub. 1667; E. Howard, *The Six Days' Adventure*, 1671; T. D'Urfey, *A Commonwealth of Women*, 1685.

side and rose to be a member of the Council of State in 1651. Associated with James Harrington in republican schemes he was banished from London by Cromwell in 1654. When, after Cromwell's death he was returned as M.P. for Reading in 1658, a determined effort was made to unseat him for 'atheism and blasphemy', but his right to sit was confirmed. He became a member of Harrington's 'Rota' Club along with Milton's friend Cyriack Skinner, John Aubrey, Roger Coke and William Petty, to discuss possible constitutional reforms. For a short time in 1663 he was imprisoned in the Tower on suspicion of implication in the Yorkshire Conspiracy. After his release he lived quietly in the country until his death. He was married but had no children. According to Anthony à Wood he was 'esteemed to be a man of good parts, yet of a factious and turbulent spirit'.

Neville's literary career was marked by extremes of levity and seriousness. In his youth he wrote lampoons on ladies of importance in their day.[22] Later he became a serious writer, making an important translation of Machiavelli's Works (1675), and producing in *Plato Redivivus* (1681) a dialogue on government in which he advocated elected councils of state responsible to Parliament. To which of these two sides of Neville's activities does *The Isle of Pines* belong?

The Isle of Pines, or A Late discovery of a fourth Island near Terra Australis, Incognita. By Henry Cornelius Van Sloetten (licensed 27 July, 1668) is a not unworthy forerunner of *Robinson Crusoe* as a fictitious narrative of shipwreck and survival. It is a tale within a tale,[23] the outer frame being the Dutch sea-captain's account of how his vessel, on the way to the East Indies in 1667, was driven by foul weather to an island north of Madagascar, where they found a nation ('speaking good English') of ten or twelve thousand persons. These were all descendants of an English book-keeper, who, sailing in 1589 with his master, a merchant hoping to set up a factory in India, had been shipwrecked on the island along with three young white women and a negress, and had thrived owing to the kindness of the climate and the fertility of the land. The inner story consists of the book-keeper's narrative, written down before his death at the age of eighty, and given to Van Sloetten by his grandson, the ruler of the place.

---

[22] *The Parliament of Women*, 1647; *News from the New Exchange, or The Commonwealth of Ladies*, 1650. He also satirized the current political situation in *Shuffling, Cutting and Dealing in a Game at Piquet*, 1659.

[23] The main story, unfortunately without the Van Sloetten framework or the second part (1668), is printed (from an eighteenth-century edition) in *Shorter Novels, Vol. 2, Jacobean and Restoration*, ed. P. Henderson, Everyman Library, 1930, pp. 225–35.

The whole thing, though brief, is well organized to obtain veri-similitude, and Van Sloetten's explanation is supported by two letters from Abraham Keek 'to a credible person in Covent Garden' vouching for his accuracy.

George Pine's narrative is marked by factual detail of a winning simplicity, as he tells how the voyage was arranged, of its progress till the storm, of the shipwreck and how he, his 'Master's Daughter, the two Maids and the *Negro*' escaped by clinging to the bowsprit, which broke off and was carried up a creek to safety. We learn of their natural fears, their salvaging of material ('great part of our lading') from the seashore, their discovery of eggs, and 'a sort of fowl much like our Ducks, which were very good meat'. Pine describes in some detail how he built a cabin and placed their hammocks in it, not expecting that they would be there long.

During the first four months they realized that they were the only survivors on the island, which was uninhabited and very pleasant, 'so that this place (had it the culture that skilful people might bestow on it) would prove a *Paradise*'.

Only after this period is the sexual theme introduced, when 'Idleness and Fulness of everything begot in me a desire of enjoying the women'. This 'Admirable Crichton' had no inhibitions, and the women accepted him without demur, first 'the two maids in private, but after, custome taking away shame (there being none but us) we did it more openly, as our Lusts gave us liberty'; then his Master's Daughter (whom he cared for most); and lastly the negro who came to him at night 'with the consent of the others',[24] 'so that in the year of our being here, all my women were with child by me, and they all coming at different seasons, were a great help to one another'.

Henceforth the story is mainly concerned with child-breeding and the arrangements Pine made for his growing family. Like a true bookkeeper he kept a tally of them, 'the Women never failing once a year at least, and none of the Children (for all the hardships we put them to) were ever sick'. 'My first Wife brought me thirteen children, my second seven, my Master's Daughter fifteen, and the *Negro* twelve, in all forty seven'—and more girls than boys.

When his eldest boy was about fourteen Pine gave him a mate; 'and

[24] Cf. Montaigne, 'Of the Cannibals': 'It is a remarkably beautiful thing about their marriages that the same jealousy our wives have to keep us from the affection and kindness of other women, theirs have to win this for them ... they strive and scheme to have as many companions as they can, since that is a sign of their husbands' valour.'

so I did to all the rest, as fast as they grew up and were capable'. 'As fast as we married them I sent them and placed them over the River by themselves severally, because we would not pester one another.' Moreover, as he got older, 'I liked not the wanton annoyances of young company'.

Pine was twenty when he was shipwrecked. When he was sixty he held an assembly of his descendants, who now numbered 'five hundred and sixty-five of both sorts'. Whereas at first he had had to allow brothers to marry their sisters, he now 'took off the Males of one Family and married them to the Females of another'.

Religion was not neglected, for he held monthly general meetings at which the Bible was read. When he was nearly eighty he made his eldest son 'King and governor of all the rest'. 'I informed them of the manners of *Europe*, and charged them to remember the Christian religion, after the manner of them that spake the same *Language*.' He held a last general assembly at which his progeny numbered one thousand, seven hundred and eighty-nine. He called his people 'the English Pines (because his chief wife's name was 'English'); and he named his wives' descendants by their mothers' names, so that there were four tribes of the nation.

Wood wrote that *The Isle of Pines* was 'look'd upon as a mere sham or piece of drollery'. Actually it was translated into several other languages and at least once as a true narrative. It was certainly a *jeu d'esprit*, but behind it was more than a promiscuous sexual fantasy or a desire to shock. I question whether Pine's statistics would stand up to close analysis, but in the light of discussions current in the sixteen-sixties it seems likely that the story was not only a parody of a traveller's tale but also a half-serious essay on population and the making of a nation.

As we have seen, Neville was associated in the 'Rota' Club with James Harrington (whose *Oceana* depicted an ideal commonwealth based on the Republic of Venice) and Sir William Petty the economist (who as an expert on taxation was interested in problems of population). Another of the group, John Graunt, made an important pioneer study in his *Natural and Political Observations upon the Bills of Mortality* (1662),[25] in which he made 'a few perspicuous *Tables*' of the statistics of births and deaths, and concluded, among other things:

[25] Third edition 1665; printed in *The Economic Writings of Sir William Petty*, ed. C. H. Hull, 2 vols., Cambridge, 1899. The treatise has been attributed to Petty, but Hull believed that Graunt wrote most of it.

That the irreligious *Proposal* of some, to multiply people by *Polygamy*, is withal irrational, and pointless. . . . That the wasting of *Males* by Wars and Colonies do not prejudice the due proportion between them and Females. (II, 320).

His statistics show that in England, contrary to a common supposition, 'There are more *Males* than Females . . . by about a thirteenth part', and that this preponderance is removed because 'More men die violent deaths or go abroad or remain celibates (as *Fellows* of *Colleges*, and Apprentices above eighteen). So every Woman may have an Husband, without the allowance of Polygamy'. (II, 375).

Graunt concludes:

> That *Christian Religion*, prohibiting *Polygamy*, is more agreeable to the *Law of Nature*, that is, the *Law of God*, than *Mahumetism* and others, that allow it: for one Man his having many Women, or Wives, by Law, signifies nothing, unless there were many Women to one Man in Nature also. (II, 374).

Later he returns to this matter:

> It is a blessing to Mankind that by this over-plus of *Males* there is this natural Bar to *Polygamy*; for in such a state Women could not live in that parity and equality of expense with their Husbands, as now and here they do.

Under polygamy the husband, in order to keep his wives in awe, tends to subject them utterly, 'the poorest Subjects, (such as this plurality of Wives must be) being most easily quelled'. (II, 378)

Graunt's suggestion that the excess of males over females meant that God approved of monogamy was frequently quoted. Maybe Neville was answering it, pointing out that whatever the custom in modern western civilization, the earth was not peopled by monogamy. His narrative was really a rationalization of Genesis, describing how, in suitable surroundings, the human race could grow and develop institutions under the benevolent autocracy of patriarchs.

His story was in line with the current view of social development summarized by Bishop Thomas Sprat in his *History of the Royal Society* (1667):[26]

> The First of all human Race, when they were dispers'd into severall Lands, were at first sustain'd by the *Fruits* of the *Earth*, which fell to their share. These at first they cherish'd, and us'd, not by any *Rules of Art*, but

[26] See the edition by J. I. Cope and H. W. Jones, St. Louis and London, 1959, p. 379.

by that *Natural sagacity*, which teaches all men to indeavor their own preservation. For the peaceable injoyment of these, they combin'd into Families, and little Leagues, which were the beginnings of *Civil Government*.

Neville illustrated how quite naturally families were subdivided as they grew and took over new territory, and how incest gave place to exogamy. The counting of Pine's descendants corresponds to the numbering of the children of Israel, and he ended with a simplified version of the naming of the tribes after the sons of Jacob.

Sprat went on to describe how barter, commerce, standards of value and money developed as an alternative to war and rapine when it was discovered 'that all places did not bring forth all things for Clothing, Food, and Defence'.

> ... in course of Time, the small Clans, and Naturall Commonwealths, were devour'd by the strength of the greater; or else some of the wiser men seduc'd the Rude multitude into one place, and persuaded them to live quietly under *Laws*. From thence Mankind began to have the face of Civility.

These very questions were touched on by Neville in a sequel printed later in 1668, first separately and then together with the first part.[27]

The story runs straight on as William Pine, the founder's grandson tells how, after his father made the people explore their country many of them went far from the original settlement, and there was a general decline in morals as their numbers grew:

> But as it is impossible, but that in multitudes disorders will grow, the stronger seeking to oppress the weaker; no tye of Religion being strong enough to chain up the depraved nature of mankinde, even so amongst them mischiefs began to rise, and they soon fell from those good orders prescribed them by my Grandfather.

The main cause of these troubles was

> the neglect of hearing the Bible read ... with all other means of Christian instruction, whereby the sence of sin being quite lost in them, they fell to whoredoms, incests and adulteries; so that what my grandfather was forced to do for necessity, they did for wantonness. ...

The second Pine put down the offenders and executed the ringleader.

---

[27] *A New and further Discovery of the Isle of Pines in a Letter from Cornelius Van Sloetten a Dutchman (who first discovered the same in the year 1667) to a Friend of his in London ... 1668.* My quotations are from the 1668 complete edition.

Then 'with the advice of some few of his Counsel', he made a few simple laws imposing severe penalties for irreverence or blasphemy, 'for not attending the Bible assembly', for rape, adultery or physical violence, for fraud, and for disobedience to the Governor.

A pleasant picture is drawn of the simple life of these people who have lived so long without any tool but an axe. The grandson invited the Dutchmen to a monthly meeting, when a wedding was celebrated, with a reading and exposition of Scripture lasting two or three hours; 'but all the rest of that day was by the people kept very strictly, abstaining from all manner of playing or pastimes'.

The second part is more solemn than the first, as if the author were insisting on the seriousness of his intention—which readers may have doubted—while continuing his account of a developing civilization. He accepts the doctrine of Original Sin and shows that George Pine's Paradise is soon lost through increase of population and a decline in religious observance. Before Van Sloetten leaves the island he has to help William Pine suppress a rebellion led by a man who has ravished a woman and defied the Governor. The islanders are sober and puritanic in outlook, and polygamy is not mentioned as practised any longer, presumably because customs change with the needs of society. When Van Sloetten reaches the Indies he finds there other curious marriage-customs which he describes, doubtless because Neville wished his readers to realize the variability of human behaviour and the relativity of moral standards.

To sum up, Renaissance theorists had recognized that there were four kinds of law operating in matrimonial behaviour as in all other human conduct: Divine law; the law of 'nature'; custom; and the law of nations. None of these was entirely free from ambiguities. Divine law was open to diverse interpretations owing to differences between the Old and New Testaments and conflicting evidence within each of them. Natural law could be regarded as either good or bad according to one's view of human nature as inherently evil, or good, or mixed. Customs differed from time to time and between societies; and the laws of nations depended on particular interpretations of social needs, with reference also to the three other kinds of law.

On the whole the Catholic authorities insisted on Divine law as laid down in the Bible and interpreted through the centuries, and drew a firm distinction between what was allowed to the patriarchs and the Christian Sacrament of marriage. Many Protestants agreed, but some saw no essential difference between the Old Dispensation and the New as regards marriage, and could therefore approve of polygamy in theory, and even, for expediency, in practice. This was roughly Milton's position.

If owing to the Fall there were a conflict between Divine law and 'natural' law, most thinkers held that the former must be obeyed. Many religious supporters of polygamy therefore sought to prove that Divine law and 'natural' law were not here antithetical. In the late seventeenth century the rigid codes of conservative Bibliolaters came under fire, as some men taught that Divine law was a shadowy general sanction to be explored by human reason rather than a completely revealed set of particular rules. And as the sense of historical change grew and interest awoke in the many cultures described by explorers, traders and missionaries, custom and systems of national law began to be examined in terms of 'natural' law. So from the sixteen-seventies onwards polygamy was one of many disputed points in the great quarrel between deists and orthodox Christians.

The new controversy was probably touched off by the writings of Johannes Lyser (a lifelong bachelor who devoted his energy to preaching the cause of polygamy in Central Europe). His *Discursus politicus de Polygamia* (Fribourg, 1674) was issued in English as *Polygamia Triumphatrix* (1682) and was often cited in the next century. This phase of the debate has been surveyed by A. O. Aldridge, who illustrates its repercussions in the work of writers so various as Matthew Tindal, Bolingbroke, Swift's friend Patrick Delany, and the novelists Mrs Manley, Samuel Richardson and Thomas Amory.[28] In the light of this development Milton's paragraphs in the *De Doctrina* may be seen as a climax of humane Reformation opinion, and Neville's slight parable as heralding the new rationalistic empirical and comparative approach to problems of morals and social development. Neville was no deist, but he saw Divine law as behind 'natural' law and he suggested that there was virtue in the lusts of the flesh if they were the means of fulfilling God's command, 'Increase and multiply!' George Pine and his harem were doing God's will in their peculiar situation, just as Abram and the other patriarchs were in theirs.

King's College, London

---

[28] A. O. Aldridge, 'Polygamy and Deism', *J.E.G.P.*, Vol. CLVIII (1949), pp. 343–60.

Marlowe's *Hero and Leander* and Chapman's Continuation

VESELIN KOSTIČ

MARLOWE'S *Hero and Leander*, left unfinished on the day when the fatal 'recknynge' was presented at Deptford, proved no less a seminal influence in its own limited field than Marlowe's dramatic works. Apart from establishing the *genre*, it made a profound impact on later poets, traceable well into the seventeenth century in various imitations and echoes, and gave rise to two continuations. Henry Petowe's sequel has never been thought worthy of more than a passing mention by literary historians, while Chapman's continuation has usually been accorded greater respect. However, the opinions of those who view Chapman's portion in relation to Marlowe's poem are not in unison. Some critics hold that the continuation is manifestly inferior to Marlowe's part and that it 'lessens . . . its fascinating effect upon the reader'.[1] This is the view that seems to have prevailed until C. S. Lewis put forward, in his brilliantly persuasive way, the thesis that the collaboration was an extremely fortunate one, for 'each poet has produced what the other could not have done, and both contributions are necessary to a worthy telling of the story'.[2]

[1] J. Ingram, *Marlowe and His Poetry*, London, 1914, pp. 145–6.
[2] 'Hero and Leander', *Proceedings of the British Academy*, Vol. XXXVIII (1952), p. 23.

C

The relative merits of the two portions of the poem are difficult to evaluate because they are not conceived on the same lines and we cannot apply the same criteria to them. But it would be perhaps more to the point to put the question in another way: since Chapman's part is a continuation of Marlowe's poem, to what extent is it suitable as a sequel to what precedes it? In other words, does it sustain, enhance or weaken the specific qualities of Marlowe's fragment? In an attempt to assess this I shall confine myself chiefly to those elements which seem to me most contributory to the peculiar effect of Marlowe's poem.

The narrative structure of Marlowe's *Hero and Leander*, as far as can be inferred from the existing part of his poem, was not to be much different from that of Musaeus's story. The chief differences in this respect result from the introduction of Ovidian decorative details and digressions, but the basic outline of the tale is the same in both poems. His treatment of characters, however, is more complex and represents an odd but singularly effective mixture of irony, idealization, detachment and inspired glorification of sensual joy. The basic characteristic of Marlowe's Hero and Leander is that they are larger than life. The interest in them is symbolic rather than merely human. They are conceived as the male and female principles of love, almost as the positive and negative poles of the erotic current: 'the aire with sparkes of living fire was spangled' at their meeting.[3] This archetypal quality of the two lovers is stressed by several elements in Marlowe's treatment of the story. The setting and time (the Adonis festival) of the action are described early in the poem, and local and temporal references intrude as little as possible in the further development of the story, so that the general impression is that Hero and Leander live in a timeless and detached world of intensified emotional experience. Moreover, they are the focal points of that world, and all minor currents in it converge on them to enlarge their significance. Marlowe constantly stresses the irresistible effect of the beauty of his lovers not only on men, but also on divine beings, on heavenly bodies, on the animal world and even on inanimate objects. This universalization of erotic appeal, known from earlier literature but given a particularly consistent and strong emphasis here, is of central importance to Marlowe's treatment of the story and accounts largely for the specific quality of his characters.

Indispensable to this achievement of the supra-human, archetypal stature of the two lovers was the creation of an appropriate unrealistic

[3] I quote from E. S. Donno's edition of the poem (*Elizabethan Minor Epics*, London, 1963).

atmosphere, or more precisely, the exclusion of details from everyday life. In this respect Marlowe's poem is a remarkably sustained *tour de force*, as C. S. Lewis pointed out. Hero and Leander are isolated beings, detached from ordinary life and human society in general. They are without any clearly defined context—social, ethical, national, intellectual—that could impose limits on them. The few everyday details, mainly of Ovidian derivation, which nevertheless found their way into the poem are distinctly jarring. When Marlowe tells us that those whose love Hero rejected turned to composing 'sharpe satyrs' (I, 127), or that Leander sent a letter after Hero (II, 14), or again that his father rebuked him (II, 136–7), this has an unpleasantly sobering effect and causes a temporary suspension of the charm of the poem.

The images, too, which Marlowe uses are in conformity with this conception of the two lovers. They usually are of the expanding type, i.e. they serve to stress their more-than-human quality, to isolate them from human society, and to link them with divine or semi-divine beings, with the forces of nature and the heavenly bodies. The few examples which might be considered metaphysical[4] are as a rule cosmic or at least geographical, so that even they do not tend to eliminate the sense of detachment or to introduce links with artefacts or abstractions of human thought—so characteristic of the genuine metaphysical style —which would implicitly relate the two lovers to other human beings or at least provide a human background for them. Throughout Marlowe's part of the poem Hero and Leander remain in splendid isolation, two superhuman beings possessed by love.

'Possessed' is perhaps the right word. A marked characteristic of almost all Renaissance poems of this type is the representation of love as an extrapersonal force. The idea, of course, was not new, but it seems to have played a particularly large role in Elizabethan epyllia. But while the other writers either describe this passion purely declaratively or show it in its consequences, Marlowe alone succeeds in presenting it *in actu*, in its irrevocable submission of the two lovers. For in spite of their semi-divine character—and this is another element in the complex fabric of Marlowe's lovers—Hero and Leander are little more than passive instruments of the operation of love. This is apparent at their first meeting when both fall in love almost at once, and, in the case of Hero, involuntarily. The persuasive speech, which Leander utters 'like a bold Sophister' has really no function in the poem since Hero 'was

---

[4] In the introduction to his edition of the poem L. C. Martin adduces three: Sest. I, ll. 361–2, Sest. II, ll. 275–6 and Sest. II, ll. 291–3.

woon before'. She is not taken in by his arguments and accepts them for what they are worth ('Who taught thee Rhethoricke to deceive a maid?'). We need not be reminded that arguments of this type were stock-in-trade in the Renaissance and represented only an elaborate and rationalized treatment of the conventional and extraordinarily persistent *collige rosas* motive. Marlowe probably introduced it as a set piece, and in view of his conception of the story it is, strictly speaking, irrelevant. Leander's speech is not functional like the similar and greater speeches in Spenser or Milton where the persuasion is presented as a problem of free and self-defining moral choice, for here the two lovers are trapped by the external forces of a world where 'it lies not in our power to love or hate'.

This conception of the erotic passion accounts for several other features of the poem. Marlowe, and for that matter the majority of the later writers of Elizabethan epyllia, represents love, symbolized in Cupid, as indifferent, irresponsible, and sometimes even directly malignant:

> Love is not ful of pittie (as men say)
> But deaffe and cruell, where he meanes to pray. (II, 287–8)

In Marlowe's poem this view of love is not evident in the relationship of Hero and Leander only, but also in the decorative and illustrative images and episodes, as in the Neptune-Leander interlude, the account of the effect of Hero on other people, and the pictures in the Temple of Venus depicting

> ... gods in sundrie shapes,
> Committing headdie ryots, incest, rapes. (I, 143–4)

C. S. Lewis has termed this as the hard quality of love and explained it as Marlowe's attempt to avoid cloying sensuality.[5] It seems rather that this is a natural outcome of the conception of the erotic passion as an irrational force which impells those smitten by it against their will. This is, at least, how a contemporary of Marlowe's understood it:

> What made the gods to trewant it from heaven,
> And shift them subtillie into sundrie shapes,
> But he that roves his shaftes at sixe and seven,
> Laughing at riot, revelling and rapes.[6]

[5] 'Hero and Leander', p. 26.
[6] Thomas Heywood, *Oenone and Paris*, 1594, st. 109.

As a result, Marlowe shows no interest in the exploration of the psychological aspects of the story. What interests him is the operation of the passion of love, its effects, and the actions and responses it exacts. The first meeting between Hero and Leander could offer an excellent opportunity for an analysis of the subtle and gradual growth of feelings between the two lovers, but Marlowe does not exploit it. What we have instead is a brief and deliberately abrupt statement of Leander's falling in love:

> There Hero sacrificing turtles blood,
> Vaild to the ground, vailing her eie-lids close,
> And modestly they opened as she rose:
> Thence flew Loves arrow with the golden head,
> And thus Leander was enamoured. (I, 158-62)

The same omission of psychological preparation, entailed by the presentation of love throughout the poem as a force operating independently of the human will, is evident, though in a less striking degree, in the description of the change in Hero's mind.

This quality, together with the almost complete detachment from any social context and lack of reference to any ordered and dignified Pantheon, produces the specific atmosphere of the poem in which the introduction of a set of ethical values would be not only unexpected but clearly incongruous. Hero and Leander cannot be held morally responsible in their own eyes since they are possessed by love; they cannot be judged as offenders against the laws of society since no social conventions exist in their world; they cannot be condemned by divinely set ethical norms since the gods are worse than themselves. We do not think of them as tinged with tragic guilt. The tragic ending of their love, like its beginning, was to be brought about by forces entirely beyond their control and responsibility. The Mercury episode at the end of the first Sestiad, though doing rather poor credit to Marlowe's mythopoeic abilities, serves to provide a purely external key to the ultimate tragic dénouement of the story and to stress the position of Hero and Leander as mere instruments, or even toys of superhuman forces.

The pathos of Marlowe's poem was probably conceived as a result of the ironic contrast between the naked elementary splendour and unbounded emotional intensity of the two lovers and their helplessness in the face of the baleful forces of destiny and divinity. In their own intensely glowing world there is not the slightest premonition of the 'golden bubble' or of the painful awakening that was to follow. The last lines that Marlowe wrote describe the brilliantly sublimated consummation of their love and the breaking of the new day.

Chapman obviously had some misgivings when he approached his task of completing Marlowe's fragment. In several passages of his continuation he implies disapproval of the way the subject was treated in the first two Sestiads. He speaks of his 'trifling' subject (Dedication), implicitly condemns the pervading sensuality of Marlowe's fragment (III, 182), and indicates that the erotic aspect of the story—the only aspect that Marlowe was interested in—will be deliberately eliminated in his continuation (III, 197–8).

This verdict on the first two Sestiads naturally resulted in a radical change in the further treatment of the legend. In order to make room for this change Chapman had to elaborate considerably the portion of the tale which fell to his share. Marlowe tells about two-thirds of Musaeus's story, and yet Chapman makes his fragment a mere introduction to his sequel. He employs digressions and episodes whose function is to transfer the story to a different plane and introduces elaborate details and situations, not found in previous writers, to bring out his conception of the legend. And this conception was so different from that of Marlowe that it necessitated the rejection of almost all the elements suggested above as contributory to the effect of the first two Sestiads.

The first thing that Chapman did was to reduce Marlowe's characters to the human status. In the third Sestiad the world of the two lovers becomes suddenly peopled and filled with limiting contexts. The first episode which is wholly destructive of the impression of Hero and Leander produced by Marlowe's portion is the Thesme passage (III, 105ff.). Ceremony, for which Thesme stands, is not even a purely ethical category which might be taken to bear some relationship to supra-human, transcendental values. It is primarily a social ritual and one, therefore, which puts Leander, who accepts Thesme's rebuke, at once on a level with any young man from Abydos. The two lovers become entangled in other relations and tinged with other sentiments; they get a wider amplitude, but they lose their exceptional significance and singleness of emotional content. With Chapman Leander is brought into action: he plans with his father the abduction of Hero and prepares a ship 'throughly rigd and mand' (III, 167). Hero is similarly engaged in everyday activities—she embroiders, performs her priestly duties, etc. Besides, their social environment is also given a much more conspicuous place than in Marlowe, so that the two lovers are set amidst a community which is living its own life:

> Day was so long, men walking fell asleepe,
> The heavie humors that their eyes did steepe,
> Made them feare mischiefs. The hard streets were beds
> For covetous churles, and for ambitious heads,
> That spite of Nature would their business plie. (III, 13–17)

These references to other human beings are not used to stress the superiority of Hero and Leander to them, as in Marlowe, but rather to establish a situation in which the behaviour of the two lovers can be viewed in relation to values accepted by other people. In the Alcmane-Mya interlude in the fourth Sestiad we have not only an episode which divests Hero and Leander of their archetypal uniqueness by providing a parallel for them, but also the implication of a social and ethical standard which they fall short of. For perhaps the most essential alteration which Chapman introduced was to transfer the source of the erotic passion from outside the lovers to within them. In this respect Chapman's continuation differs not only from Marlowe's fragment, but also from the majority of Elizabethan epyllia. By doing so Chapman makes his Hero and Leander responsible for their feelings and acts, and justifies his change of tone—'delights . . . being enjoyd aske judgement' (III, 8–9). The two lovers are not governed by external forces, as in the first two Sestiads, and their tragedy is chiefly the result of their failure to discipline their inward passion and subject it to society-made norms. They are guilty of giving in to their sensuality before it was sanctioned by marriage rites. From the beginning of Chapman's continuation the reader is aware that the amoral, frankly sensual world of Hero and Leander is being transformed into something different in which the two lovers become subjected to quite different pressures and influences, and are sometimes treated as mere moral *exempla*:

> And now, ye wanton loves, and young desires,
> Pied vanities, the mint of strange Attires;
> Ye lisping Flatteries, and obsequious Glances,
> Relentfull Musicks, and attractive Dances,
> And you detested Charmes constraining love,
> Shun loves stolne sports by that these Lovers prove. (III, 11–16)

In harmony with this, the accounts of the actions and feelings of Hero and Leander are accompanied by sententious comments whose function is to generalize the ethical content of the story:

31

Joy graven in sence, like snow in water wasts;
Without preserve of vertue nothing lasts. (III, 35–6)
Another instance of this is to be found in the excellent description of
Hero's repentance in the third Sestiad, which, with its running commentary in general terms, produces an impression that Hero is just a
case out of many that might have been chosen to illustrate the great
moral law.

It would be perhaps wrong to class the metaphysical, or rather
protometaphysical conceits which Chapman uses so abundantly among
the merely stylistic elements which mark the difference between the
two parts of the poem, since their function is not only ornamental, and
contributes to the more essential differences which have been already
noted. A conceit often strikes a note of particularization and exclusive-
ness; it interposes the author's ingenuity between the reader and the
poem, and introduces a personal note—the poem becomes as it were a
private experience shared by the poet and the reader: the one seeks to
establish an unexpected and recondite analogy, the other is anxious to
retrace his steps and grasp the full meaning of it. In this sense Chapman's style accounts greatly for the elimination of the many qualities
from the first two Sestiads whose effect depends on direct and im-
personal statement. His images are involved and represent obviously
the result of a primarily rational effort; besides, they are not drawn
from the world of natural phenomena, but rather from the social and
political spheres, from man-made objects and scientific concepts. It
does not follow, of course, that one style is better than the other, but
there can be little doubt that Chapman's way of presenting the story
eliminates the specific 'unearthly' overtones which Marlowe gave to
his paraphrase of the legend.

Moreover, since a metaphor is in itself a comment on its context,
Chapman's imagery contributes considerably to the 'degradation' of
the two lovers. For example, Leander is compared to a London gallant
(VI, 108ff.), Hero to a counterfeit coin (IV, 250), and their love to
'bils unsignd' and 'meates unseason' (III, 148–9). Such stylistic
treatment serves to relate the story to the fabric of human society, and
to divest the characters of their previous mythical quality by using concrete and contracting images instead of general and expanding ones. It
would be easy to compile a long list of instances of this type and show
that they colour the whole of Chapman's continuation.

The basic tragic pattern in Chapman is complex and not quite clear.
He does not preserve the same outlook throughout. At V, 24 he says

that the two lovers must die because Death has stopped the ears of the Fates so that they cannot hear the supplication of gods; in the final section of the poem Leander's death seems almost an accident; and yet the overall impression the last four Sestiads are meant to convey is that the lovers are punished for their neglect of moral laws and marriage rites. It is perhaps partly because of this divided conception that the tragic forebodings are much more effective in Chapman than the tragedy itself. When he comes to the final scene of Leander's drowning he obviously cannot rise to the occasion and resorts instead to ineffectual rhetoric and irrelevant *sententiae*:

> ... the Seas mixt with the skie,
> And tost distrest Leander, being in hell,
> As high as heaven. ... (VI, 182–4)

> The more kinde Neptune raged, the more he raste
> His loves lives fort, and kild as he embraste.
> Anger doeth still his owne mishap encrease;
> If any comfort live, it is in peace. (VI, 230–4)

In the light of this analysis there is only one point of view which enables us to see Chapman's continuation as an eminently suitable continuation of Marlowe's poem and that is if we take the legend of Hero and Leander to be meant for an indirect glorification of marital love. From this standpoint Chapman's continuation is not only extremely effective, but also necessary. But then this is a highly individual view of the legend which Marlowe almost certainly did not share. Indeed, the very length of the continuation is indicative of the manœuvring space Chapman needed to re-direct the story and impress his own interpretation on it. In all other respects Chapman's portion can be said to be a rather unsuitable sequel to Marlowe's poem.

Of course, to suggest that Chapman's continuation considerably obliterates the impression produced by the first two Sestiads, and that its characters are only namesakes of Marlowe's Hero and Leander is not to say that it has no poetic merits. It contains superb passages which range from inset pieces and longer episodes such as the Epithalamion Teratos and the description of Hero's repentance in the third Sestiad, to pictorial presentation of allegorical figures such as that of Venus (IV, 239–43), and to single richly evocative phrases and epithets. Nevertheless, to assert that the story gets told between the two poets better than if either of them had told it himself means not only neglecting the essential differences, amounting sometimes to incongruities, in the approaches of the two poets, but also comparing the existing portions of the poem with their imaginary counterparts. It is a statement that stimulates thought, but the validity of critical conclusions reached on the basis of such speculations is perhaps open to doubt. One conclusion, however, which seems to be warranted by the texts themselves, is that neither would Chapman have begun the tale of Hero and Leander as Marlowe did, nor would Marlowe have continued his poem in Chapman's way. The poem as it is usually printed today consists of a good beginning and a good continuation which nevertheless do not make up a good and harmonious whole.

University of Belgrade

The Monstrous Regiment of Women

Sources for the Satiric View of the Court Lady in English Drama

ROBERT BRUSTEIN

SATIRE on the court lady, like satire on the Italianate courtier, does not appear in English drama to any great extent until 1599.[1] But in that year and after, Marston, Shakespeare, Tourneur, Webster, Middleton and many minor dramatists subject the court lady to a condemnation more scathing than anything encountered previously. The Elizabethan-Jacobean dramatists assume, as it were, the function of medieval troubadours, but with a crucial change in doctrine: they sing not of love but of lust. The upper-class female character is most frequently depicted as a sink of evils, a stews, a loathsome pit of rottenness, a painted image, a gilded pill, a decked idol of May-tide, a skin-full of lust, a school of uncleanness. Her painted good looks are a snare for the innocent, her lascivious fashions an invitation to lechery, her wanton eye a bait for adultery. Her total lack of moral stamina quickens man's appetite. He can either submit to the sinful pleasures she easily tenders —in this case he is damned—or take refuge in misogyny and bitter abuse. Only by contemplating beauty in decay can he counteract the power of this beauty. The worms are his most potent allies.

[1] See Eudo C. Mason, 'Satire on Woman and Sex in Elizabethan Tragedy,' *English Studies*, Vol. XXXI (February 1950), pp. 1–10—a brief article but just about the only one to bear directly on this subject.

The date of this misogynistic onslaught is significant: it is the date of the Bishops' Edict of 1599 when satire, banned from the presses, entered the drama. Like many of the conventions of the Italianate court play, the convention of the wanton court lady thus reached the drama by way of formal satire and homiletic tracts. Among formative dramatic influences on the Elizabethans, only Seneca seems to have affected their views of women directly (that is, not first through satire), and even his influence does not seem particularly strong in this area. It is true that a good many evil highborn ladies appear in Seneca's plays (Clytemnestra, for example, and Medea and Phaedra), but only his *Phaedra* contains an extended diatribe against such women which suggests the tone and substance of Elizabethan attacks, though his *Hercules Oetaus* also has scattered anti-feminist passages. Juvenal probably has a stronger impact here, and his misogyny is absorbed first through the English satiric tradition. In his sixth satire, Juvenal rebukes women (primarily married women) for their lust, ill-temper, vulgar tastes and passions, debauchery, loquacity, gaudy apparel, painting, superstition and treachery to their husbands—the very female vices that are so to exercise the Elizabethans.[2]

Juvenal's scathing realism provides an effective antidote for Elizabethan satirists to the Platonism of their courtly contemporaries; but the most palpable tradition of anti-feminism available to them comes through the patristic strain of medieval preaching and medieval complaint, currently manifesting itself in the sermons of contemporary Puritans. Christianity from its beginnings had entertained a semi-misogynist quality—the connection between women and the temptations of the flesh is too obvious for comment. Whereas Paul found matrimony preferable to burning in hell, many Christian thinkers thought even marriage to be a very weak alternative to the celibate life. The Puritans inclined more towards Paul's view on the subject of marriage, but they intensified attacks on pre-marital sexuality, and they believed that woman, fundamentally, was man's moral inferior. As the Puritans never tired of reminding everyone, their own strictures on

[2] The Elizabethans absorbed Juvenal through his own satires and also through Italian satires written in a Juvenalian tradition, so it might be well to mention just a few of these. Boccaccio satirized women in his *Corbaccio*, and Alberti, in *Amiria* and *Deifiria*, attacked them for their cosmetics, skin preservers, hair dyes, eye lotions, lip salves, ointments and rouges. Ariosto satirized women for their basic dishonesty and inconstancy in his satires; and Aretino accused court ladies of murder, poisoning, infanticide and adultery in *La Cortegiana*, while, in his *Dialogues*, he burlesqued the Platonists by representing a brothel-madam and a novice-prostitute engaged in Platonic dialogues.

women had been laid down by the Church fathers (Chrysostom, Tertullian, Cyprian, Ambrose, Jerome, Augustine, Gregory) and the medieval preachers. And, to be sure, the earlier preachers and the Puritans agree on these points entirely: women are obstinate and perverse, they talk too much, they have an excessive love of superfluous finery, and they are prone to lies, deceit and dissembling. Above all, they are weak of will, highly erotic and perpetually tempting.[3]

Woman's instrument of temptation is her physical beauty. For this reason, the preachers and homilists—both medieval and Puritan—developed a passionate hatred for female allure, treating it as a mere surface which blinds men to the rottenness beneath. Endeavouring to warn against this, woman's most powerful weapon, the preachers emphasized the filth that lies beneath the outer layer and the decay that illness and old age can visit on the finest complexion. As Chrysostom, the author of this strategy, wrote:

> Take her skin from her face and thou shalt see the loathsomeness under it
> ... within she is full of phlegm, stinking, putrid, excremental stuff.[4]

Artificial beauty was even more vigorously attacked by preachers who detested anything that diverged from the natural.

These terms, formulated during the early period of Christianity and in the Middle Ages, remained fairly consistent up until the time they were picked up by the Puritans and the satirists. But the sixteenth-century animus against womankind not only has religious roots but social ones as well: it coincides with the increasing status of women, a development that more properly belongs to the Renaissance than to the Middle Ages.

Female independence certainly reached new heights in the latter part of the sixteenth century, partly because Elizabeth was on the throne during that time. The example of this great queen, and the reverence in which she was held, undoubtedly affected women throughout the realm. Whether as a direct result of this or not, the Elizabethan woman was certainly assuming a more active position in her household. No longer confined exclusively to the kitchen and the childbed, she now

---

[3] For extended discussions of this particular subject, consult: G. R. Owst, *Literature and Pulpit in Medieval England*, Cambridge, 1933, pp. 375–404; Margaret Adlum Gist, *Love and War in the Middle English Romances*, London, 1947, *passim*; Louis B. Wright, *Middle Class Culture in Elizabethan England*, Chapel Hill, 1933, pp. 465–507; Carroll Camden, *The Elizabethan Woman*, New York, 1952, pp. 25ff.; and Chilton Latham Powell, *English Domestic Relations 1487–1653*, New York, 1917, pp. 147–78.

[4] Quoted in Mason, 'Satire on Woman and Sex', p. 4.

enjoyed—in her relations with her husband, her freedom of movement throughout the city, and her access to the latest fashions and cosmetics—a liberty unparalleled in former times or in other countries (this trend was much noted by foreign travellers in England).[5] The satirists observed an increase in the authority wielded over her husband by the English wife—for them this reflected an obstinate and dominating nature. Instead of welcoming female independence as a manifestation of progress and enlightenment, such guardians of social virtue began to stigmatize it as a sign of reversal of degree and good order. It was simple insolence, flagrant libertinism and usurpation of the privileges of the male.

Throughout the sixteenth century, therefore, woman was being charged, primarily, with masculinity and vice. Both charges have a Puritan coloration, but the attack on female masculinity especially was closely related to a Puritan red herring: the attack on female government. Calvin himself had linked female government with original sin, writing that since it 'was a deviation from the original and proper order of nature, it was to be ranked ... among the punishments consequent upon the fall of man'.[6] This, however, was a private view, voiced in a letter and held with more conviction when the Roman Catholic Mary was on the English throne than when the Protestant Elizabeth succeeded. Calvin, as a matter of fact, was angered when John Knox published *The First Blast of the Trumpet Against the Monstrous Regiment of Women* (1558)—not because he disagreed with its contents but rather because the book was so ill-timed (Elizabeth was crowned later that year). Knox was penitent, but never made a retraction, and although Elizabeth was henceforth spared any direct criticism, Knox's views became general Puritan doctrine. Knox had written:

> I am assured, that God hath reveled to some in this our age, that it is more than a monstre in nature that a Woman should reigne and have empire above Man.[7]

Knox's remarks were soon to have more application in the home than

[5] Frederick, Duke of Wirtemberg, for example, visiting England in 1592, noted the famous saying then circulating among men of other nations: ' "England is a paradise for women, a prison for servants, and a hell or purgatory for horses"—for the females have great liberty and are almost like masters, whilst the poor horses are worked very hard.' See William Brenchley Rye, *England as Seen by Foreigners in the Days of Elizabeth and James I*, London, 1865, p. 14. It is not an isolated observation.

[6] Letter from Calvin to Sir William Cecil, quoted in John Knox, *The Works*, ed. David Laing, Edinburgh, 1864, Vol. IV, p. 357.

[7] Knox, *Works*, Vol. IV, pp. 366–7.

in the court: Puritans vigorously criticized all women exercising control over their husbands and households, for such women had usurped the proper sovereignty of man.

The English satirists, operating on the same assumptions, concentrated on female masculinity as evidenced in mannish clothes. In *The Steele Glas* (1576), George Gascoigne complained of his inability to distinguish women, now dressed in jerkins and doublets, from men;[8] and William Harrison, repelled by the same sort of fashions, wrote in 1577 of having 'met with some of these trulls in London so disguised that it hath passed my skill to discern whether they were men or women.'[9] Marston also registered a protest, in his satires (1598), against the mannish modes of women:

> Nay then, I'll never rail at those
> That wear a codpis, thereby to disclose
> What sex they are, since strumpets breeches use. . . .[10]

But women were satirized for wearing the breeches in a metaphorical sense as well as a literal one. Thomas Dekker (?) (1603) called it 'a generall imperfection of women, bee they never so honest, never so kindly used, and have never so much wealth and ease, to strive for the breeches'.[11] Like the effeminate male, the mannish woman was to receive in 1620 a generic name, *hic-mulier*, in a series of pamphlets which recapitulated all the sixteenth-century fulminations against her type.[12]

The satire against the *hic-mulier* type was probably a Renaissance modification of the old medieval charge against female obstinacy and perversity. Another medieval charge echoed in the sixteenth century questioned woman's nature even when she remained feminine. Depending on whether she was thought to be consciously evil or

[8] George Gascoigne, *The Steele Glas*, Vol. II, pp. 173–4.

[9] William Harrison, *Descriptions of Britaine and England*, p. 110.

[10] John Marston, *Certain Satires*, in *The Works*, ed. A. H. Bullen, Boston, 1887, Vol. III, pp. 273–4.

[11] Thomas Dekker (?), *The Batchelors Banquet*, London, 1603, unsigned.

[12] The pamphlets were called *Hic-Mulier*, *Haec-Vir* and *Muld Sacke*, and were all three published in 1620. *Hic-Mulier* was the first and most comprehensive of the lot. Subtitled 'a Medecine to cure the Coltish Disease of the Staggers in the Masculine-Feminines of Our Times', it attempted to prove that this strange reversal of degree was a vice of great magnitude: 'Since the daies of *Adam* women were never so masculine, Masculine in their genders and whole generation, from the Mother, to the youngest daughter; Masculine in their number, from one to multitudes; Masculine in Case, even from the head to foot; Masculine in Moode, from bold speech, to impudent action; Masculine in Tense: for (without redresse) they were, are, and will be still most Masculine, most man-kinde, and most monstrous' (*Hic-Mulier*, London, 1620, unsigned).

merely at the mercy of her own weak nature, woman was regarded either as a devil or as a beast.

The analogy between women and beasts is easily explained: just as animals were assumed to have no rational soul, so women were assumed to have so little rational soul as to be almost negligible. Women permitted their appetites to dominate their reason, their concupiscible soul (or affections) to take control. When a woman went mad, her reason was presumed to be totally defeated, her affections reigning supreme, and like the beasts, she was then given over completely to sexual passion. (This accounts for the sex-obsessions of such madwomen as Ophelia in *Hamlet* and the Jailer's Daughter in *The Two Noble Kinsmen*.) As for man, his control over his affections was supposed to be a good deal stronger (though even this assumption was sometimes doubted), but he was always subject to temptation. Thus, woman's beauty and lust were man's prime obstacles to salvation. Having lost her own battle with restraint, the temptress Eve enjoined man to lose his as well.

If consciously evil, woman was assumed to be in consort with the devil, a kind of devil's apprentice. Sometimes she was confused with actual devils. In Middleton's *A Mad World My Masters* (1604), for example, Sir Penitent Brothel exhorts the lecherous Mistress Harebrain to virtue after a devil has appeared in her shape:

> Be honest, then the devil will ne'er assume thee:
> He has no pleasure in that shape t'abide
> Where these two sisters reign not, lust or pride.[13]

Lust was assumed to be the chief weapon of Satan, who adorned women with beauty in order to make desire more sharp.

In the satiric view, therefore, virtue and constancy were products less of self-control than of lack of opportunity.[14] As Marston wrote (c. 1609); 'Faire women play: she's chaste whom none will have.'[15] Men could guarantee a woman's chastity only by removing her from the source of temptation, by sending her, say, to a nunnery or to the country, where she would not be a hapless breeder of sinners. The view

[13] Thomas Middleton, *A Mad World My Masters*, IV, iv, 46–9, in *The Works*, ed. A. H. Bullen, Vol. III, p. 329.

[14] This is not a new notion about women, of course. In Ovid's *Amores*, for example, the old bawd Dipsas tells Corinna that the chaste woman is the one who has not been asked, adding that if a woman is not completely countrified she will usually do the asking herself.

[15] Marston, *The Insatiate Countess*, I, i, 58, in *The Plays*, ed. H. Harvey Wood, London, 1934, Vol. III, p. 6.

is cynical, but satirists and moralists, in this time, were almost univer-
sally convinced that most women were untrustworthy. Recorded in
Manningham's *Diary* (1603) is this choice bit of sermonizing:

> Mr Hemmings, sometimes of Trinity College in Cambridge, in his sermon
> at Paul's Cross, speaking of women, said that if a man marry, it were a
> thousand to one but he should light upon a bad one, there were so
> many naught; and if he should chance to find a good one, yet he were not
> sure to hold her so. . . .[16]

The odds were high because woman's lightness and inconstancy were
proverbial, the result of some primeval curse. And such writers as
John Donne—even when he was defending women, as in his *Paradoxes and Problemes*—assumed that these unfinished creatures were
morally inert and fundamentally unstable.[17]

Women, therefore, were assumed to be in constant danger of losing
their chastity, but the inconstancy of widows was thought to be almost
inevitable. For if virgins—those strangers to pleasure—could be easily
seduced, how much more easily would widows, habituated to the sex
act, lend themselves to concupiscence. St Paul, meditating on the
impossibility of widows remaining chaste, had urged them to remarry
and avoid the risk of eternal damnation. Elizabethan moralists, however, were more stony-hearted, and disapproved of second marriages.
For them, remarriage was, at best, a kind of legal adultery, at worst, an
overt form of lust. 'Marry?' cries the Duke Ferdinand in Webster's
Duchess of Malfi (1613), 'they are most luxurious will wed twice.'[18]
If, on the other hand, the young widow heeded the dictates of such
moralists, she was caught between her natural desires and the moral
code, and it is no wonder that she found herself frequently involved in
illicit affairs. Whichever path she chose, she was simply adding more
proof of woman's hereditary bent toward whoredom.

Most satirists, then, and many satiric dramatists, were in agreement
that women were inconstant, weak-willed and amorous. By the end of
the first decade of the seventeenth century, in fact, this had become such
a familiar accusation that playwrights were at a loss to articulate it with
originality: 'Oh who would trust deceiving woman!' says a character

[16] Quoted in G. B. Harrison, *A Jacobean Journal*, 1603–6, New York, 1941, p. 13.

[17] See Donne's ironic 'Defence of Women for their Inconstancy & Their Paintings',
where he affirms: 'That Women are *Inconstant*, I with any man confesse, but that Inconstancy is a bad quality, I against any man will maintaine.' In *Paradoxes and Problemes*,
ed. Geoffrey Keynes, London, 1923, p. 5.

[18] John Webster, *The Duchess of Malfi*, I, i, 325–6. Webster, of course, is much more
indulgent towards second marriages in this play than his character.

in Massinger and Fletcher's *The Custom of the Country.* 'I could rail now against the sex, and curse it; but the theam and way's too Common....'[19] The *degree* of woman's sinfulness, however, remained a subject for some argument, for it depended on a number of things. An ugly woman, for example, might be more virtuous than a fair one, because she did not have as many opportunities to indulge her nature. Similarly, a busy woman could be more chaste than an idle one because her mind was occupied with more important matters than love. But a woman who—like the court lady—was *both* beautiful *and* idle had as little chance of preserving her virtue as a widow. It was not to be thought that such women could withstand the energetic assaults of ardent suitors.

Consequently, at the same time that the Platonists were emphasizing the harmony between inner and outer beauty, the satirists were severely doubting the moral honesty of handsome women. John Florio puts these doubts into dialogue form in 1591, when they appear in a debate between the Platonist Silvestro and the satirist Pandulpho:

S. Why defame you the fayrest with the foulest blot? since in a crooked bodie you seldome see an upright minde, and there is more care in keeping, what is more worth the keeping.
P. Because beautie and honesty seldome agree, for of beautie comes temptation, of temptation dishonour; and as an other saith of beauty comes pride, and pride makes way for letchery.[20]

The more famous discussion of this question, of course, occurs in the dialogue between Hamlet and Ophelia:

Ham. Ha, ha, are you honest?
Oph. My lord!
Ham. Are you fair?
Oph. What means your lordship?
Ham. That if you be honest and fair, your honesty should admit no discourse to your beauty.
Oph. Could beauty, my lord, have better commerce than with honesty?
Ham. Ay, truly, for, the power of beauty will sooner transform honesty from what it is to a bawd, than the force of honesty can translate beauty into his likeness. This was sometime a paradox, but now the age gives it proof. ...[21]

[19] Massinger and Fletcher, *The Custom of the Country,* V, i, in *The Works of Beaumont and Fletcher,* ed. Arnold Glover and A. R. Waller, Cambridge, 1905–12, Vol. I, p. 369.
[20] John Florio, *Second Fruites,* ed. R. C. Simonini, Jr., Gainesville, Fla., 1953, pp. 191–3.
[21] *Hamlet,* III, i, 103–15.

Ophelia, ignorant of the age's 'paradox', is here upholding the old Platonic view of beauty as the handmaiden of a virtuous spirit; but Hamlet, like the satirists he echoes, is discontented with Platonism.[22] And so is John Donne, whose expression of the contradiction of terms implicit in the phrase 'a woman true and faire' is almost as famous as Shakespeare's.[23]

Natural beauty could not justifiably be considered the fault of woman, but the artificial enhancement of this beauty by means of cosmetics and sumptuous attire was quite another thing. Since such beauty aids were thought to encourage immorality, woman was belittled for them persistently throughout this period. Women, of course, had been decking themselves out in finery ever since the discovery of the silkworm, and even before, but court fashions at this time seem to have become unprecedented in their extravagance. Imitations by upstart gentlewomen had also reached a new high. The majority of Englishwomen were proving the literal truth of Ben Jonson's assertion about the court: 'In thee, the whole kingdome dresseth it selfe, and is ambitious to use thee as her glasse.'[24] As a result, upstart gentlewomen were soon subjected to satiric abuse as violent as that directed towards upstart courtiers. The satirist Edward Hake, for example, in *News Out of Powles Churchyarde* (1579) admonished the middle-class woman for dressing in the fashion of great ladies so as to 'walcke about the streate with hir true Lover deere',[25] and Stephen Gosson wrote an entire pamphlet against these female upstarts.[26]

Perhaps to preserve her distance from her middle-class imitators, the English court lady was changing the vogues as quickly as they were copied—and making her gowns as costly as possible. John Lyly, usually a defender of the English court lady, could not stomach her abuse of fashions, and he attacked this vice in *Euphues*;[27] but although he diplomatically tried to absolve Elizabeth of the overdressing of her ladies, there is little doubt that Elizabeth's love of finery was equal

---

[22] A later satirical rephrasing of this theme can be found in Robert Burton's *Anatomy of Melancholy* (1621), p. 597: 'If she be fair, as the saying is, she is commonly a fool; if proud, scornful . . . or dishonest, *rara est concordia formae atque pudicitae*, "can she be fair and honest too?"'

[23] See John Donne, 'Song', ll. 10–18.

[24] Jonson, *Cynthia's Revels*, 1601, Dedication, ll. 6–8.

[25] Edward Hake, *News out of Powles Churchyarde*, 1579, ed. Charles Edmonds, London, 1872, sig. Diii.

[26] Stephen Gosson (?), *Pleasant Quippes for Upstart Newfangled Gentlewomen: or a Glasse to View the Pride of Vainglorious Women*, 1595, London, 1841.

[27] See John Lyly, *Euphues*, 1578, Pt. I, p. 319; Pt. II, pp. 22–9.

to, if not greater than, that of her waiting women. At her death, the Queen had a wardrobe numbering two thousand gowns, all of them (if her portraits are accurate) made of the most expensive materials. Even were materials less costly—or wardrobes less huge—female attire would obviously have proved expensive. Each lady carried on her back a smock, a petticoat, a bodice, a farthingale, a kirtle and a gown; on her head, she wore a coif and a hat.[28] Some of these articles of dress were—and would seem even to our more sophisticated age—extremely daring. A doublet had been designed which exposed the breasts almost entirely, a fashion that started contemporary critics fulminating over 'novelty' (even though it had been in existence since the Middle Ages).[29] In the middle of the century, Robert Crowley noted, in his *One and Thirtye Epigrammes*, that 'Nice Wyves' laid their 'bosome all bare, and more whorelyke dight'.[30] And Puritans and satirists were also quick to observe that only courtesans had hitherto exposed their breasts in the street, leaving their readers to make the obvious inferences. Barnabe Rich was outraged by the sight of women's 'open breasts, their naked stomaches';[31] Stephen Gosson wrote of 'these naked paps, the Devils ginnes';[32] and Thomas Nashe complained that women 'theyr round Roseate buds immodestly lay foorth, to shew at theyr handes there is fruit to be hoped'.[33] Had we any doubt that such a style had become modish at court, we have only to remember how Queen Elizabeth, by appearing before a French dignitary with her breasts exposed, forced him to keep his eyes on the floor all through the interview.

The satiric railing against clothes reflected a general feeling, inherited from the Middle Ages, that fashions were the appurtenances of sin, magnets to draw men and women into adultery. Moralists generally believed with Montaigne that the function of clothes was to excite desire in the opposite sex.[34] Some, like Phillip Stubbes, even preferred a modified nudity to the clothes then in fashion.[35] No Elizabethan, of

[28] See Camden, *Elizabethan Woman*, pp. 220ff.
[29] See Owst, *Literature and Pulpit*, pp. 396–7.
[30] Robert Crowley, *One and Thirtye Epigrammes*, 1550, in Select Works, ed. J. M. Cowper, London, 1872, p. 45.
[31] Barnabe Rich, *Faultes, Faultes, and Nothing Else but Faultes*, London, 1606, p. 23.
[32] Gosson (?), *Pleasant Quippes*, p. 6.
[33] Thomas Nashe, *Christs Teares over Jerusalem* in *The Works*, ed. R. B. McKerrow, London, 1904–10, Vol. II, p. 137.
[34] See Montaigne, 'Upon Some Verses of Vergil.'
[35] Phillip Stubbes, *The Anatomy of Abuses*, 1583, ed. Frederick J. Furnivall, London, 1877–9, p. 82.

course, with the possible exception of John Donne,[36] would have championed *complete* nakedness. But the fig-leaf simplicity of Adam and Eve was frequently invoked as a rebuke to the vanity of the proud modish lady.

Another form of lily-gilding that revolted the English moralists was the art of painting. In *Euphues and his England*, John Lyly affirmed that only the Italian lady used cosmetics;[37] but if painting was limited to Italy in 1580 (which we can safely doubt), it certainly spread quickly through England. In 1593, Thomas Nashe was writing:

> Gorgeous Ladies of the Court, never was I admitted so neere any of you, as to see how you torture poore old Time with spunging, pynning, and pounsing. . . .[38]

Elizabeth, who used cosmetics herself, seems once again to have supplied the sanction for the practice. In her old age, particularly, the Queen became very vain. As Jonson told Drummond,

> Queen Elizabeth never saw her self after she became old in a true Glas. They painted her & sometymes would vermilion her nose.[39]

As for the rest of the ladies, they followed suit until, by the Jacobean age, a natural complexion at court had become as rare as a winter pomegranate. A letter from John Chamberlain in 1613 is witness to this, where he speaks of the wife of the Earl of Bedford:

> Mary, she is somewhat reformed in her attire, and forbeares painting, which they say makes her look somewhat straungely among so many visards, which together with theyre frisled, powdred hair, makes them looke all alike, so that you can scant know one from another at first view.[40]

The frizzling and powdering of the hair about which Chamberlain writes was another extreme cosmetic practice prevalent in the court and the city. The Elizabethan-Jacobean woman manifested a marked impatience with her own locks, either curling them, dying them or wearing a wig.

Once again, the English moralists made the inevitable connections with immorality. Barnabe Rich asserted (1606) that 'painting . . . is as

---

[36] See Donne, Elegie XX, 'Going to Bed', ll. 33ff.: 'Full nakedness! All joyes are due to thee,/As souls unbodied, bodies uncloth'd must be,/To taste whole joyes.'

[37] See Lyly, *Euphues and his England*, Pt. II, pp. 200–1.

[38] Nashe, *Christs Teares*, in *Works*, Vol. II, p. 138.

[39] Jonson, *Conversations with Drummond of Hawthornden*, in *Works*, Appendix I, Vol. I, pp. 141–4.

[40] Letter from John Chamberlain to Dudley Carleton August, 1613, in *The Letters of John Chamberlain*, ed. Norman Egbert McClure, Vol. I, p. 470.

generall amongst a number of women (that faine would be accounted honest) as it is to the most noted and common strumpet'.[41] Marston, in 1599, wrote with blistering irony of a 'celestial angel' who was approaching him so laden down with vizards, masks and paint that he could not see her face.[42] And all the satirists assumed that painted beauty could only cover spiritual corruption. An image passed from satire into a number of plays—including Chettle's *Hoffman* (1602), Chapman's *All Fools* (1604?), and Middleton's *Women Beware Women* (*c.* 1621)—comparing women to a gilded tomb or luxurious temple, handsome without, but within full of rottenness, evil and disease.[43]

As a result, a surprising number of writers began to speak, with obvious relish, of the destruction wrought by old age, disease and death on the female flesh.[44] When Barnabe Barnes, for example, kills his heroine in *The Devil's Charter* (1607), he fashions the scene as a visual illustration of the transience of beauty and the vanity of female pride. Lucretia Borgia, after a prolonged session before her mirror, is poisoned by her cosmetics, crying 'Who painted my faire face with these foule spots,/You see them in my soule deformed blots'.[45] One can imagine the satisfaction with which moralistic spectators watched a lady being struck down by Nemesis in the very act of painting.

Other authors were more explicit, though no less sensational, in showing beauty in decay. Attempting to turn man's thoughts from worldly temptations, they depreciated the objects of his attention, emphasizing particularly the effects of illness and old age on female beauty. Vindice's remarks to the skull of his mistress in *The Revenger's Tragedy* ('Does every proud and selfe-affecting Dame/Camphire her face for this. . . .?')[46] are typical of this approach, and so are Hamlet's remarks to the skull of Yorick:

> Now get you to my lady's chamber, and tell her, let her paint an inch thick, to this favour she must come.[47]

[41] Rich, *Faultes*, p. 21.

[42] Marston, *Scourge of Villainie*, ed. G. B. Harrison, London, 1925, Sat. VII, ll. 164–83.

[43] See Henry Chettle, *The Tragedy of Hoffman*, Oxford, 1951, II, iii; Chapman, *All Fools*, I, i, 84–91; Middleton, *Women Beware Women*, III, i, 95–9.

[44] See M. C. Bradbrook, *Themes and Conventions of Elizabethan Tragedy*, Cambridge, 1952, pp. 170–1. Professor Bradbrook explains the connection in the Elizabethan mind between painting the face and the decaying of a corpse as due to 'the habit of painting to hide disease or merely to hide dirt (as clean rushes were strewn over dirty ones)'.

[45] Barnabe Barnes, *The Devil's Charter* (1607), IV, iii.

[46] Cyril Tourneur, *The Revenger's Tragedy*, (1607), III, v, in *The Plays and Poems of Cyril Tourneur*, ed. John Churton Collins, London, 1878, Vol. II, pp. 84–5.

[47] *Hamlet*, VI, i, 212–15.

Even minor playwrights, such as the unknown author of *The Second Maiden's Tragedy* (1611), achieved something like intensity of expression when singing of beauty in decay.[48] All reminded women that beauty was only a sliding shadow that quickly vanishes, and that all their vanity would end in the grave or, worse, in the infernal fires. 'How will you attyre your selves,' asked Thomas Nashe in 1593, 'what gowne, what head-tyre will you put on, when you shall lyve in Hell amongst Hagges and devils?'[49] Or as Richard Braithwaite asked, as late as 1631,

> Why doe ye embellish and adorne your flesh with such port and grace, which within some fewe dayes wormes will devoure in the grave?[50]

These female vices—from masculine obstinacy to artificial beauty—were common to women of all orders, and satiric attacks were aimed at the kitchen maid as much as at the court lady. But certain charges were directed at upper-class women alone. Chief among these was the charge that the English court lady—like the English courtier—had fallen under vicious Italian influences, and particularly the scandalous Italian fashion of Platonic love.

Always anxious to compare the Italian lady unfavourably with the English, John Lyly had assumed, in 1580, that the Italian version of courtly love was not to be found at the English court—but it had already been institutionalized there. With court scandals multiplying,[51] and with the Ovidians and sonneteers at the height of their popularity, the satirists of the nineties were far more reluctant than Lyly to absolve the English lady of sin. Their insinuations, however, were, for obvious reasons, always rather guarded. 'The Court I dare not touch,' wrote Nashe in 1592, 'but surely there (as in the heavens) be many falling starres, and but one true Diana.'[52] One late sixteenth-century moralist preferred to remain anonymous when he wrote:

> The women of the Courte have also their vices. For alwaie we see manie endowed with goodly giftes of the body, fayre, preatie, handsome and

[48] *The Second Maiden's Tragedy* (1611), V, ii, in *The Old English Drama: A Selection of Plays from the Old English Dramatists*, London, 1825, Vol. I, pp. 82–3.

[49] Nashe, *Christs Teares*, in *Works*, Vol. II, p. 138.

[50] Richard Braithwaite, *The English Gentlewoman*, London, 1631, p. 17.

[51] Elizabeth's reluctance to permit her maids to marry resulted in many illicit affairs which might otherwise have proved legitimate marriages. There were, in addition, genuine scandals like that caused by Penelope Rich and Charles Blount. Plagued by an unhappy marriage, Penelope carried on an extra-marital liaison with the Earl of Devonshire, and bore him five illegitimate children. In 1605, she scandalized the nation and the court by marrying her lover while her husband was still alive.

[52] Nashe, *Pierce Penilesse*, in *Works*, Vol. I, p. 216.

comely. Moreover, richly attired in purple, golde, jewels, and ryches; but all men cannot see what filthy monsters do often lurke under those faire skinnes. . . .[53]

Ben Jonson's Moria, in *Cynthia's Revels* (1600–1) is much more outspoken about courtly immorality:

> I would tell you, which Madame lov'd a *Monsieur*, which a player, which a page; who slept with her husband, who with her friend, who with her gentleman-usher, who with her horse-keeper, who with her monkie, who with all. Yes, and who jigg'd the cocke too.[54]

Satirists conveyed their disdain for the courtly mistress by taking a closer look at her features. Under their pitiless magnifying glass, these satirists saw every imperfection in the female face, characterizing the revered lady of the Petrarchan lover as 'Lady Swin-snout, his yeolow fac'd Mistress.'[55] One print from later times (1654), created by a satirist with artistic talent, literally represented the 'lady' as the woebegone 'servant' pretended to see her: a remarkably ugly and grotesque creature with a Cupid sitting on her forehead, hearts sticking absurdly from her head, roses plastered on her cheeks, bows glued to her eyebrows, hemispheres for breasts, suns for eyes and pearls for teeth.[56]

Besides this, the satirist found the courtly mistress to be a masculine *hic-mulier* type, encouraged by the Platonic lover (who continually spoke of her superiority) to usurp the rights of men. Women demonstrated their masculinity, sometimes, by taking an active part in the love relationship; the pursued became the pursuer. This reversal of roles was perhaps the most distasteful of all female vices to the satirists, for they found such seducing women to constitute a genuine threat to masculine vigorousness. Like drink, aggressive wooing by a woman was thought to diminish man's power of sexual performance. This fear, in fact, partly accounts for the satirists' hatred of Ovidian poetry for, as Hallet Smith has informed us,[57] the central Ovidian myth is one (Salmacis and Hermaphroditus) in which a forward nymph woos a reluctant boy. Certainly, in the drama, forward women are very often lascivious women: Livia in Middleton's *Women Beware Women*, Isabella in Marston's *The Insatiate Countess*, Vittoria Corombona in

[53] Quoted in Georgiana Hill, *Women in English Life*, London, 1896, Vol. I, pp. 163–4.
[54] Jonson, *Cynthia's Revels*, IV, i, 140–56, in *Works*, Vol. IV, p. 119.
[55] Nashe, *Pierce, Penilesse*, in *Works*, Vol. I, p. 168.
[56] Reproduced in Camden, *Elizabethan Woman*, p. 185.
[57] Hallet Smith, *Elizabethan Poetry: A Study in Conventions, Meaning, and Expression*, Cambridge, Mass., 1952, pp. 64–130.

Webster's *The White Devil*, the Duchess in Tourneur's *The Revenger's Tragedy*—even though an active wooer like Shakespeare's Rosalind is free from taint.

Even passive court ladies, however, were thought to be instinctively immoral, though not as immoral as the masculine *hic-mulier*. The enticements of court life, and her own weak nature, made it imperative that she fly the court for her own safety. Her chances of preserving her chastity, if she remained, were considered very slim indeed. If the end of Platonic love was, as the satirists believed, seduction, then the court lady was always at the mercy of lecherous courtiers. And it was assumed to be extremely difficult to resist the advances of finely dressed men who wooed with honeyed flattery and sugared sonnets, who proffered expensive gifts, and who made false promises of marriage. Furthermore, the rich meats, wines and aphrodisiacs consumed at court tables were thought to swell the court lady's veins with lust, thus helping to weaken her powers of resistance (such foods are prescribed by Sir Epicure Mammon in *The Alchemist*).[58] And finally, such court functions as the masque threw the sexes into each other's arms where they had the opportunity for amorous play and lustful badinage: 'For what clipping, what culling, what kissing and bussing, what smouching & slabbering one of another, what filthie groping and uncleane handling is not practised everywher in these dauncings?' asked the moralist Stubbes, who found this 'horrible vice' to be a certain prelude to carnal copulation.[59]

Such conditions led moralists to believe that a woman, vulnerable anywhere, was particularly likely to fall at court. And this belief enters late Elizabethan and Stuart drama as a set conviction. Perhaps the best and fullest expression of this kind is found in Marston's *The Malcontent* (1604) where Malevole asserts that he would rather leave his lady in a whorehouse than leave her to the wicked temptations of the court:

> When in an *Italian* lascivious Pallace, a Lady gardianlesse,
> Left to the push of all allurement,
> The strongest incitements to immodestie,

[58] See Jonson, *The Alchemist*, IV, i, 155–66, in *Works*, Vol. V, p. 364.
[59] Stubbes, *Anatomy*, pp. 154–5. Some court observers came to the same conclusions about dancing. In the diary of Lady Anne Clifford, there is an entry (1603): 'Now ther was much talk of a maske wch the Queene had at Winchester, and how all the Ladies about the Court had gotten such ill names that it was growen a scandalous place; and the Queene hir selfe was much fallen from hir former greatnes and reputation. . . .' Quoted in Violet A. Wilson, *Society Women of Shakespeare's Time*, London, 1924, Vol. I, p. 160.

To have her bound, incensed with wanton sweetes,
Her veines fild hie with heating delicates,
Soft rest, sweete Musick, amorous Masquerers,
lascivious banquets, sinne it selfe gilt ore,
strong phantasie tricking up strange delights,
presenting it dressed pleasingly to sence, sence
leading it unto the soule, confirmed with potent
example, impudent customs inticed by that great bawd
opportunitie, thus being prepar'd, clap to her easie
eare, youth in good clothes, well shapt, rich, faire-spoken,
promising-noble, ardent bloud-full, wittie, flattering:
Ulisses absent, O *Ithacan*, chastest *Penelope*, hold out.[60]

These are the allurements which, as we have seen, were thought to be characteristic not only of the '*Italian* lascivious Pallace' but of the English court as well, and, before these temptations, it was not to be expected that Penelope's virtue would hold out. Thus, the wanton court lady enters the drama, a character just as conventional as the villainous Italianate courtier, the blunt plain-dealing soldier, or the malcontent hero, and based just as strongly on contemporary satiric attitudes. To reside in court was, to these satirists, tantamount to being in a state of sin; for the taint of the court's corruption spread like an evil sore over innocent and guilty alike.

Columbia University

---

[60] Marston, *The Malcontent*, III, i, 190–207, in *Plays*, Vol. I, p. 179.

Rochester: Augustan or Explorer?

HOWARD ERSKINE-HILL

I

ROCHESTER, the man and his work, is a major landmark in the terrain of Restoration poetry. That he should come to be recognized as such, in the last fifty years, is due largely to the enthusiasm of the writings and teaching of Vivian de Sola Pinto.[1] But if Rochester's place is assured, the nature of his achievement is in dispute. Pinto, while recognizing Augustan qualities in his work, has also drawn analogies between Rochester and such un-Augustan authors as Marlowe and Blake. David M. Vieth, in an important recent study, considers him fully an Augustan, and finds a strong affinity between his satire and Pope's in respect both of literary techniques and underlying values.[2] The question is whether Rochester's poetry is chiefly that of an explorer through the '*Perplexity* of endless *Thought*', or of a man confident in a stable and ultimately satisfying world-view, by which he can judge the follies of his fellow men.[3]

---

[1] See V. de S. Pinto, *Rochester: Portrait of a Restoration Poet*, 1935, pp. x, 136, for his acknowledgement to earlier critics.

[2] Pinto, op. cit., pp. 257–8; *Enthusiast in Wit*, 1962, p. 226; Rochester, *Poems*, ed. V. de S. Pinto, 1953, pp. xxxviii–xl; D. M. Vieth, *Attribution in Restoration Poetry*, 1963, pp. 106, 221, 271–2. Since the Rochester cannon is still in some cases in dispute, I propose to confine my references to poems which Pinto and Vieth agree in attributing to him. Quotations from Rochester's poetry are from the above-mentioned edition.

[3] *The Works of John Earl of Rochester . . . Printed for Jacob Tonson*, 1714, p. 156.

Without doubt there are interesting and important affinities between Rochester and Pope in respect of qualities which may reasonably be called Augustan. *An Allusion to Horace* is the first Augustan imitation in English and is comparable to Pope's *Epistle to Augustus*.[4] *Tunbridge-Wells* has resemblances to Pope's *Fourth Satire of Dr Donne*, owing to the common descent from the Ninth Satire of Horace's First Book. *Artemisa to Cloe*, in its intimate and delicate modulation of the familiar, Horatian style of formal satire, strikingly anticipates Pope's *Epistle to a Lady*. All these poems of Rochester Pope knew; their relation with Pope's work deserves exploration; but it is not primarily on these that Vieth rests his case.[5] He concentrates rather on the more ironical satires of Rochester: *Upon Nothing*, *A Very Heroical Epistle*, *An Epistolary Essay*, and deduces from them, in course of a detailed explication of their irony, an underlying attitude towards man and his relation to the cosmos similar to that which he finds explicit in Pope's *Essay on Man*.[6]

There is, however, a poem where Rochester makes explicit his 'general map of man', and which is in this respect the comparable poem to Pope's *Essay*. This is *A Satyr against Mankind*, of which it is surprising Vieth takes so little account. For while it resembles *An Essay* in its concern with humankind in general (differing from Satire VIII of Boileau, on which it is partly based, in its exclusion of social satire) it expresses a view of the natural order almost diametrically opposed to Pope's. An investigation of the Augustan nature of Rochester's work must take into account *A Satyr against Mankind*; I propose to comment on it here, with two other related poems, as a prelude to discussing *A Very Heroical Epistle* and *An Epistolary Essay*.

II

A Satyr against Mankind, like *An Essay on Man*, is a polemic against human pride, proceeding from a consideration of man's place in the universe to his behaviour to his fellow men. Each poem declares

---

[4] See Harold F. Brooks, 'The "Imitation" in English Poetry', *Review of English Studies*, 25 (1949), pp. 138–9.

[5] Pope's knowledge of Rochester: see Joseph Spence, *Anecdotes*, ed. S. W. Singer, 1820, p. 281; *Imitations of Horace, To Mr Murray*, ll. 126–31 (cf. *Artemisa to Cloe*, ll. 44–5); *A New Collection of Poems Relating to State Affairs*, 1705, p. 258 in the British Museum copy, where Pope's manuscript annotation shows he knew *Tunbridge-Wells* but attributed it to another hand.

[6] D. M. Vieth, op. cit., pp. 109–26.

man's proper concern to be his immediate 'environment'; Rochester maintains that

> Our *Sphere* of Action, is life's happiness,
> And he who thinks Beyond, thinks like an *Ass* (ll. 96–7)

while Pope takes as his apparent premise the following lines:

> Say first, of God above, or Man below,
> What can we reason, but from what we know?
> Of Man what see we, but his station here,
> From which to reason, or to which refer? (I, ll. 17–20)

and at the beginning of Book IV he apostrophizes 'Happiness' as 'our being's end and aim!/Good, Pleasure, Ease, Content! whate'er thy name' (ll. 1–2). But the fundamental conception of Pope's poem is that of the general yet particularly and vividly conceived hierarchy of creation, extending far above man and below, in which the wise, humble and pious person will know the proper place of his kind. It is a paradox from a modern positivist viewpoint that Pope, holding that we can reason only from what we know, should affirm the existence of this partly metaphysical hierarchy with such confident and splendid particularity. In Rochester no such paradox is found. In *A Satyr against Mankind*, the assertion of the hierarchy, of 'the whole connected creation', is left to the Adversary whose very intervention (and here I would differ from Pinto) Rochester has made subtly ridiculous, and whose views he strongly rebuts in other parts of the poem.[7] The divine is gratified at Rochester's attack on wit, but is sufficiently unmoved by the terrible force of the preceding lines to get in a hint at the irony of it's being *Wilmot* who makes such an attack: '. . . *but you take care,/Upon this point, not to be too severe.*' He then ludicrously displays his own vanity in wit:

> *Perhaps my* Muse, *were fitter for this part,*
> *For I profess, I can be very smart*
> *On* Wit, *which I abhor with all my heart:* (ll. 52–4)

following this up with the use of a metaphor (the 'Tide of Ink'—l. 57) both clumsy and rather archaically metaphysical. The divine now proceeds with his counter-assertion of the dignity of man and of his connection with his Creator. There is a bland facility in his expression which speaks for itself.

---

[7] Pope, *An Essay on Man*, Argument of the First Epistle. Pinto, *Enthusiast in Wit*, p. 154.

Blest glorious Man! *to whom alone kind* Heav'n,
An everlasting Soul *has freely giv'n;*
Whom his great Maker *took such care to make,*
That from himself he did the Image *take;*
And this fair frame, in shining Reason *drest,*
To dignifie his Nature, *above* Beast. (ll. 60–5)

Next he praises Reason for enabling man to quest beyond material sense for knowledge of the cosmos, and imitates (as Pinto notes) a line from Lucretius's *De Rerum Natura* in praise of Epicurus.[8] This is a subtle passage. The ideas it advances are of so traditional a kind that it seems at first sight possible that Rochester is allowing the divine to put them over to us straight. A closer look reveals a disturbing quality in the language of the divine. A man who can throw together so lightly the two adjectives '*Blest glorious*' does not seem to be weighing his words, but to have a mechanically dutiful sense of the wonder of his theme. The vacuousness of the line: '*Whom his great* Maker *took such care to make*' strengthens this impression and the whole passage, laden as it is with laudatory epithets, seems to be saying something altogether too good to be true. The line from Lucretius is interesting, and is perhaps ironical. If the divine is attempting to argue *ad hominem*, and enlist Rochester's favourite Lucretius in the defence of Reason, he only displays ignorance of his source. As Rochester well knew, Reason operating beyond the guidance of '*material sense*' was precisely what Lucretius distrusted, concepts such as '*Heav'n and Hell*' precisely what he praised Epicurus for exploding.[9] Nearer to what would probably have won the approval of Lucretius is Rochester's own account of 'right *Reason*' in the latter part of this poem. Yet *A Satyr* is not entirely Lucretian; even the value of exploring the material universe, which Lucretius glories in, is doubted by Rochester's scepticism.

Thus the whole intervention of the divine, with its attempt to assert human dignity by reference to a divinely and benevolently ordered cosmic structure relating man to God, has been satirically undermined. What remains is the grim strength with which Rochester had described the human situation, before this ineffectual challenge was made:

Reason, an *Ignis fatuus*, in the *Mind*,
Which leaving light of Nature, sense behind;
Pathless and dang'rous wandring ways it takes,

[8] Cf. *A Satyr*, l. 69; *De Rerum Natura*, I, ll. 72–4 especially 73; Pinto, *Enthusiast in Wit*, p. 153–4.
[9] *De Rerum Natura*, I, ll. 62–79, 102–11. See Rochester, *Poems*, pp. 49–50.

Through errors, Fenny-*Boggs*, and Thorny *Brakes*;
Whilst the misguided follower, climbs with pain,
Mountains of Whimseys, heap'd in his own *Brain*:
Stumbling from thought to thought, falls head-long down,
Into doubts boundless Sea, where like to drown,
Books bear him up awhile, and makes him try,
To swim with Bladders of *Philosophy*;
In hopes still t'oretake the 'escaping light,
The *Vapour* dances in his dazled sight,
Till spent, it leaves him to eternal Night. (ll. 12–24)

The verse of this passage enacts the failure to erect structures of knowledge or belief in which human life has a significant place. It justifies Pinto's insistence that Rochester is a poet of exploration; the imagery is almost that of pilgrimage, pilgrimage not towards a goal but in search of one. But the quest fails; man is left confronting 'eternal Night'. This 'Night' is the darkness not of the unknown but of nullity, with which, on the extinction of Reason's deceptive light, human life is seen to be rounded. More specifically, and bearing in mind the possible parallel with Lucretius, 'Night' may express the extinction of the individual soul, and ultimately that of the universe.[10] Yet the poem is not entirely nihilistic. 'Our *Sphere* of Action, is life's happiness'—this still remains; within this sphere moral distinctions are still meaningful. It is here that Rochester's unfavourable comparisons of man to the lower animals, which come from Montaigne's *Apologie de Raimond Sébond* as well as from Boileau, are effectively introduced. Their force is greater than in Montaigne, for while he introduced them experimentally, as a kind of salutary medicine for human pride, within the wider and firm context of orthodox Christian belief, Rochester shows no such wider belief.[11] Thus while *A Satyr against Mankind* and *An Essay on Man* both seek to humble human vanity, they do so in opposite ways. Pope does so by depicting the divinely ordered hierarchy of creation of which man is merely a part; Rochester does so, in perhaps more devastating fashion, by showing the absence of such a hierarchy, the failure of man to fill and systematize the surrounding void. Pope's cosmos teems with life; Rochester's is almost empty. It is clear from this comparison that if D. M. Vieth is correct when he states that Rochester's 'innermost values were as conservative as Pope's and more conservative, perhaps,

---

[10] Ibid., III, ll. 445–58, 926–30; V, ll. 235–46, 373–5.
[11] See especially Montaigne's opening defence of Sébond for seeking to establish religious truths with reason. For specific parallels, see Rochester, *Poems*, pp. 215–19.

than Dryden's', conservatism must mean a fundamentally different thing in each case.[12]

The human predicament which Rochester expressed dramatically in *A Satyr against Mankind* he returned to in different ways in two probably later poems: *Upon Nothing* and the imitation from Seneca's *Troades*.[13] The connections between *A Satyr* and *Upon Nothing* are clear; man's '*Sphere* of Action' is surrounded by 'eternal Night' in the earlier poem, as here all things are snatched from Nothing only to be driven back to her 'hungry Womb' like slaves.[14] It is the principle of the 'Great Negative' that Rochester is concerned to express, and it is both logically and poetically appropriate that a poem which enacts the collapse of man's attempt to erect a system or find a faith should be followed up by an ironical encomium upon Nothing. Rochester continues his polemic against the purveyors of religious or philosophical metaphysics:

> Tho' Mysteries are barr'd from Laick Eyes,
> And the Divine alone, with Warrant, pryes
> Into thy Bosom, where the truth in private lies, . . .
>
> Great Negative, how vainly would the Wise,
> Enquire, define, distinguish, teach, devise?
> Didst thou not stand to point their dull Philosophies.[15]

The truth sought after by Divines does not exist; the only significance of philosophy lies in the very void which it seeks to fill and rationalize. These statements are too close to the unambiguous passages of *A Satyr against Mankind* to be regarded as the reverse of what Rochester really means. This poem springs from the experience of scepticism and unbelief. Unless we are prepared to detach it from the rest of Rochester's work, in particular from the preceding *Satyr against Mankind* and the

[12] D. M. Vieth, op. cit., p. 221.

[13] *A Satyr against Mankind* seems to have been written between 1674 and early 1676 (*Poems*, p. 214; Vieth, op. cit., p. 293). The earliest date we have for *Upon Nothing* is May 1678 (Vieth, op. cit., p. 399); it is probable though not certain that it post-dates *A Satyr*. Even were it contemporaneous, however, it would be hard to detach its attitudes from those of the longer, more explicit poem. The imitation from Seneca was probably written early in 1680 (*Poems*, pp. 179–80; Pinto, *Enthusiast in Wit*, pp. 187–90).

[14] Thus *Upon Nothing* is not a strictly Lucretian poem; Lucretius rejects the idea that the universe emerged from nothing, as likely to foster theories of divine creation (*De Rerum Natura*, I, ll. 146–58). But from the human viewpoint a disintegration of the universe to its primary particles is as near a return to nothing as makes no matter.

[15] Stanzas 8 and 10. The 1680 edition of Rochester's *Poems on Several Occasions* gives 'thy truth' for the last line of stanza 8 (ed. James Thorpe, 1950, p. 52) but the substantial sense remains the same.

succeeding imitation of Seneca, we must have care how readily we accept it as the 'most nearly archetypal expression' of 'the inverted world of Augustan satire' and 'an ironic eulogy of an Uncreation opposite to God's original act'.[16] That Rochester had the deepest doubts about God's original act should be clear from the foregoing discussion.

Where then is the irony? It pervades the poem, but is of a less thorough-going kind than that, say, of Swift's *Modest Proposal*. It lies in the elevation of nullity to the status of a mock-positive deity, and in the tributes the poet makes to this goddess. Just as in Erasmus's *Encomium Moriae* a claim directly true is often served up in the guise of irony, so here statements in mock-praise of the goddess. Nothing contain a kernel of literal truth. Rochester has changed the manner with which he expresses an unchanged predicament. He has replaced the powerful directness of *A Satyr* by a complex mock-heroic mode, whose humorous ingenuity of wit and word keeps the grim truth at bay. This poem, elevating nothingness into a deity as it does, certainly resembles in method such Augustan mock-heroic poems as *Mac Flecknoe*, *The Rape of the Lock* and *The Dunciad*; Pinto notes that 'the Triumph of Dullness at the end of The *Dunciad* probably owes a good deal to Rochester's Triumph of Nothing'.[17] That Pope learned much from this poem there can be no doubt; his imitation *On Silence*, of which two early manuscript versions exist, was begun in 1702 and underwent drastic revision before its publication in 1712. These early versions show that over a period of years the young Pope absorbed, understood and reflected on Rochester's poem.[18] We can see that Nothing, Folly and Dullness are connected in the minds of both poets; also that both poems employ a manner at once comic and grand. But most significantly it is the conception of the 'Great Negative'—Dullness or Nothing—that the two poems have in common. In the complexity of literary influences synthesized in Pope's mind to create *The Dunciad*, Rochester's *Upon Nothing*, with Milton's Chaos in the background, was the only one to suggest the mock-philosophical implications with which Dullness might be poetically endowed. At the beginning and end of *Dunciad* IV Dullness assumes an awesome generality; it is addressed as 'eternal Night', 'Uncreating word', 'Universal Darkness', (ll. 2,654,656)

[16] Vieth, op. cit., p. 106.

[17] V. de S. Pinto, 'John Wilmot and the Right Veine of Satire', *Essays and Studies*, 1953, p. 64.

[18] The first manuscript version is printed in Pope, *Minor Poems*, ed. Norman Ault and John Butt, 1954, pp. 463–4; the second (almost certainly not in Pope's hand) is to be found in the British Museum, Add. MSS. 28253, ff. 135–6.

and in this elevated blend of irony and fear we do indeed, I believe, find Pope close to Rochester. At the same time we must remember that long and complex poem *The Dunciad* as a whole. One of its unifying factors, strong in the earlier books but increasingly submerged as Dullness moves to her triumph, is the mock-parallel to the action of Virgil's *Aeneid*. While it is expressively significant that the parallel should be submerged in this way, its presence in the poem is an assurance that there is a positive standard to which Pope adheres. There is no such factor in *Upon Nothing*. Though Matter, Form and 'Rebel Light', set up like Lucifer in opposition to the original deity, the ultimate victory belongs to Nothing, as in Milton Lucifer must finally submit to God. 'Turn-Coat Time' is on her side; it is in the nature of things that Nothing, which permeates all, should in the end claim all. It is not in the nature of things for Pope that Dullness must *inevitably* triumph. That she does triumph in the poem is a consequence of the actions of men. These inferences are strengthened when we look beyond the two individual poems; Rochester had but recently written *A Satyr against Mankind*, while Pope had not long written *An Essay on Man*. In short, *Upon Nothing* is a sceptical and nihilistic work, lacking the moral assurance we associate with the term Augustan in English literature.

Rochester's outlook emerges even more plainly in his imitation from Seneca's *Troades*. Not only does he follow Seneca in denying the immortality of the soul, but he also totally transforms the calm and quiescent tone of his original; he imputes to the nature of things an energy and violence with which he also animates his poem. He has given it a contemptuous and hostile spirit; Seneca pities those who hope for immortality, Rochester sees through them and despises them. That Rochester should have made this poem so much his own and of his time (Seneca's *avidi* becoming the 'proud' and 'ambitious Zealot', that is the Puritan) shows that the view he expressed in *A Satyr* he continued to hold into the last winter of his life. This is a poem written outside and against the Christian tradition as to the nature of man and the wider context in which the Christian believes mortal life is led. While Pope does not treat specifically of immortality in *An Essay on Man* he is, despite his protests, an unashamed metaphysician, viewing man and his relation to the created order in a way with which Hooker, for example, would have sympathized.[19] The Augustan assurance which Rochester displays in the limited sphere of *An Allusion to Horace*—

[19] Cf. *Of the Laws of Ecclesiastical Polity*. I, iii, 2 with *An Essay on Man*, I, ll. 233–58.

that of a man confident in a stable and satisfying pattern of values—is not found in the poems where Rochester writes of man in general and his relation to the natural order.

III

When we compare Pope's and Rochester's presentation of man in general, we see the stark contrast between a poet of unbelief and a poet of belief.[20] This is even apparent in the relation between *Upon Nothing* and *The Dunciad*, where in satiric conception and procedure Pope had so much to learn from Rochester. This conclusion is relevant to an assessment of *A Very Heroical Epistle* and *An Epistolary Essay*.[21] These poems were once taken as direct expressions of Rochester's egoistic hedonism; Vieth's interpretation, on the other hand, parallels his interpretation of *Upon Nothing* and rests on the detection in each poem of 'a distinctive Augustan poetical technique': the use of systematic irony in a manner generally resembling *The Dunciad*, whose

> structure functions through ironic approval of a spectrum of disvalues
> ... diametrically opposed to the traditional Christian-classical standards
> shared by most of the contemporary audience. Whether the speaker of the
> poem is a *persona* who is himself satirized—a favorite device with
> Rochester—or remains anonymously omniscient, the satire operates by
> ironically replacing traditional norms with their direct contraries....
>
> (op. cit., p. 105)

Let us look at a passage from *A Very Heroical Epistle*. The speaker 'Bajazet' (Mulgrave) grandly absolves himself from any obligation to be constant in love:

> You may as justly at the *Sun*, repine,
> Because alike it does not always shine:
> No glorious thing, was ever made to stay,
> My blazing *Star*, but visits and away.
> As fatal to it shines, as those 'ith'*Skyes*,
> 'Tis never seen but some great *Lady* dyes.
> The boasted favor, you so precious hold,
> To me's no more than changing of my Gold
> What e're you gave, I paid you back in Bliss. . . . (ll. 18–26)

Clearly these lines express the mentality of egoism and pride; the

[20] A distinction applied by Pinto to Rochester and Milton (*Enthusiast in Wit*, p. 114).
[21] Vieth dates them respectively late summer 1675, and November or December 1679 (op. cit., pp. 107, 135).

crucial question, however, concerns Rochester's and our moral relation to the *persona*. If the poem is indeed systematically ironical then he is inviting us to ridicule and condemn. Yet this passage has a certain ambiguity. Though the notion of 'degree' is sufficiently flouted by the speaker to give us the measure of his egoism, and his vanity comically underlined in lines 22–3 particularly, the passage is subtly contrived to invite to some degree the reader's identification and sympathy. The speaker's protestations are not entirely ridiculous: constancy is *not* the rule in nature, glorious things *are* transient, the image of the gold is a compliment as well as an insult, there is a certain justice in the last line. Much of this Vieth ingeniously admits: the 'ironic inversion of traditional values undergoes a full 360 degrees rotation, so that passages taken out of context may seem to read quite straightforwardly' (op. cit., p. 128). The plain truth is that the irony is not consistent, but weaker at some times than others, and often temporarily absent. Rochester has balanced our critical detachment against a chance to identify with the speaker; this accounts for the quality of exultation in the passage. To find a similar type of satire to this, we shall do better to look back to Rochester's admired Ben Jonson than forward to Pope. Volpone's opening address to his gold has a similar complex effect.[22] Later in Rochester's poem the ironic ridicule grows stronger, and one thinks of Epicure Mammon rather than Volpone, but only at one point (the phrase: 'Secure in solid Sloth'—l. 41) does a comparison with *The Dunciad* seem appropriate. I conclude that this poem is not a work of consistent satirical irony but one which seeks to explore a world of egoism in a less committed way. It is not surprising to find such ambiguity since we know from *A Satyr against Mankind*, written about this time, that the 'Christian-classical' conception of the metaphysical hierarchy of degree, which Rochester does allude to in the present poem, did not command his allegiance.

Rochester's *Epistolary Essay From M.G. to O.B. Upon their mutual Poems* is more ambiguous than *A Very Heroical Epistle*. Vieth is the first critic to read it, not as a kind of confession, but a work systematically deploying an ironical *persona*. It is on this interpretation of the poem itself that he builds his theory that 'M.G.' is *Mul*Grave, 'O.B.' '*Old Bays*' (i.e. Dryden); that the 'mutual Poem' is Mulgrave's and Dryden's collaborative *Essay upon Satyr*; and that the date of composi-

[22] Act I, Scene I, ll. 1–27; Rochester *An Allusion*, l. 81. Though Jonson does subscribe to the metaphysic of 'degree' he lets too much exultation into Volpone's tone for the passage to be termed 'ironical'.

tion must therefore be 1679 rather than 1669 (op. cit., pp. 119–35). Certainly, many lines in this poem resemble the egoistic statements of *A Very Heroical Epistle*; but when read in their context they also have a cogency which does much to modify what might otherwise have been simple irony. Consider the following passage:

> And this is all I'le say in my defence
> T'obtain one Line of your well-worded sense,
> I'le be content t'have writ the *British Prince*,
> I'me none of those who think themselves inspir'd,
> Nor write with the vain hope to be admir'd;
> But from a Rule I have (upon long tryal)
> T'avoid with care all sort of self-denyal.
> Which way soe're, desire and fancy lead,
> (Contemning Fame) that Path I boldly tread;
> And if exposing what I take for wit,
> To my dear self a Pleasure I beget,
> No matter though the cens'ring *Criticks* fret.
> These whom my *Muse* displeases are at strife,
> With equal spleen against my course of life,
> The least Delight of which I'le not forgo,
> For all the flatt'ring praise *Man* can bestow. (ll. 9–24)

We are struck first by the compliment to Dryden; here at least is a plausible judgement. To disclaim inspiration (l. 12) is not a mark of arrogance, nor is an indifference to admiration (l. 13); in fact 'admiration' probably does not carry the modern sense of well-grounded approval, but the older Horatian sense of uncritical adulation which we find in the Sixth Epistle of Horace's First Book (*Nil admirari*) and which Pope was to use some fifty years later: 'With foolish *Pride* my Heart was never fir'd,/Nor the vain Itch *t'admire*, or *be admir'd*.'[23] M.G.'s contempt for 'Fame', which Vieth sees as a violation of the Augustan norm of deference to educated good taste, is in fact a perhaps equally Augustan scorn of capricious and uninformed public opinion. Such phrases as: 'saucy Censurers', 'dull age', 'cens'ring Criticks', 'flatt'ring praise' seem to confirm this reading. It is not clear that such ordinary sentiments must be ironically intended. But perhaps the challenging and egoistic statements make them so? Yet unlike those in *A Very Heroical Epistle* these lack any kind of comic inflation; in fact they are rather soberly put. Again Rochester is careful to blend the egoistic with the acceptable, so that each modifies the reader's reaction

---

[23] *Imitations of Horace, The Fourth Satire of John Donne*, ll. 9–10.

to the other. Having struck this balance in the earlier part of the poem, Rochester can introduce his comparison of writing verse to physical excretion without totally banishing our doubt that there could be some seriousness in its surface-meaning. Any identification with M.G. is reduced to the barest minimum by the sense of revulsion created, yet is there not some truth in the comparison? Is the poet, who in *A Satyr against Mankind* preferred the animals' life of desire and satisfaction to the human life of questing and pretension, incapable of suggesting that self-expression at its lowest may be a sufficient reason for writing verse? As an earlier critic points out, 'his chase had a beast in view, the "happy beast" '.[24] Vieth defends his judgement that this passage is one of undiluted irony by reference to at first sight similar passages in Pope's *Peri Bathous* and *Dunciad* II 'whose irony is beyond question' (op. cit., p. 124). But Augustanism is not a set of absolute attitudes and conventions which all poets of the period use in the same way; that Pope wrote one way in 1728 does not mean that Rochester must have done exactly the same in 1679. *The Epistolary Essay* has now passed its climax; M.G.'s egoism has passed through its most objectionable phase, which is succeeded by a rearguard argument in his own defence. God is hardly generous in providing for man's needs; like a proud but impoverished Lord He keeps more creatures than He can maintain. Only of wit is this not held so, since no man could hold an opinion if he distrusted his own wit. Thus, says M.G., self-esteem is the only 'fame' that is meaningful. Again Vieth finds unmodified irony; these propositions violate the concept of the 'great chain of being' and the principle of plenitude to which, he argues, Rochester as a man of his age must subscribe. But *A Satyr against Mankind* and the imitation from Seneca show that these are precisely the notions to which Rochester did not subscribe; far from directing his irony towards a final condemnation of M.G.'s views, he seems to be following the argument to its conclusion with impartial interest. The speaker now regains a degree of assent from the reader; the quotation from Descartes in line 64, which Pope noted in the margin of his edition of Rochester, seems to clinch this; so does M.G.'s return, at the end of the poem, to the theme of his contempt for 'common Fame' and 'Idle Rumour'.[25] I do not dispute that Rochester is using a *persona* in this poem, nor that M.G. is probably his enemy Mulgrave, and O. B. Dryden. These are valuable and to me convincing

[24] Francis Whitfield, *A Beast in View: A Study of the Earl of Rochester's Poetry*, 1936, pp. 56–7. Cf. *Tunbridge-Wells*, ll. 171–80; *A Satyr against Mankind*, ll. 1–7, 114–44.
[25] See Vieth, op. cit., pp. 126–7.

suggestions. My contention is rather that the irony of this poem is not a simple '180 degree reversal' of traditional 'norms'; it is spasmodic rather than systematic; the *persona* is made deliberately ambiguous so that Rochester is less attacking a complex of attitudes he already disapproves of than exploring a state of mind through the poem, and prompting approval or disapproval from the reader as each seems appropriate. Fittingly enough for a poet who did not subscribe to the 'Christian-classical' norms implicit *and* explicit in the work of Dryden and Pope, Rochester is less the resolved satirist here, than the satirically inclined explorer. There is thus some truth in the comments of those critics who, in this poem and *A Very Heroical Epistle*, sensed Rochester talking of himself.[26] There is nothing comparable to this effect in the formal satire of Pope whose subtler and more delicate *personae* invariably express different moods of himself *as satirist*. True, *The Dunciad* does explore as well as satirise the world of Folly, and Swift, in a manner closer to Rochester, uses *personae* to this end in *A Tale of a Tub*; to this extent the two poems of Rochester have affinities with these major achievements of Augustan satire.[27] But to find a better pattern for the way Rochester's satire works here we should look back, through the ambiguously satirical oratory of his own Alexander Bendo's Bill, to such protean satirical figures as Erasmus's Folly, Rabelais's Panurge or Cervantes's Quixote; Rochester's mood might sometimes be described as the soul of these satirists in a desolate world of doubt.[28]

I have been led, in this essay, to apply the term 'exploration' to the poems discussed. Exploration should be regarded as one of the characteristic features of Rochester's poetry. Even if we turn to one of the formal satires most resembling Pope, *Artemisa to Cloe*, we notice that the 'Fine Lady' who tells among other things the story of Corinna is twice observed by Artemisa to be 'So very wise, yet so impertinent' (ll. 148–9, 256–7). Rochester thus introduces into the satire a note of ambiguity similar to that more strongly present in *A Very Heroical Epistle* and *An Epistolary Essay*. In the world of Rochester's satire

[26] See, e.g. Pinto, 'John Wilmot and the Right Veine of Satire', loc. cit., p. 62; *Enthusiast in Wit*, pp. 148–9.

[27] On the *exploration* of folly in *The Dunciad*, see my article 'The "New World" of Pope's *Dunciad*', *Essential Articles for the Study of Alexander Pope*, ed. Maynard Mack, 1964, pp. 739–60.

[28] See Thomas Alcock and Rochester, *The Famous Pathologist . . .*, ed. V. de S. Pinto, Nottingham University Miscellany No. 1, 1961, pp. 32–8. It is relevant to note Alcock's description of Bendo '. . . in an old overgrown Green Gown which he religiously wore in memory of Rabelais his Master . . .', op. cit., p. 29.

wisdom and folly are often less distinct than in the formal satire of Pope; hence the quality of exploration. We get the same impression from the songs, still more from the biography: the picture of a man caught in a '*Perplexity* of endless *Thought*', pleasing or otherwise; a man who in many respects lacked a stable pattern of any but the most elementary values, yet who was never without an obscure sense that there ought to have been more that he could believe. The contemptuous phrase 'Lumber of the World', in the imitation from Seneca, probably gets its bite from an opinion he confessed to Burnet about this time: 'He said, They were happy that believed: for it was not in every man's power'.[29]

The choice lies between regarding Rochester as a complete Augustan in the sense that Pope is an Augustan, or as a poet who, while Augustan and like Pope in some respects, has more in him of the adventurer through experience than Dryden or Pope. It is the choice between Rochester as a poet who, like Pope and Dryden, subscribed to a complex inheritance of 'Christian-classical' values, or as a poet in very many respects of scepticism and unbelief. The first view is that of D. M. Vieth, the second that of Pinto. The second, I suggest, is the more accurate of the two.

University College, Swansea

---

[29] Gilbert Burnet, *Some Passages of the Life and Death of the Right Honourable John Earl of Rochester* . . ., 1680, p. 71. Rochester's basic values were summed up in what he told Burnet at the end of his life: the 'Two *Maxims* of his *Morality* then were, that he should do nothing to the hurt of any other, or that might prejudice his own health. . . .', ibid., p. 38, to which we should add his contempt for self-importance and pretension.

Goldsmith and Sheridan: Satirists of Sentiment

ALLAN RODWAY

I F the latter half of this title is ambiguous, it is then the more apposite
to the work of Goldsmith and Sheridan. For their anti-sentimental
plays must seem, to anyone familiar with the Restoration mode they
purported to revive, to be themselves affected by the usurping Genteel
or Sentimental mode they purported to attack. Perhaps it is significant
that Goldsmith, the initiator of the attack, particularly admired
Farquhar—whose *Beaux Stratagem* (referred to in *She Stoops to
Conquer*, Act III) may be stylistically late-Restoration but is surely
early-Sentimental in terms of plot.

This ambiguity of attitude, present in all their comedies, though
not to the same degree, may well go far to explain their holding the
stage so much better than the more consistent work of Jonson and the
Restoration dramatists; for the age symbolically initiated by the accession of a Protestant Dutchman has not yet closed. No doubt the
naïve-bourgeois period is dead, and Goldsmith and Sheridan deserve
some credit for helping to pull the pillows away; but the aristocratic
sophistication of Restoration theatre has hardly yet been replaced by
a sophistication of the intelligentsia—seemingly the only possible
audience for a comedy truly unsentimental without being merely
cynical.

The taste of the Hanoverian age is sufficiently indicated by the fact that Goldsmith was forced to omit his bailiffs scene from performances of *The Good-Natur'd Man* (1768), as unpardonably 'low'. Similarly Sheridan, as manager of Drury Lane, feeling unable to present Vanbrugh's *Relapse* as a straight revival, reduced it to his *Trip to Scarborough* (1777). Both, then, had literary cause for disliking the dominant sentimental comedy (to say nothing of justifiable envy provoked by the greater rewards of inferior writers). However, Goldsmith is to be found in opposition before he ever wrote a play, witness his essay on 'Sentimental Comedy' (*Essays 1758–65*, No. 32):

> Which deserves the preference,—the weeping sentimental comedy so much in fashion at present, or the laughing and even low comedy which seems to have been last exhibited by Vanbrugh and Cibber?
> ...
> But there is one argument in favour of sentimental comedy which will keep it on the stage in spite of all that can be said against it. It is, of all others, the most easily written. Those abilities that can hammer out a novel are fully sufficient for the production of a sentimental comedy.

(True enough, at any rate, of the abilities which could hammer out a novel like *The Vicar of Wakefield*.) In *Retaliation* (1774), even after the success of his own plays, he complains of Cumberland:

> His gallants are all faultless, his women divine,
> And comedy wonders at being so fine;
> Like a tragedy-queen he has dizened her out,
> Or rather like tragedy giving a rout.
> His fools have their follies so lost in a crowd
> Of virtues and feelings that folly grows proud. ...

It comes as no surprise, then, to find the Preface to *The Good-Natur'd Man* opening with a confession of the author's prepossession 'in favour of the poets of the last age', or the Prologue to *She Stoops to Conquer* (1773) lamenting the death of Comedy:

> Pray would you know the reason why I'm crying?
> The Comic muse, long sick, is now a-dying!
> To *her* a mawkish drab of spurious breed,
> Who deals in *sentimentals* will succeed!

—an idea Sheridan borrows for his Prologue to *The Rivals* (1775):

> Look on her well—does she seem formed to teach?
> Should you expect to hear this lady—preach?
> Is grey experience suited to her youth?

> Do solemn sentiments become that mouth?
> Bid her be grave, those lips should rebel prove
> To every theme that slanders mirth or love.
> Yet thus adorn'd with every graceful art
> To charm the fancy and yet reach the heart—
> Must we displace her? And instead advance
> The goddess of the woful countenance—
> The sentimental muse!—Her emblems view,
> The Pilgrim's Progress, and a sprig of rue!
> View her—too chaste to look like flesh and blood—
> Primly portrayed on emblematic wood!

Yet, for all this, the first of these dramas—and the most strongly anti-sentimental in purport—betrays most clearly an underlying sentimental motive. True enough, Honeywood, the protagonist of *The Good-Natur'd Man* seems to be a vehicle for satire upon unintelligent, and ultimately calamitous, benevolence, since he is censured from beginning to end:

> *Sir William:* Don't let us ascribe his faults to his philosophy, I entreat you. No, Jarvis, his good nature arises rather from his fears of offending the importunate, than his desire of making the deserving happy

---

> *Sir William:* ... I saw, with indignation, the errors of a mind that only sought applause from others; that easiness of disposition which, though inclined to the right, had not courage to condemn the wrong. I saw with regret those splendid errors, that still took name from some neighbouring duty. Your charity that was but injustice; your benevolence that was but weakness; and your friendship but credulity.

These censures are from the opening and the concluding scenes of the play, and there are plenty like them in between—together with many examples of foolish behaviour, notably Honeywood's courting Miss Richland, whom he loves and is loved by, on behalf of someone else. But there is never any doubt that he is precisely one of those delineated in the essay on 'Sentimental Comedy' whose 'Faults and Foibles the Spectator is taught not only to pardon, but to applaud ... in consideration of the goodness of their hearts'. Perhaps this is because Goldsmith was trying to do something fairly subtle. Sir William Honeywood is not only opening the dyke to sentimentality, but is also making an intelligent point, when he says:

> Yet we must touch his weakness with a delicate hand. There are some faults so nearly allied to excellence, that we can scarce weed out the vice without eradicating the virtue.

As if to emphasize the element of underlying virtue Honeywood is allowed some rather skilled verbal fencing with the acute Miss Richland (whose love for him, of course, also implies more merit in Honeywood than is good for satire). Unhappily, the result is not so much a complex character as an improbable one, nor so much refined satire as satire adulterated. Not only is almost every speech of censure qualified in some way, but the plot—in defiance of the facts of finance and feminine psychology—allows the victim to wind up with wealth and a prize among women.

Sheridan has a harder edge. Sentimentality of a romantic kind is genuinely satirized in Lydia Languish and, of a moral kind, in Joseph Surface; both are ruthlessly and amusingly exposed. There is no double feeling here. But is it not a species of sentimentality to ask admiration for Charles Surface, just the type that has never lacked sympathy—nor ever deserved it ('God's life, don't talk about it: poor Stanley's wants are pressing, and if you don't make haste, we shall have some one call that has a better right to the money')? Again, could anything be less principled or more deserving satire than Sir Oliver's generosity and forgiveness, all because Charles has sentimentally spared his picture in the auction. Indeed, the introduction of Sir Oliver at all to make 'a test of [the brothers'] hearts' is a piece of structural sentimentality. Restoration dramatists found no need for a moral arbiter and judge, but trusted to their own and the audience's intelligence to see that the characters were properly 'placed'.

In satirizing one brother Sheridan elevates the other beyond his deserts. Thus scapegrace sentimentality is the price of moral satire. However, this may be a matter of conscious preference; but Sheridan's attitude to the scandalmongers is ambivalent beyond doubt. They are strongly condemned yet greatly relished, a whole scene being lovingly devoted to their epigrammatic dissections; so that the pleasure of righteous indignation at scandal is combined with that of indulging in it.

Of course, much of the superiority of *The School for Scandal* over any other of Sheridan's plays comes from the interlocking of two stories: that of Lady Sneerwell and her circle and that of the Teazles and Maria; and since both are so much involved in scandalmongering, it may well be felt that any question of intrusive sentimentality is of little importance beside the ambivalent attitude to scandalmongering. But the two brothers—Joseph in particular—are so important, as link characters that in fact the sentimentality weighs by far the more heavily. The keener edge of Sheridan's dialogue may give the illusion that he was less prone to this fault than Goldsmith. But a man capable of taking the preposterous *Pizzaro* seriously, was obviously just as soft-centred as the perpetrator of *The Vicar of Wakefield* and *The Deserted Village*:

> The truth is, Sheridan's taste in the sublime was uncertain—he could not be trusted to distinguish the true from the false. As long as his wit had the upper hand he was safe, but when his heart took charge the case was very different (Lewis Gibbs, *Sheridan*, 1947, p. 198).

Gibbs is right about Sheridan's wit; it is all important. Not only was he prone to be sentimental while attacking sentiment, but also he lacked invention—even the much-laboured *School for Scandal* having some difficulty in keeping the action going. Goldsmith, on the other hand, a quicker and slacker writer, relies much more on situation—though the distinction is not absolute. Sheridan has his masterly 'screen' scene, Goldsmith his moments of wit, like Croaker's 'A man is tired of getting the better before his wife is tired of losing the victory'. Too ambiguous to be distinct, they are too individual not to be different.

However, since Goldsmith's is basically drama of situation, his characters are often 'humour' characters, but (Honeywood excepted) not of the Jonsonian kind. Their humours tend to be seen as funny but not absurd. *She Stoops to Conquer*, indeed, is farce pure and simple, and not comedy-manqué, like *The Good-Natur'd Man*. And as its humour characters are thus tenderly treated, it straightway inclines towards sentimentality. Hardcastle—like Honeywood and Croaker, like Marlowe—is a character one might hear of from raconteurs but would never meet:

> I love everything that's old: old friends, old times, old manners, old books, old wine; and I believe, Dorothy (*taking her hand*), you'll own I've been pretty fond of an old wife.

He is what he is, not because Goldsmith is making some comic point, but merely to raise a laugh by his oddity and subserve the funny situation to come, when Marlowe takes him for an old-fashioned inn keeper. Nevertheless, in the minor figures Goldsmith often dispenses with the 'idea' of a character; and even the major ones—perhaps in proportion as they are *not* Jonsonian—do have some life. In part, no doubt, because they are infused with feeling (as they are not armoured in epigram, the sentimentality doesn't have to go into the action as in Sheridan), and in part because they are allowed a certain unexpectedness. Hardcastle turns out to be sensible and honest as well as crusty, Tony Lumpkin to be good-natured and keen-witted as well as spoilt. In a sense, the characters have an existence apart from that facet necessary for the plot of recurrent situation—a plot in which even the stagiest device (such as Lumpkin's real age being concealed to make a concluding denouement) seems not out of keeping. Such plots do not depend on character; that is why they need it so desperately.

In Sheridan, there is less feeling for idiosyncracy and idiom of character, but less need for it, as there is more wit. Unlike Honeywood and the others, Sheridan's characters start off as possible beings. But as characters of wit, they remain fixed; that is, they do not evolve or display unexpected facets, so as to become as rounded as the requirements of plot might allow, but occasionally they do speak out of character, becoming the writer's mouthpiece for some felicity unlikely in them; witness Fag's explanatory metaphor, nicely—and more plausibly—capped by his master:

> *Absolute:* You blockhead, never say more than is necessary.
> *Fag:* I beg pardon, sir—I beg pardon—but, with submission, a lie is nothing unless one supports it. Sir, whenever I draw on my invention for a good current lie, I always forge endorsements as well as the bill.
> *Absolute:* Well take care you don't hurt your credit by offering too much security.

However, being fixed characters, they take themselves seriously, so to speak, and are stripped of their rags of seeming (or, like Faulkland and Charles Surface, are excused) without awareness of the audience; Sheridan *does* have a point; the *Rivals* and *School for Scandal* are both comedies, not farces. Goldsmith's characters—in *She Stoops to Conquer* anyway—know they are only there for fun and often play up to, rather than play, their allotted parts. They display, as it were, a private feeling that after all there is more in them than first met the author's eye. Hence, they are able to throw a retrospective mock-heroic feeling over their troubles by concluding scenes with a Shakespearian tag ('Would it were bedtime and all were well' I, i) or to make sudden renunciations without embarrassment.

In Sheridan this is not possible; the characters must play their part and nothing but their part in his satiric world. As he is skilled only in the witty style, this can lead to some dichotomy. Faulkland's character is clearly and acutely analysed, but in a rather computer-like manner:

Unused to the fopperies of love, he is negligent of the little duties expected of a lover—but being unhackneyed in his passion, his affectation is ardent and sincere; and as it engrosses his whole soul, he expects every thought and emotion of his mistress to move in unison with his. Yet though his pride calls for this full return, his humility makes him undervalue those qualities in him, which would entitle him to it; and not feeling why he should be loved to the degree he wishes he still suspects that he is not loved enough. This temper I must own. . . .

When Faulkland himself appears, however, his language is that of the lover of typical sentimental comedies, and it is difficult to know whether this is meant satirically (in which case Julia's analysis was just a psychological show-off by Sheridan) or realistically as a passionate lover (in which case his idiom is very unfortunate for a play containing Lydia Languish). In short, it is difficult not to accuse Sheridan of opportunism here. Again, where he does attempt to adapt his wit to the character there is often failure

Mrs Malaprop may be more often funny than tiresome (and some of her mistakes are meaningful—the right wrong words for an implication), but David's 'Oons! some lion-headed fellow, I warrant, with his d——d double-barrelled swords and cut-and-thrust pistols!' is wit far too broad for its context. Sheridan is at his best as a pure stylist. The polish of Sir Benjamin Backbite's 'beautiful quarto page, where a neat rivulet of text shall meander through a meadow of margin' is no more *characteristic* than, say, the polish of Sir Peter Teazle's big speech on marriage (I, ii), which is out of keeping with his roughness of character but not with its stylistic context:

> 'Tis now six months since Lady Teazle made me the happiest of men— and I have been the most miserable dog ever since. . . . I had lost all comfort in life before my friends had done wishing me joy.

Sheridan's personages, in fact, are not humour-characters so much as wit-characters. And where, comparatively rarely, there *is* amusement from character, it is not of Goldsmith's sort. He shows absurd character in *action*—in a situation springing from, and dependent on the 'humour'—Sheridan shows it in *speech*. But not all the glittering protection of an even surface of wit—'No, no; the merit of these is the inveterate likeness—all stiff and awkward as the originals', 'an old *gouty* chair', 'and a damned disinheriting countenance'—nor all the intelligence that can bring Lady Teazle, by logical steps, to admit 'I must sin in my own defence, and part with my virtue to secure my reputation', can keep sentiment from seeping in.[1] In the event, Lady Teazle does not part with her virtue—any more than Marlowe can finally bring himself to betray the supposed chambermaid—and, what is worse, Sir Peter after all his ill-usage, and quite unasked, goes loudly making over money to her, while she listens, and reforms, behind the screen. And Charles, like Honeywood, is rewarded rather for virtue of soul than deed—just as in any sentimental comedy.

University of Nottingham

[1] The following item—for which I am indebted to Professor Boulton—is a small but psychologically significant instance:

> *Rowley:* . . . and believe me, sir, you will find in the youngest brother one who, in the midst of folly and dissipation, has still, as our immortal bard expresses it,—'a heart to pity, and a hand, open as day, for melting charity'. (III, i)

The immortal bard in question is Charles Churchill, who doesn't presume to flatter his subject, Wilkes, with the sentimental phrase 'for melting charity'. And in context the difference becomes still more marked:

> And strictly weighs, in apprehension clear,
> Things as they are, and not as they appear.
> With thee, Good-Humour tempers lively Wit,
> Enthron'd with Judgement, Candour loves to sit,
> And Nature gave thee, open to distress
> A heart to pity, and a hand to bless. (*Prophecy of Famine*)

Edmund Burke's *Letter to a Noble Lord:*
Apologia and Manifesto

JAMES T. BOULTON

THE century of aristocratic privilege was also that of men like Defoe, Pope, Johnson or Garrick; men whose reputation derived not from hereditary rank but solely from personal talents. Burke was of their number and shared their pride. Indeed Pope's scornful repudiation of the privileged litterateur in his *Letter to a Noble Lord*—

> You, who are no sooner born, but in the lap of the Graces; no sooner at school, but in the arms of the Muses; no sooner in the World, but you practised all the skill of it . . . you may well give up the poor talent of turning a Distich.[1]

and the famous rejection of aristocratic patronage in Johnson's letter to Chesterfield, find their counterpart in Burke's *Letter to a Noble Lord*. 'I was not, like his grace of Bedford, swaddled, and rocked, and dandled into a legislator; "*Nitor in adversum*" is the motto for a man like me.'[2] Burke always readily admitted about men 'of great families and hereditary Trusts and fortunes': 'if their conduct and example hands down their principles to their successors', then they are like 'the great Oaks

[1] *Works*, ed. Joseph Warton, 1797, Vol. III, p. 342.
[2] *Works*, 1815–27, Vol. VIII, p. 27.

that shade a Country and perpetuate [their] benefits from Generation to Generation'. By comparison, Burke and his kind were 'but annual plants that perish with [their] Season and leave no sort of Traces behind them'.[3] But the conditional 'if' was used advisedly; veneration was not automatically extended to hereditary rank. The new man too had his pride, the result of 'doing [his] duty agreably to [his] own Ideas, within the Laws of the land, and the Rules and orders of the Body to which [he belonged]'.[4] And the moral integrity, achievement and consequent reputation became in their turn his distinctive legacy for his children. Burke expressed such aspirations—in a way that strikingly anticipated part of his reason for writing the *Letter to a Noble Lord*—in a private letter to the Bishop of Chester twenty-five years before. The Bishop had attacked Burke and his reputation; on behalf of his son Burke rejected the accusations:

> My Lord, I may have very little to leave him but the Character, the freinds, I would add . . . the example of his Father. It is most essential to him that these should not be rendered vile, or cheap, or odious in the opinion of mankind.[5]

This was in 1771 after only five years in the Commons; in 1794 Burke retired after nearly thirty years as a parliamentarian, and within a few months his only child, Richard, was dead. At a blow his hopes to have become 'a sort of founder of a family'[6] were shattered; and Pitt's intention to ennoble his family (with Burke as Lord Beaconsfield) was abandoned. However, Pitt at once proposed (on 30 August 1794) to grant Burke a Civil List pension of £1200 and to introduce a bill into Parliament to increase that provision. On the second proposal he changed his mind. Possibly because of the growing unpopularity of Burke's fervent advocacy of the anti-French war and the likelihood of personal attacks on the grief-stricken man, Pitt arranged for a further grant to be made to him from the West Indian 4½% duties at the disposal of the Crown. Parliament's consent was not necessary; its approval was not invited.

Pitt's tactics—though they secured Burke a much-needed pension totalling £3700—were probably humiliating to one of the most sensitive as well as celebrated parliamentarians of the day. But worse was to follow. During a debate in the Lords on the Treason Bill (13 November 1795) the Duke of Bedford denounced ministerial cor-

---

[3] *The Correspondence of Edmund Burke*, ed. L. S. Sutherland, Cambridge, 1960, Vol. II, p. 377.
[4] Ibid., p. 269.   [5] Ibid., p. 257.   [6] *Works*, Vol. VIII, p. 45.

ruption of the kind he thought was illustrated 'by the places they have created for the accommodation of their friends; by the pensions they have bestowed on their minions, and on those very persons who were the Advocates of economy'.[7] This oblique reference to Burke and his attempts in 1780 to curb the royal power exerted through patronage and pensions, became an explicit condemnation in the speech of the Earl of Lauderdale. He inquired:

> What were the people of this country, oppressed and impoverished as they are, to think, when they saw enormous grants heaped on such a man as Mr Burke, who, at one period of his life, had inveighed against the practice of allowing considerations of such magnitude as he had now received, to any person whatever, let his merit be what it would, and a man who had been the instrument of involving this country in a war, which had exhausted the revenues of the State and which threatened in its consequences to annihilate the rights of the people.[8]

Any public attack on his pension was galling; that it should originate in the Lords, the sanctuary of hereditary privilege which Burke had sought to uphold against (what Lord Grenville, in his defence, described as) 'the rude assaults of dangerous innovations', was bitterly ironic; and that in the case of Bedford his assailant's fortune should ultimately derive from Crown grants, gave the final provocation. Both as a statesman and as a distinguished commoner Burke's reputation was at stake.

Within four days of the beginning of the debate Burke wrote to his friend William Windham who had defended him in the Commons: '... I had made some progress in a Letter to Lord Grenville, who behaved handsomely in the House of Lords; in that I took some Notice (as much as he deserved) of the Duke of Bedford.'[9] The *Letter to a*

[7] *Parliamentary Register*, Vol. XLV (1796), p. 108.
[8] Ibid., p. 110.
[9] B.M. Add. MS. 37,843, fol. 85, quoted by kind permission of the Trustees of the British Museum. The identity of the 'Noble Lord' to whom the letter was addressed remains a matter of dispute. Since Robert Bisset's *Life of Burke* (1800) many writers have identified Earl Fitzwilliam as the addressee. The letter quoted above, however, seems to support Thomas W. Copeland (*Checklist of the Correspondence of Edmund Burke*, Cambridge, 1955, p. 234), Carl Cone (*Burke and the Nature of Politics*, Lexington, 1964, p. 450), and William B. Todd (*Bibliography of Burke*, 1964, p. 296) in their claim that Grenville was the 'Noble Lord'. But changes obviously occurred during the writing of the *Letter*. Bedford looms much larger in the published work than is suggested by Burke's remark; and the fact that Grenville is mentioned in the third person during the *Letter* makes it less likely that the work was being addressed to him. The truth may be that, though Burke set out with Grenville as the addressee, he gradually came to associate 'Noble Lord' not exclusively with one individual but generally with all men to whom both terms (in his view) would apply.

Noble Lord was published on 24 February 1796 and achieved immediate popularity. The ninth impression was on sale a week later; thirteen English impressions bear the date 1796.[10]

'A stab was attempted on my reputation, and on the goods of my creditors. Dukes and earls chose to be the assassins. I have appealed to the people against their pretended friends.'[11] In this passage from a letter to Mrs Crewe, Burke gave a clue to his purpose in the published work. He clearly intended to defend his reputation against open and the constitution against insidious attack. What is not clear from the remark to Mrs Crewe was his intention to vindicate the 'Novus Homo' (as he once described himself[12])—the man who had no status except that achieved through public service but whose political maturity gave him the right to uphold the constitution against men whose eminence depended solely on inherited rank. The evidence to support this claim will be considered later. It is relevant, however, to quote again from the letter to Windham, 17 November 1795. Of Bedford Burke remarked there: 'As to him I may say—Tecum est mihi Sermo Rubelli.' This was no mere Latin tag; Burke was surely conscious of the poem from which the words came. Juvenal's *Eighth Satire*, beginning 'Stemmata quid faciunt', was highly relevant to the gist of his pamphlet. In the context of the dispute over the French Revolution and the attack on himself as the defender of the established order, Burke too had the right to ask:

> quis enim generosum dixerit hunc qui
> indignus genere et praeclaro nomine tantum
> insignis? (ll. 30–2)

Bedford and Lauderdale, in his view, were unworthy of the aristocracy and its significant role in the social hierarchy. Burke himself was like the eloquent but low-class Roman who, Juvenal claims, would urge the cause of the ignorant nobleman. This was his intention: in the face of denigration from nobles who were blind to their own best interests, he had to plead the cause of aristocracy and to rebut the contempt they lavished on his reward for unstinting service to the state. For this reason Burke was much concerned in the *Letter* with 'nobility' both as an essential feature of the constitution and as a moral quality which did not inevitably accompany high rank.

---

[10] See William B. Todd, *Bibliography of Burke*, pp. 192–3.

[11] *The Correspondence of Edmund Burke*, ed. Fitzwilliam and Bourke, 1844, Vol. IV, p. 335.

[12] *The Correspondence of Edmund Burke*, ed. L. S. Sutherland, Vol. II, p. 128.

His choice of the eighteenth-century 'genre', the 'Letter to a Noble Lord', was thoroughly appropriate. It was—as used by Defoe, Pope or Johnson—associated both with the defence of the writer's reputation and the denunciation of his enemies; it allowed him to be personal without seeming egocentric; and, in Burke's hands, the letter encouraged the reader not only to feel that he was being addressed individually but also to identify himself with the 'Noble Lord' who shared the writer's views on the topics discussed. Rhetorically, therefore, the form was well chosen. Moreover Bedford provided a unifying focus of attention that forced Burke to concentrate on the particulars of an actual situation which was important to every reader. His quarrel was more than a personal tiff; its significance was bound up with a real political world that Burke knew through rigorous experience. His readers were reminded at every turn of its reality through the abundant imagery.

Time, and the wisdom that results from long experience, are important ideas from the outset. They are involved in Burke's personal apologia, his attack on Bedford, his defence of the constitution, and his view of the French Revolution. 'Before this of France, the annals of all time have not furnished an instance of a *complete* revolution'; 'eternal battle' must be waged against it; indeed only a tradition symbolized by the historic keep of Windsor was powerful enough to resist its catastrophic influence.[13] Such a situation was not for boys; not for a child in politics like Bedford who had 'never learned the rule of three in the arithmetick of policy and state'. This infant with his 'few and idle years' was not competent to pass judgment on national affairs or on the aged Burke, a man of 'long and laborious life'.[14] Contempt was thus excited for Burke's brash, inexperienced antagonist, and confidence in the author himself; sympathy too was aroused for the bereaved statesman—'the sorrows of a desolate old man'. And when Burke quoted Gray's line (from *The Descent of Odin*)—'Leave me, [oh] leave me to repose'—though he applied it to the dead whom the revolutionaries refused to leave undisturbed, his contemporaries would respond to his own deep world-weariness.[15]

Yet the writer of the *Letter* was no sentimentalist seeking to obtain easy sympathy. The element of personal apologia was inextricably involved with the rejoinder to Bedford and the political creed he represented. 'The awful state of the time, and not myself or my own

13 *Works*, Vol. VIII, pp. 5, 49–50.
14 Ibid., pp. 9–10.
15 Ibid., p. 6.

justification, is my true subject'; what he says of himself or Bedford 'is nothing more than a vehicle' to convey his sentiments on 'matters far more worthy' his readers' attention.[16] And the theme which fused the apologia with the attack on Bedford and on the revolutionary threat from France was that of the complete inversion of the natural order of things.

> I live in an inverted order. They who ought to have succeeded me have gone before me. They who should have been to me as posterity are in the place of ancestors.[17]

Instead of his being able to transmit a worthy name to his son, Burke was compelled to defend his reputation as an 'act of piety' to his son's memory. But the opening remark here was thematic with wide connotations. The French believed, for example, that '*the whole duty of man* consists in destruction'; Bedford's assault on Burke was the attempt of a child to reprimand an adult; his social eminence depended entirely on 'the herald's college' but this 'the philosophy of the sans culottes' (to which he apparently adhered) would 'abolish with contumely and scorn'; and, the most ironic inversion of all, the commoner Burke had diligently defended the aristocratic system against republicanism while Bedford had been his traducer.[18] This paradox evidently fascinated Burke; he toys with it ironically for nearly eight pages. He speculates on the fate of Bedford who, preying on Burke, would be himself the prey of the revolutionaries, that 'misallied and disparaged branch of the house of Nimrod. They are the duke of Bedford's natural hunters; and he is their natural game'.[19] He reduces Bedford to the level of a mouse watched by 'the grave, demure, insidious, spring-nailed, velvet-pawed, green-eyed philosophers'; he describes the way in which the French would conduct their '*agrarian* experiment' on the duke's vast estates, or reduce his buildings to rubble in order to obtain 'true democratick explosive insurrectionary nitre'. The speculation culminates in an excellently sardonic passage in which Bedford becomes a carcase in a butcher's shop:

> Is it not a singular phenomenon, that whilst the sans-culotte carcase-butchers, and the philosophers of the shambles, are pricking their dotted lines upon his hide, and like the print of the poor ox that we see at the

[16] Ibid., p. 34.
[17] Ibid., p. 47.
[18] Ibid., pp. 37, 52.
[19] Ibid., p. 52. Cf. Milton: 'men not beasts shall be his [Nimrod's] game', *Paradise Lost*, Bk. XII, l. 30.

shop-windows at Charing-cross, alive as he is, and thinking no harm in the world, he is divided into rumps, and sirloins, and briskets, and into all sorts of pieces for roasting, boiling, and stewing, that all the while they are measuring *him*, his Grace is measuring *me*; is invidiously comparing the bounty of the crown with the deserts of the defender of his order, and in the same moment fawning on those who have the knife half out of the sheath—poor innocent!

> *Pleas'd to the last, he crops the flow'ry food,*
> *And licks the hand just rais'd to shed his blood.*[20]

The theme of inversion is admirably clinched in this passage; the irony of the situation is conveyed through what is essentially a cartoonist's vision.

Bedford served to focus Burke's contempt; but he did more than that. For, throughout, associated with him are ideas of destruction, tyranny, and rapacity; and these ideas are indelibly linked with the revolutionaries to whose philosophy he subscribed. Language and imagery identify the man with the group. Burke traced the origin of Bedford's wealth to the first Russell's support for Henry VIII, a 'jackall in waiting' to 'a *levelling* tyrant'; Russell thrived in consequence of pillage, wretchedness and injustice; and, like the tyrant Macbeth, he merited 'curses, not loud but deep' (a quotation whose original context confirms Burke's awareness of the theme of inverted order previously discussed).[21] The French are described through animal imagery— 'They have tygers to fall upon animated strength. They have hyenas to prey upon carcasses'; they are hunters of men; and 'the revolution harpies . . . are foul and ravenous birds of prey'.[22] Both through statement and imaginative suggestion Bedford and the French were identified with disorder and destruction; the man was representative of the movement.

Burke invariably associated himself in the *Letter* with an order of things which was at once traditional, creative, and continuous. At the time of Lord North he was connected with men who pursued 'a liberty inseparable from order, from virtue, from morals, and from religion'; his Economical Reform Bill was designed to apply 'a remedy to the grievance complained of', to be 'healing and mediatorial'; he detested 'a cold penury' that may 'blast the abilities of a nation, and stunt the growth of its active energies'; and in the comparison between his merits

---

[20] *Works*, Vol. VIII, p. 63.
[21] Ibid., pp. 38, 42.
[22] Ibid., pp. 5–6, 21.

and those of the first Russell, Burke stressed his own concern with economic health and growth, and with freedom.[23] This theme of creative order culminates in the introduction of Lord Keppel who dominates the final ten pages of the pamphlet. Keppel—the uncle of Bedford, and the popular (and thus rhetorically valuable) idol of seventeen years earlier when he was acquitted by a court-martial—is Burke's mouthpiece; he is, as it were, Burke's 'Man of Ross', unsophisticated but of the highest integrity, intellectually and emotionally honest. Imagery of natural growth is used of him; and his authority is adduced for Burke's conception of aristocracy, 'not as an excuse for inglorious sloth, but as an incitement to virtuous activity'.

> He considered . . . that a man born in an elevated place, in himself was nothing, but every thing in what went before, and what was to come after him . . . he felt that no great commonwealth could by any possibility long subsist, without a body of some kind or other of nobility, decorated with honour, and fortified by privilege. . . . He felt that no political fabrick could be well made without some such order of things as might, through a series of time, afford a rational hope of securing unity, coherence, consistency, and stability to the state.[24]

Judged by these values Bedford was an inglorious failure and the revolutionary philosophy a disastrous agent of disintegration.

There is no doubt that, within the framework of his repudiation of that philosophy, Burke was primarily concerned with the second strand in 'the triple cord'—of King, Lords, and Commons—'which no man can break'. Yet, despite his advocacy of an hereditary nobility, there runs through the *Letter* an unmistakable pride in the worth of the man who, without a title, has done his 'country important service'. Burke did not claim outright superiority for his kind over all aristocrats; however, alongside his defence of the aristocratic principle, he affirmed his belief in the essential 'nobility' of the 'Novus Homo'. And it is important to remember one current attitude to the talented but landless politician:

> If a man is famous for opposition, eloquence, ministerial compliance, or any thing else un-united with a pretty considerable property, he does not meet with the same attention as much inferior speakers, from the circumstance of their more considerable estates.[25]

[23] Ibid., pp. 15, 20, 23, 29, 39–43.
[24] Ibid., pp. 66–7.
[25] *Middlesex Journal*, 1774. Quoted by Donald C. Bryant in 'A Note on Burke's Parliamentary Character, 1774', *The Burke Newsletter*, Vol. V (1963), No. 1, p. 240.

The least degree of truth in this statement, in addition to the attack on him by the noble lords, was sufficient to provoke Burke's defence of the self-made man. His defence is expressed with the same fervour as drew from him, in the Commons in 1770, the Ciceronian retort: 'Novorum Hominum Industriam odisti.'[26] Burke affirms his complete independence—'I was not made for a minion [the term used of him in the Lords by Bedford] or a tool'; he had made his progress against adversity along a road barred with obstacles; and his political knowledge and experience alone afforded him the 'honour of being useful to [his] Country'.[27] The contrasts with Bedford are sharp. This 'overgrown duke' presumes 'to oppress the industry of humble men'; he is 'the leviathan among all creatures of the crown'; and Burke develops this memorable image to stress that the Crown had indeed *created* the Bedfords.

> It would not be gross adulation, but uncivil irony, to say, that he has any publick merit of his own to keep alive the idea of the services by which his vast landed pensions were obtained. My merits, whatever they are, are *original and personal*; his are *derivative*.[28]

Here is the central contrast: the man whose sole repute was inherited with his title, balanced and found wanting against the man whose nobility essentially resided in distinguished moral and intellectual qualities and political skills. Burke was claiming that the beneficiaries of the hereditary principle could not necessarily be entrusted with its defence; its proper defenders were those whose conviction of its rightness had been tested by adversity and experience. At the heart of one of the clearest vindications of hereditary nobility, then, lay a manifesto of the 'Novus Homo'; paradoxically appropriate to an age of revolution it could be expressed in Juvenal's line: 'nobilitas sola est atque unica virtus'.[29]

University of Nottingham

---

[26] *The Correspondence of Edmund Burke*, ed. L. S. Sutherland, Vol. II, p. 128.
[27] *Works*, Vol. VIII, p. 28.
[28] Ibid., pp. 31, 35, 36 (my italics).
[29] *Satires*, VIII, 20.

Crabbe and Shakespeare

G. R. HIBBARD

REGARDING the heroic as the highest form of poetry, the great
Augustans had more sense than to write it. Instead of seeking to rival
Homer, Vergil and Milton, Dryden and Pope preferred to translate the
Ancients into the idiom of their own time, to utilize the work of all
three, in no belittling spirit, for the purposes of mock-epic, and, above
all, to enrich their own poetry by studied and purposeful allusion to the
works of those whom they admired. The great Romantics substituted
Shakespearean tragedy for the epic as the supreme kind of poetic achievement. Rasher in enterprise and less restrained by self-criticism than the
Augustans had been, they also tried to write it. Ignoring the fact that
the theatre was moribund, oblivious of Dryden's warning that all that
could be accomplished in the Elizabethan manner had been done by the
Elizabethans themselves and that there were 'no bays to be expected
in their walks',[1] they set out to resurrect blank verse tragedy and
resuscitate Elizabethan diction. The consequence was a series of mis-
carriages, still births and monsters. In Shelley's *The Cenci*, which is
probably the best known of these misguided undertakings, the Augustan habit of significant allusion is replaced by a mingle-mangle of loose
evocative echoes, so that figures as different as Hamlet, King Lear and

---

[1] *Essays of John Dryden*, ed. W. P. Ker, Oxford, 1900, Vol. I, p. 99.

the Claudio of *Measure for Measure* jostle each other for attention in the same speech and, indeed, in a dozen lines or so of it.[2]

Yet, at the very time that all this was happening, George Crabbe was quietly demonstrating just how Shakespeare could be profitably utilized by a poet writing in the early nineteenth century. He made no attempt to write a blank verse tragedy. He stuck to the tale which he understood, to the couplet which he could handle and to a diction that had nothing of the archaic about it. But he alludes to Shakespeare, as Pope had alluded to Homer and to Horace. He takes material from the plays and adapts it to his own age and to the life and society that he knew. And, in the process of doing so, he lays himself open to a larger influence: something of Shakespeare's attitude, and especially of his humanity, passes into his own work with a broadening and fertilizing effect. While his poetry remains narrative, it also becomes more dramatic; a sense of the tragic now gives depth and resonance to the moralizing; reproof is sweetened with compassion.

Crabbe's knowledge of the plays, beginning apparently in early childhood,[3] became full and close. The readiest index to it is to be found in the epigraphs prefixed to each of the poems in the *Tales* of 1812. Without exception the quotations are taken from Shakespeare. They are always apt and are culled from a wide field, giving the impression that Crabbe had most of the plays at his finger-tips. Until he turned to Shakespeare for them, the choice of epigraphs had given him some trouble. At the end of his Preface to *The Borough* (1810) he writes with characteristic candour both about his motives in using them and the methods he employed to find them:

> I know not whether to some readers the placing two or three Latin quotations to a Letter may not appear pedantic and ostentatious, while both they and the English ones may be thought unnecessary. For the necessity I have not much to advance; but if they be allowable (and certainly the best writers have adopted them), then, where two or three different subjects occur, so many of these mottoes seem to be required: nor will a charge of pedantry remain, when it is considered that these things are generally taken from some books familiar to the school-boy, and the selecting them is facilitated by the use of a book of common-place. Yet with this help, the task of motto-hunting has been so unpleasant to me, that I have in various instances given up the quotation I was in pursuit of,

---

[2] *The Cenci*, V, iv, 48–60.
[3] See 'Silford Hall', *Posthumous Tales*, Tale I, ll. 135–40.

and substituted such English verse or prose as I could find or invent for my purpose.[4]

The true Augustan poet never found himself in this difficulty. It is one of the marks of difference between Crabbe and those whom he most admired and imitated—Dryden, Pope and Dr Johnson—that he was less at home with Latin poetry than they had been. The tradition he belonged to was essentially native, and he did his best work when he recognized this fact. It was with the writing of *The Borough* that he really found himself as a poet, and his turning to English sources for some of the epigraphs is a pointer to the way he was taking.

There was a further advantage to be gained from substituting Shakespeare for the classics as a source of allusion. Writing for a wide audience, Crabbe could not assume that they would all be familiar with the ancient writers. He could, and did, take it for granted that they would know Shakespeare. His later tales are studded with references to the plays. In 'Silford Hall', for example, he describes the temptation to run away from home, that comes over the hard-worked boy, Peter, by glancing at *The Merchant of Venice*:

> To him the Fiend, as once to Launcelot, cried,
> 'Run from thy wrongs!'—'Run where?' his fear replied.
> 'Run!'—said the Tempter; 'if but hard thy fare,
> Hard is it now—it may be mended there.' (ll. 63–6)

The method is utterly different from Shelley's. The allusion is precise and pointed, not a piece of unconscious plagiarism. It endorses the fact that Peter is something of a servant in his own home, it helps to establish the comic tone of the tale in which it occurs and it lends a touch of drama to the narrative.

In this instance, however, the effect of the allusion is passing and local; it does not colour the tale as a whole. But there are cases in Crabbe's poetry where the reference is on a much larger scale and serves to establish a kind of dialectical relationship between a tale and a play. All four epigraphs prefixed to 'The Wager' (*Tales*, XVIII) are drawn from *The Taming of the Shrew*. They strongly suggest that it was the last act of that play which provided Crabbe with the basic idea for his tale, and they compel one to read it with the play in mind. The result is a kind of dialogue between two ages which is also an appreciation of Shakespeare's drama. Crabbe strips the story of all its Elizabethan qualities. Petruchio

---

[4] *Poems by George Crabbe*, ed. A. W. Ward, Cambridge, 1905–7, Vol. I, p. 282. All subsequent quotations from Crabbe's works are taken from this edition.

and Lucentio become Clubb and Counter, not young gallants in search of a wife and a fortune, but sober partners in business. The linguistic exuberance and the elaborate intrigues of the original disappear. The world of the tale is the world that Crabbe knew: East Anglia, not Italy. But the essential differences in character between the two women involved are carefully preserved and even sharpened. Clubb's wife is independent by nature; like Katharina, she prefers to have her own way; but she can distinguish between the unimportant and the serious. Consequently, when her husband tells her that, in a moment of rashness and under provocation from Counter, he has laid a wager on her obedience, she raises no difficulties, but says:

> If I in trifles be the wilful wife,
> Still for your credit I would lose my life. (ll. 179–80)

Counter's wife, carefully chosen by him for her submissiveness, is the opposite type. Apparently soft and yielding, she uses her weakness to tyrannize over her husband. Clubb's wife sums up her and her kind in some quietly devastating lines at the end of the tale:

> These weeping willows, though they seem inclined
> By every breeze, yet not the strongest wind
> Can from their bent divert this weak but stubborn kind;
> Drooping they seek your pity to excite,
> But 'tis at once their nature and delight.
> Such women feel not; while they sigh and weep,
> 'Tis but their habit—their affections sleep;
> They are like ice that in the hand we hold,
> So very melting, yet so very cold;
> On such affection let no man rely:
> The husbands suffer, and the ladies sigh. (ll. 283–93)

For Crabbe *The Shrew* was clearly a play about marriage and about the kinds of relationship between husband and wife that make for success or failure in it. 'The Wager' is a piece of Shakespeare criticism as well as a domestic tale.

Although he knew the comedies particularly well—the only one to which I have not found a reference of some kind in his work is *Love's Labour's Lost*—it was the tragedies and the dark comedies which most affected Crabbe's own art. This influence first makes itself felt in *The Borough*, where, in a number of tales, he shows a deeper sympathy with human failings than he had done hitherto and an understanding of abnormal states of mind that had appeared in only one previous poem of his, *Sir Eustace Gray* (1807). The most powerful tale in the collection is 'Peter Grimes'. It is prefaced by three epigraphs: one from Scott's *Marmion*, one from *Richard III* and one from *Macbeth*. It is possible, of course, that Crabbe wrote the tale first and found the quotations afterwards, but the correspondences between the poem and the two plays are so close that it is hard not to believe that the plays were somewhere at the back of his consciousness while he was writing. Huchon is clearly of this opinion. Referring to the fact that the tale was, in part at least, based on actual events that Crabbe knew about, he writes:

> As for 'Peter Grimes', his name was plain Tom Brown, and if he did lose his apprentices in a very suspicious manner, he never saw the spectres rise from the water. The perusal of *Richard III* and the quest of pathos alone procured us those horrors.[5]

The connection between the spectres and *Richard III* is plain enough. The passage from the play that Crabbe quotes is part of Richard's soliloquy in V. 3:

> Methought the souls of all that I had murder'd
> Came to my tent, and every one did threat.

But far more is involved than these two lines indicate. The entire soliloquy seems to have been in Crabbe's mind, for what Richard expresses in it is his discovery that he has, after all, a conscience, and also his realization that the ultimate victim of all his crimes is himself. By his actions he has deliberately cut himself off from the society of men. He now learns what it really means to be completely alone. This is the realization that comes to Grimes also, but it does so in a way that owes something to *Macbeth*. The epigraph taken from that play is also concerned with a spectre, the ghost of Banquo in III. 4. But Crabbe had, I would suggest, consciously, or unconsciously, perceived that Macbeth, like Richard, is the victim of his own actions. But in Macbeth's case Shakespeare depicts the whole process in far greater depth and detail. Realization of what he has done to himself comes late to Richard; it comes early to Macbeth. He moves into a waste land of spiritual death in which life becomes merely a pointless sequence of events in time. It is precisely this sense of futility that is so splendidly embodied in the central section of Crabbe's tale, where he uses the flat East Anglian landscape of mud and marsh-banks to mirror his character's state of

---

[5] R. Huchon, *George Crabbe and His Times*, London, 1907, p. 310.

mind. Peter sitting idly in his boat, incapable of any action, except to

> view the lazy tide
> In its hot slimy channel slowly glide, (ll. 186–7)

is, at his own more commonplace level, in the same condition as Macbeth when he says:

> To-morrow, and to-morrow, and to-morrow,
> Creeps in this petty pace from day to day.

Huchon was right to see *Richard III* behind 'Peter Grimes', but wrong to limit Shakespeare's influence on the tale merely to the appearance of the spectres, and still more mistaken in describing it as productive only of horrors. *Richard III* and *Macbeth* helped to free Crabbe's imagination, enabling him to write with sympathy, as well as with understanding, about the psychology of crime, the lust for power over others and the effects of a self-inflicted exile from society.

King Lear also left its mark on Crabbe's poetry. It is plain in 'Resentment' (*Tales*, XVII), where one of the epigraphs is Lear's address to the Fool before he enters the hovel in II. 2:

> How dost. . . . Art cold?
> I'm cold myself, etc.

In this tale of the wife who is charitable in other things, but continues to harbour resentment against the husband who betrayed her trust by defrauding her of money, there are deliberate and telling echoes of Shakespeare's play. Becoming affluent again after the disaster of bankruptcy, the wife treats her husband, from whom she is separated and who has fallen into poverty and misery, rather as Goneril and Regan treat Lear. Just as Goneril says of her father, when he rushes out into the storm at the end of II. 4:

> 'Tis his own blame; hath put himself from rest,
> And must needs taste his folly,

so the wife says of her husband, from the warmth and security of her fire-side:

> Wilful was rich, and he the storm defied;
> Wilful is poor, and must the storm abide. (ll. 417–18)

Opposing this attitude is the maid, Susan, who has had far more reason than her mistress to distrust all men, but has remained good and charitable, despite all that has happened to her. It is she who states the wretched predicament of the husband, old, penniless, living in a hovel and exposed to a cruel winter. She does it in lines that recall in a suitably muted fashion the scenes on the heath:

> 'The snow,' quoth Susan, 'falls upon his bed—
> It blows beside the thatch—it melts upon his head.
> . . .
> Through his bare dress appears his shrivell'd skin,
> And ill he fares without, and worse within;
> . . .   In pity do behold
> The man affrighten'd, weeping, trembling, cold.
> Oh! how those flakes of snow their entrance win
> Through the poor rags, and keep the frost within. (ll. 366–90)

In the end the maid wins. She forces her mistress to allow her to take succour to the husband. But the parallel with *Lear* still holds; she comes too late. When she arrives at the hovel, the old man is dead. Thereupon Susan blames not her mistress but herself for hardness of heart. It was not only the truth of *Lear* that excited Crabbe's interest, but also its compassion, which he embodies in the figure of the maid.

Perhaps the most interesting of all Crabbe's debts to Shakespeare is to be found in his use of *Measure for Measure*. It affects two tales: 'The Confidant' (*Tales*, XVI) and 'Smugglers and Poachers' (*Tales of the Hall*, XXI). 'The Confidant' is a story of blackmail, and Crabbe's main concern in it is explained by the last of the three epigraphs to it, a passage from Isabella's plea to Angelo in II. 2:

> It is excellent
> To have a giant's strength, but it is tyrannous
> To use it like a giant.

The confidant uses her knowledge of the wife's past to tyrannize over her, until the husband, who behaves like the Duke in Shakespeare's play and employs indirect courses to find out the truth, reveals to her, through an inset story he tells, that he is aware of what is going on. The similarity between the husband and the Duke is endorsed by the fact that the husband forgives his wife and even tempers justice with mercy in his dealings with the confidant. Like the play, the tale is brought to a happy conclusion.

But there were other possibilities in *Measure for Measure*. Realist as he was, Crabbe must have asked himself what would have happened in the play had there been no Duke to control the action. He gives his answer in 'Smugglers and Poachers'. The impression created by the opening of this particular tale is that Crabbe began it without any realization that *Measure for Measure* was relevant to it, but that as he wrote the parallel forced itself irresistibly upon him. According to Huchon, the story is based on fact and was suggested to Crabbe by Sir Samuel Romilly.[6] It deals with two foundling brothers, James and Robert. James, the elder, is grave, upright and law-abiding, with just a touch of the prig about him. Robert is livelier and more lovable, but also more adventurous and irresponsible. The elder becomes a game-keeper, the younger a smuggler and eventually a poacher. Nevertheless, though they have their differences, the two remain on good terms with each other until they both fall in love with the same girl, Rachel. At this point differences of character and principle change into animosity. James sees more of Rachel than Robert does, since she works at the Hall where he is employed. But Rachel loves Robert and, though James tries to influence her by blackening his brother's character, she continues to love him.

Matters come to a head and the poem gathers dramatic force when James and his men capture four of the poachers, including Robert. The penalty for poaching is death. James, trusted implicitly by his master, has Robert's life in his hands. Though the precise relationships of the characters involved are different, the basic situation is that of *Measure for Measure* and it is developed with a firm moral grasp and with psychological subtlety. From this point onwards the play can be felt behind the tale, penetrating into its fabric and enriching it. James's first move is to acquaint Rachel with his power. He tells her:

> He could his witness, if he pleased, withdraw,
> Or he could arm with certain death the law. (ll. 293–4)

At first, like Isabella when Angelo makes his first overtures to her, Rachel does not see James's meaning. Convinced that Robert must die, she decides to die with him. James, however, becomes more explicit; and Crabbe places his abuse of power firmly in a single couplet:

> James knew his power—his feelings were not nice—
> Mercy he sold, and she must pay the price. (ll. 317–18)

In some ways Rachel's situation is even more harrowing than Isabella's. It is her lover's life that is at stake, not her brother's; and the price of it is not a single act of unchastity, but a lifetime of dull misery, married to a man she does not love and who has shown his lack of respect for

---

[6] Ibid., p. 459.

her by resorting to blackmail. She decides to visit Robert in prison out of motives which seem to me finer than those that take Isabella to Claudio. It is the desire to be absolutely fair that impels her to take this course, rather than the hope of freeing herself from the burden of choice.

> Rachel was meek, but she had firmness too,
> And reason'd much on what she ought to do.
> In Robert's place, she knew what she would choose—
> But life was not the thing she fear'd to lose.
> She knew that she could not their contract break,
> Nor for her life a new engagement make;
> But he was man, and guilty—death so near
> Might not to his as to her mind appear;
> And he might wish, to spare that forfeit life,
> The maid he loved might be his brother's wife
> Although that brother was his bitter foe,
> And he must all the sweets of life forego. (ll. 325-36)

The meeting between the two is handled with great dramatic skill. Rachel puts the proposition to Robert, whose immediate reaction, like Claudio's, is to refuse it. She is relieved, but asks him to think again, so that there may be no doubt. At this point his weakness begins to show. He suspects her of wishing to marry James. She repels the suspicion and tells him that she has already made it clear to James that if she marries him it will not be for love:

> 'I ask'd thy brother, "James, would'st thou command,
> Without the loving heart, the obedient hand?"
> I ask thee, Robert, lover, canst thou part
> With this poor hand, when master of the heart?
> He answer'd, "Yes!"—I tarry thy reply,
> Resign'd with him to live, content with thee to die.' (ll. 373-8)

The temptation proves too much for Robert. The possibility of life on these terms allows the terror of death to flood into his mind, and with it the relationship of the tale to *Measure for Measure* becomes full and explicit. The echoes of Claudio's great speech, 'Ay, but to die, and go we know not where', are deliberate, adding the weight of Shakespeare's scene to the situation:

> Assured of this, with spirits low and tame:
> Here, life so purchased—there, a death of shame;
> Death, once his merriment, but now his dread—

91

And he with terror thought upon the dead:
'[Oh]! sure 'tis better to endure the care
And pain of life, than go we know not where!—
And is there not the dreaded hell for sin,
Or is it only this I feel within,
That, if it lasted, no man would sustain,
But would by any change relieve the pain?
Forgive me, love! it is a loathsome thing
To live not thine; but still this dreaded sting
Of death torments me—I to nature cling—
Go, and be his—but love him not, be sure—
Go, love him not—and I will life endure:
He, too, is mortal!'—Rachel deeply sigh'd,
But would no more converse: she had complied,
And was no longer free—she was his brother's bride.

(ll. 379–96)

Rachel is no Isabella. She lacks the heroic fibre and the masculine spirit; but she is also free from Isabella's self-regarding fanaticism. A nicer and more tolerant being altogether than her Shakespearean prototype, she conveys in her quiet acceptance of the situation Crabbe's implicit criticism of Isabella's violent outburst against Claudio.

The rest of the tale is *Measure for Measure* as it might have been without the Duke. James and Rachel marry. Robert is freed from gaol by some of his companions, not without connivance from the authorities. But, once he is free, the irrevocable nature of the bargain he has made fills him with the desire to see James dead. Another poaching expedition is planned. James, who has his spies abroad, gets wind of it. The two brothers clash in the woods at night and each kills the other. Rachel, through whose consciousness the last stages of the story are portrayed, is left alone with an experience that has made the rest of life seem remote and unimportant to her.

But, while the end of the tale is quite different from the end of *Measure for Measure* and, in a way, much more realistic, the Shakespearean vitality, that forces its way into Robert's speech about death, continues to affect Crabbe's writing. He is concerned not only with violent actions, but also with strong and passionate feelings, and he renders these feelings in the verse. The passages in which he describes the night on which the final disaster takes place are some of the most vivid and imaginative that he ever wrote, and they link up with and image the state of mind of the characters. When Robert and his companions decide to go poaching once more, Crabbe sets his scene thus:

It was a night such bold desires to move:
Strong winds and wintry torrents fill'd the grove;
The crackling boughs that in the forest fell,
The cawing rooks, the cur's affrighten'd yell,
The scenes above the wood, the floods below,
Were mix'd, and none the single sound could know;
'Loud blow the blasts', they cried, 'and call us as they blow'.

(ll. 472–8)

And when Rachel, awakening from a dream of murder, sets off into the woods to discover what is happening, her terrors and uncertainties are reflected in the scene:

The moon was risen, and it sometimes shone
Through thick white clouds, that flew tumultuous on,
Passing beneath her with an eagle's speed,
That her soft light imprison'd and then freed;
The fitful glimmering through the hedge-row green
Gave a strange beauty to the changing scene;
And roaring winds and rushing waters lent
Their mingled voice that to the spirit went. (ll. 559-66)

In the end, Crabbe being Crabbe, the tale makes its moral points that the game laws are too hard, that poaching is wrong and that, ' 'Tis wisdom to be good, 'tis virtue to obey'. But before this conclusion is arrived at he comes closer to tragedy than he does almost anywhere else in his work, and especially in the way in which he creates a sense of tumult and storm in the elements, imaging and running parallel to the tumult and storm in the minds of his characters. It is hard to resist the conclusion that the Shakespearean afflatus, pouring in through Robert's speech on death, liberated Crabbe's imagination and enabled it to rise well above its usual level.

University of Nottingham

Horace Walpole's Young Poet

EDMUND BLUNDEN

'PENTYCROSS, Rev. William, versifier, ix 396; visits Strawberry Hill, xv 411; described by H. W. 416–18.' This not very startling extract comes from the index to *The Letters of Horace Walpole*, 1905, edited by Mrs Paget Toynbee. It is possible to say something more about Thomas—not William—Pentycross than that edition gave; and allowing him to be seen rather more in this world than he is there might have the luck of bringing to light some long forgotten papers of the eighteenth century. But first of all Horace Walpole must be quoted. Writing to the Rev. William Cole on 24 July 1776 he talked of some melancholy ideas of his. 'I doubt Mr Essex'—James Essex was the architect at Strawberry Hill—'perceived that my mind was greatly bewildered. He gave me a direction to Mr Penticross, who I recollect Mr Gray, not you, told me was turned a methodist teacher. He was a blue-coat boy, and came hither then to some of my servants, having at that age a poetic turn. As he has reverted to it, I hope the enthusiasm will take a more agreeable plea. I have not heard of him for many years, and thought he was settled somewhere near Cambridge: I find it is at Wallingford.'

Thomas Pentycross was the son of John Pentycross, a citizen of London and a founder by trade. He was baptized on 8 January 1748, and admitted at the age of nine to Christ's Hospital, London. In that great school, which was going through an undistinguished period, he grew up with several boys who became well known in the City or beyond; he was of an age with Charles Edward de Coetlogon, afterwards a celebrated preacher and incessant author, and Matthew Field the indulgent teacher of Charles Lamb and a prebendary of St Paul's Cathedral. Somewhat younger were John Prince, an eminent chaplain and secretary to the Magdalen Hospital, and George Dyer who will be beloved as long as the Essays of Elia are read—a poet too.

These all became university men, rare as it was then for Blues to do so. Their usual chance was to enter Pembroke College, Cambridge, and in 1766 de Coetlogon and Pentycross were elected Exhibitioners of Christ's Hospital and admitted at Pembroke. One of the principal personages there was the Rev. James Brown who had been a Bluecoat boy himself, and there was the poet Thomas Gray, ever Brown's cordial friend. So, almost certainly, Gray got to know a little of Pentycross.

A historian of Christ's Hospital, J. I. Wilson, tells us that Pentycross 'in his earlier years was particularly fond of theatrical representations, and headed a party of his schoolfellows in getting up plays. Upon being made Grecian (one of the sixth form) he from player turned preacher, and obtained the name of *bishop*.' At Cambridge, on the same authority, 'he does not appear to have been much influenced by religious feelings,' yet having done well enough in his studies to be Third Junior Optime in 1771 (the year of his B.A. degree) he was appointed curate of Horley in the county of Surrey. Horley is one of the livings in the gift of Christ's Hospital, and Pentycross's vicar was one well known to him, being the Upper Grammar Master of the school, Peter Whalley, who so indifferently edited the plays of Ben Jonson.

'Subsequently [Pentycross's] intimacy with his friend de Coetlogon and Mr Rowland Hill [founder of the independent Surrey Chapel] confirmed his bias to the Evangelical party in the Church.' It might be maintained that this bias was fairly frequent among Christ's Hospital boys of the period; at all events, Thomas Pentycross became a special favourite of the Countess of Huntingdon, who encouraged the Calvinists. Her private chaplain was the Rev. George Whitfield, and on his death in 1770 Pentycross composed a monody on him. He published, in 1776 and in 1777, a different sort of poem, one of the many topographical contemplations enjoyed by the eighteenth-century, 'Wittenham Hills'. Walpole preserved a copy of it.

Pentycross, becoming rector of St Mary, Wallingford, in Berkshire, managed to be a productive religious author. In 1774 and 1775 he was editing *The Gospel Magazine*. In 1782 he edited and prefaced a selection from the 'Journals of Several Ministers of the Gospels'. His friend de Coetlogon conducted *The Theological Miscellany* from 1784 to 1789 and naturally Pentycross gave him all assistance. Many printed sermons might be listed, and odds and ends of verse, now, like a great proportion of eighteenth-century provincial efforts, almost defying discoverers.

There is at the British Museum, however, bound together with other fugitive pieces of the same period, one quarto leaf preserving a special poem by Pentycross. It is dated 1780, though Walpole's bibliographer strongly argues that the true date of the printing at the Strawberry Hill Press was 1797. It seems like a schoolboy's effort.

VERSES TO HORACE WALPOLE

I

Thro' the bosom of yon trees
Dies away the panting breeze!
Thro' the long-drawn cloysters pale,
Trembling to the busy gale,
Silv'ring sweeps the moon along,
And suggests sweet-soothing song.
Nature sleeps, and all is still,
But the lyre that wakes at will,
WALPOLE does the strings inspire,
To WALPOLE wakes and swells the lyre.

II

Health, thou rosy-dimpled maid,
Roving gay the sylvan glade,
On the hospitable gate
With thy choicest blessings wait.
Peace, with learned Ease, attend
On the Patron and the Friend.
Smiling Candour join the train,
And protect this artless strain.
To generous WALPOLE haste away,
And at his feet subject the Bard's unpolish'd lay.

T. Pentycross

'By no means despicable' was Walpole's comment years later.

Walpole, who kept his guineas safe from the boy Chatterton, may have let one or two drift out to this other Bluecoat encomiast. At Christ's Hospital Pentycross was to have an exciting successor in the exalted rank of Grecians, one who wrote a poem concerning his school surroundings in London.

Adieu, adieu, ye much loved cloisters pale!

But Pentycross mentions trees as well as the celebrated cloisters, and at Christ's Hospital, Newgate Street, trees were few, or Coleridge would have mentioned them in his song of farewell.

When next the master of Strawberry Hill had any dealings with Pentycross—so far as I have found information—he was an old man. He was far from being in his dotage. On 7 August 1796 he wrote to his chaplain Daniel Lysons, the topographer, desiring his help concerning an imminent visitor: 'a person whom I have not seen in near thirty years'. It was Pentycross. He had called at Walpole's town house at Christmas 1795, when Walpole was too ill to see anyone, and had left a letter which moved the old hero to invite him at the return of summer to Strawberry Hill. Would Lysons come and share the occasion? Some notes about it went from Walpole to Mary Berry on 16 August 1796; it was quite an event,

> a Mr. Pentycross, a clergyman and schoolmaster of Wallingford, of whom I had heard nothing for eight-and-twenty years, and then having only known him as a Blue-coat boy from Kingston; and how that happened, he gave me this account last week.
>
> He was born with a poetic impetus, and walked over here with a copy of verses by no means despicable, which he begged old Margaret to bring up to me. She refused; he supplicated. At last she told him that her master was very learned, and that if he would write something in the learned languages, especially in French, she would present his poem to me. In the meantime she yielded; I saw him, and let her show him the house. I think he sent me an ode or two afterwards, and I never heard his name again till this winter, when I received a letter from him from his place of residence, and high compliments on some of my editions, and beseeching me to give him a print of myself, which I did send to him.

Respecting the meeting on 10 August 1796, Walpole wrote,

> I considered that to pass a whole day with this unknown being might be rather too much. I got Lysons, the parson, from Putney, to meet him; but it would not have been necessary, for I found my Blue-coat boy grown to a very sensible, rational, learned, and remaining a most modest

personage, with an excellent taste for poetry—for he is an enthusiast for Dr Darwin: but, alas! infinitely too learned for me; for in the evening, upon questioning him about his own vein of poetry, he humbly drew out a paper, with proposition forty-seven of Euclid turned into Latin verse. I shrunk back and cried, 'Oh, dear Sir, how little you know me!...' and here luckily ends, with my paper, my Penticrusade.

This was one of Walpole's last letters.

Thomas Pentycross is truly a shade, but one or two more particulars about him may be given. In 1809 Henry Clarke, LL.D. Professor of Astronomy and Experimental Philosophy at Marlow, published *Virgil Re-vindicated ... written in the year 1807, in a letter to the Rev. Mr Pentycross of Wallingford.* But Pentycross had died at that town on 11 February 1808. His funeral sermon was delivered by a man of great reputation, Thomas Scott, the author of *The Force of Truth*, rector of Aston Sandford. It was issued in pamphlet form as *The Duty and Advantage of Remembering deceased Ministers, ... preached at the Church of St Mary, Wallingford, for the Rev. Thomas Pentycross.* In 1810 Mr Rusher of Reading sent out his bookseller's catalogue of Pentycross's ample library, presumably including his Walpoliana.

In writing this brief article I have had the help, like all who approach the circle of Horace Walpole, of Mr W. S. Lewis; and my old pupil Mr Chau Wah Ching has given me some of his transcripts.

Long Melford, Suffolk

Byron and Foscolo

MARIO PRAZ

A FEW years ago Erwin Panofsky[1] drew attention to a recurring phenomenon in history which we would not dare to call 'a law', cautioned as we are by the discredit which bold generalizations usually meet with in the eyes of scholars. "The acme of mediaeval classicism', writes Panofsky, 'was reached within the general framework of the Gothic style, much as the acme of seventeenth-century classicism, as represented by Poussin, was reached within the general framework of the Baroque, and that of late eighteenth- and early nineteenth-century classicism, as represented by Flaxman, David or Asmus Carstens, within the general framework of "Romantic sensibility".' Panofsky takes into consideration only the field of art, but if we turn to poetry, we shall see that his contention holds good at least for the last of the periods he mentions. Keats, Hölderlin and Foscolo actually represent the acme of late eighteenth- and early nineteenth-century classicism reached within the general framework of Romantic sensibility.

With a difference, though, between Foscolo and the two northern classicists just mentioned. Because for Foscolo the striving after Greek serenity takes the shape of a very personal inner process of osmosis. It is not, as in the other two, a yearning after an alien world, remote and

[1] *Renaissance and Renascences in Western Art*, Stockholm, Almqvist & Wiksell, 1960, p. 68.

hopelessly elusive. In Hölderlin Greek landscapes flash like mirages and hallucinations. Keats, in his *Ode to a Nightingale* contrasts 'the weariness, the fever and the fret Here, where men sit and hear each other groan' with the serene delight of the 'light-winged Dryad of the trees', as the poet calls the nightingale using an epithet which sums up the happiness of a vanished pagan world. 'Darkling I listen', says Keats; in the dark he listens to the song of the nightingale, in the dark he smells the perfume of the flowers at his feet, and cannot discern 'what soft incense hangs upon the boughs'; he is a worshipper in the dark, yearning after a Beauty and a Permanence which are not of this world. Hölderlin's classical aspiration is equally shot through with yearning:

> Aber Freund! wir kommen zu spät. Zwar leben die Götter,
> Aber über dem Haupt droben in anderer Welt.

> *(Brot und Wein, vii)*

Hölderlin also is a poet who speaks of the abyss, an abyss of deprivation; he sings his own version of the dark night of the soul, a Saint John of the Cross of neohellenism, a priest of Dionysus roaming from land to land, driven by his sense of loss between an olympic past for ever vanished and a fondly idolized Utopian future. His invocatory and exclamatory poetry rises in pillars and columns solemn, but shadowy; his dark epiphany is at best, as in his great poem just quoted (*Brot und Wein*), only a photographic negative of the 'daylight of the gods.' These northern poets, clinging in the dark, look towards Olympus, but with such dizziness that they seem to be bending over an abyss instead of turning to an empyrean, as in the situation described in Blake's *Marriage of Heaven and Hell*: 'Down the winding cavern we groped our tedious way, till a void boundless as a nether sky appear'd beneath us, and we held by the roots of trees, and hung over this immensity.'

Foscolo, on the other hand, born in that 'island of gold, flower of the Levant', as Chateaubriand called Zante, just because of the 'native sacred air' (*nativo aer sacro*) found in himself that Apollinean temper which Hölderlin and Keats tried to conjure up on earth. Foscolo too says that men are 'born to cry and toil' (*nati al pianto e alla fatica*), but adds: 'if they are led by virtue, comfort arises from the fount of sorrow':

> O nati al pianto
> E alla fatica, se virtù vi è guida
> Dalla fonte del duol sorge il conforto.

Sorrow and comfort, a troublesome life and Olympic serenity, were in him close to each other, so much so that from the twisted roots of his novel, *Ortis*, the flower of the *Grazie* seemed to blossom naturally. Hippolyte Taine might have pushed the inference from the milieu even further, to the point of discovering a foreshadowing of Foscolo's temper in the famous pitch springs of Zante, and perhaps in its frequent earthquakes. Let us read the description of a nineteenth-century traveller, Richard Ridley Farrer,[2] not because we see in those phenomena a decisive factor, but because of their symbolic import:

> The wells are situated hard by the sea. They are two in number.... An iridescent film covers water of the most transparent clearness. At a depth of about a foot is the pitch, its surface swollen by great bubbles that slowly grow and burst, sending up a murky liquid to join the film above. Between the two wells is a hole sunk some time ago in order to obtain petroleum ... A light dropped into this cavity soon blazed up and produced a bonfire lasting some ten minutes.

The deep load of passion that lay at the bottom of Foscolo's heart, 'that warlike spirit which roars within me' (*quello spirto guerrier ch'entro mi rugge*) found in his awareness of a Greek origin a season of grace which tempered, soothed, and calmed; that was the clear water in which the pitch was dissolved, though leaving an iridescent film on the surface. There is no violent contrast between two worlds—the terrestrial and the elysian—in this entirely interior transfiguration, as in those northern poets; but a slow expansion, sublimation and refinement of impulses, until, cleansed of all impurities, they become clothed in a serene light. Foscolo does not proclaim with Keats that unheard melodies are the sweetest; his ear, his whole being can perceive the supra-sensible melody, the voluptuousness carried away beyond the senses. His Graces are not 'three ladies who have come round his heart and sit outside' (to use Dante's words), rather they have sat within his heart from the very beginning, and it was left to his intellect to isolate and free them from the surplus through a refining process not unlike the one which Michelangelo attributes to the excellent artist. In short, Foscolo's Greek inspiration is immanent, not transcendent. Hence its peculiar human throb, the accessibility and urbanity of the divine element in Foscolo, so that, for instance, in the one of the Graces who

le carole che lenta disegna
Affretta rapidissima, e s'invola

[2] *A Tour in Greece*, *1880*, Edinburgh and London, W. Blackwood and Sons, 1882, pp. 204–5.

Sorvolando su'fiori; appena veggio
Il vel fuggente biancheggiar fra'mirti—[3]

as the Italian critic Giuseppe De Robertis has well noticed, it is easy to recognize Teresa of the *Ortis*, who disappears along the avenue in the moonlight, where amid the dark shadows of the trees the poet dimly sees 'her swaying robes which shone white even from afar'. The graceful motion recollected out of the past has now sublimated itself into a ritual dance.

A godlike presence manifests itself in Foscolo through the natural combination of three elements which appeal to the senses: light, scent, music. Three eminently liturgical elements, but Foscolo's religion necessarily identifies itself with ritual. Hebe of the *Grazie*, resembling Canova's celebrated statue, her thick and curly hair constrained by a graceful diadem of gold, crowns with a ritual libation the hymns in which human passions are quieted, in the same way as Winckelmann had seen Apollo's passion contain itself in the famous Belvedere marble: 'His eye is delicately arched like Venus's, but without showing her desires: it only expresses innocence: his mouth breathes emotions from within the narrow circle of its contours, but seems not to feel them.' 'One does not see pleasure manifest itself through a smile in the expression of ancient statues: it only shows the serenity of the inner contemplation. On the face of a Bacchante there appears only the dawn of voluptuousness. Both in sadness and indignation those figures offer an image of the sea, whose bottom is still, while the surface begins to stir. Niobe, even in her intensest pain, appears like a heroine who does not want to yield to Leto.' Compare with Foscolo's: 'An immoderate gaiety and deep sorrow are unknown to the Graces; these deities smile sometimes with temperate delight, sometimes they sigh with gentle pity'.

Thus tempered, and softened, human passions assume ritual attitudes, express ritual symbols: and you have the dance of Youth down a slope nobody ascends again; the turtle doves straying between shadow and sunshine out of a myrtle grove, billing and cooing; the Genius who crowns the first cups to the exiles. . . . In this ritual every figure is satisfied and complete in itself, as in a dance in which each dancer has a memorable attitude to offer. Through such exquisite mannerism Foscolo, who was born near the Greek sea, did not resume the Hellenic tradition, rather he continued it: like Callimachus, like Catullus, his

---

[3] 'her slow dancing steps she hastens of a sudden, and flees away sweeping over the flowers; I dimly see her floating veil vanishing white among the myrtles'.

mind had a Greek cast, even if it expressed itself in imitative Tuscan modes.

The elegance of attitudes was not meant to be, in Foscolo's intention, an aim in itself: it was rather intended to form the most suitable medium to express moral truths: beauty and truth, for him as for Keats, formed an inseparable whole. He aimed at the art of the ancient poets, who 'drew from the most abstract thoughts sensible allegories and pictures, which were better calculated to persuade than syllogisms and numbers: what most appeals to the senses, best conquers the minds'. These words belong to that discourse *Della ragione poetica di Callimaco* which, while stating Foscolo's artistic intentions, shows him in the act of deliberately linking himself to the Alexandrian tradition. There was a philosophy which especially stressed the presence of the spirit in matter, often with genuine poetical intuition: the Platonic philosophy, which had greatly been in vogue during the Renaissance and contributed considerably to fix the character of Italian art. This philosophy, alongside the influence of classical models, is responsible for the universal character of Italian art, which succeeded best in expressing the serenity of an ideal world (Raphael), and remained universal and heroical also when it wanted to express struggle and pain (Michelangelo). There is a general aspect of Platonic philosophy which has caused some critics (for instance Sir Herbert Grierson) to see Plato's dialogues as the first document of a Romantic tendency in the West; one might argue that seeing in the world of sensible things a reflection, a foreshadowing of supra-sensible ones, is a trait common to Plato and to the great Romantic poets and thinkers, to Wordsworth, Shelley and the philosophers Schelling and Fichte. Winckelmann's ideal beauty was particularly instinct with Platonism.

But the way in which the epiphany of the supra-sensible was elicited from the world of material things during the Renaissance was very different from the vague suggestions and intimations of the Romantics. These latter would say with Blake:

> To see a World in a Grain of Sand,
> And a Heaven in a Wild Flower,
> Hold Infinity in the palm of your hand,
> And Eternity in an hour.

But the men of the Renaissance sought for more precise correspondences, they created a system of symbols which claimed the extravagant authority of a dream-book: they had learned from antiquity that hieroglyphs had been invented in order to protect myths from profanation, that the Cabala and the Orphics pursued similar aims, i.e. to clothe profound mysteries in the shape of myths, that substantially the doctrine of the Cabala and the figurations of the Pagans could be useful instruments of Christian theology. Thus classical myths became loaded with a doctrinal element, and canonical doctrines assumed a halo of poetry. The chief representative of this cultural tendency was Pico della Mirandola, who derived from the syncretism of the late classical age; and also Marsilio Ficino derived from the lucubrations of the Hellenistic commentators. One of the most popular figurations of classical art, which passed on to the Renaissance and was taken up again during the neoclassical period, was that of the Graces. Foscolo strove to invest their beautiful forms with deep meanings, and in doing so he merely went back to a tradition illustrated in Seneca's *De beneficiis*, which had particularly appealed to the artists of the Renaissance. Seneca had explained why the Graces are three, why they are sisters, why they entwine their hands: it is the triple rhythm of liberality, whose phases are giving, receiving and returning. This rather trite Stoic morality struck people's fancies as being clothed with beauty: one of the so many examples of the principle which dominated ancient art: to mix the useful with the pleasant. But that was not all: the smallest details of the group of the three beautiful female figures were controlled by a punctilious and exacting ceremonial, so that the turning of the head here or there, the placing of the foot nearer or farther, the position of the veils, the type of head-dresses, everything had an esoteric meaning as in a religious rite. To the Graces were associated Eros, the perpetual knot of the universe, blindfolded in order to signify the mystery of celestial bliss which transcends every perception of the intellect; and Venus who regulates the harmonious exchange of gifts. These divinities were organized like a planetary system, a moral precept was conceived figuratively like a constellation, in the same way as a few luminous points in the sky were seen to represent the Wain or Cassiopea. Painters would imagine it as a tableau vivant: hence the so-called *Primavera* by Botticelli, a painting which also stressed the grouping by triads, which fascinated Christian thought mindful of the Trinity, and bent on finding its traces everywhere. Edgar Wind[4] has clearly shown how Botticelli's plan in painting that famous picture was based on ideas which were discussed in Florentine learned circles; 'the marvel is that', he concludes, 'in Botticelli's treatment, philosophical

[4] *Pagan Mysteries in the Renaissance*, London, Faber & Faber, 1958.

pedantry has become so infused with lyrical sentiment that, for many generations of beholders, the sentiment of the picture has extinguished the thought, with the result that the mood itself has been too loosely interpreted'.[5] Now Foscolo in his poem, *The Graces*, intended to breathe 'a lovely fancy and a secret melody, and images calculated to benefit the students of fine arts' (*amabile fantasia e melodia segreta, ed immagini da giovare agli alunni delle belle Arti*), but, not being enough of a pedant to give his figurations precisely articulated meanings like those of Seneca, he only succeeded in creating a succession of delightful episodes, of dance figures, incapable of organizing themselves into a consistent whole. The conclusion is something of a paradox: Foscolo's art, designed to carry a civil and ethical message, to lead to Truth through Beauty, came to resemble the art of those Alexandrian poets who, in order to exalt the Ptolemies, tried to recall Homer's deities to life, and revived the cult rather than the god, the symbol rather than the myth: theirs being an art which Foscolo actually condemned when he wrote: 'If the poet's song is not addressed to real nations, but to royal families and large vulgar herds, then the exile ordained by Plato seems just' (*Che se non a nazioni vere, ma a regali famiglie ed a grandi volghi tende il canto del poeta, allora pare giusto l'esilio che decretava Platone*).

While the message, a message in solemn and insipid capital letters, remained vague and general, the arabesque, the attitude, the rhythm, carried weight. Foscolo's poetry mostly identified itself with a phenomenon of taste, and was typical of that Alexandrian mannerism which is seen in paintings like François Gérard's *Eros and Psyche*, a great success of the 1798 salon, though a few found fault with it as being too affected and *métaphysique*, or like *Venus, Cupid, Folly and Time* by Angelo Bronzino, the mannerist who has been appropriately defined 'a Platonic painter'. There predominates in both these paintings a furtive sensuality—the hand lightly touching the breast, the mouth just touching the face—the same resolution of a feeling into an exquisite pattern of flowing lines without any abrupt interruption—flowing though motionless. Both paintings breathe a statue-like immobility. Flesh is as smooth and polished as semi-precious stones; the firmness of the contours joined with the tenderness of the tints, conveys a strange effect like the pulp of iced fruits.

> These delicates he heap'd with glowing hand
> On golden dishes and in baskets bright
> Of wreathed silver: sumptuous they stand

[5] Ibid., p. 110.

In the retired quiet of the night
Filling the chilly room with perfume light. . . .

Indeed the suspended, spell-bound image of love in those paintings could not be better described than with certain lines of Keats's ode *On a Grecian Urn*:

More happy love! more happy, happy love!
For ever warm and still to be enjoy'd,
  For ever panting and for ever young;
All breathing human passion far above,
  That leaves a heart high-sorrowful and cloy'd,
  A burning forehead, and a parching tongue.

And a few lines further on Keats speaks of 'fair attitude' and 'cold pastoral': phrases that would fit well with both Bronzino's and Gérard's paintings and with Foscolo's poem.

'Try to reduce your inquiry to figures', wrote Cusanus in *De coniecturis* (I, xi), 'so that under the guidance of sensibility (*sensibili manuductione*) you may turn your conjecture toward the arcana'. Leon Battista Alberti, for having invented his device of the winged eye with the motto *Quid tum?* to signify the all-seeing eye of God and the fear of the Day of Judgment, was better pleased than if he had written a philosophical treatise. It was a kind of elegant, solemn game. For the men of the Renaissance to express a thought through an image appealing to the senses was tantamount to the discovery of a truth. Foscolo thought the same. But the difference between his Platonism and that of the romantics was the difference between allegory and symbol. The danger of neo-Platonism, just as the danger of imitating the classics, was that it offered a facile solution to all problems, ignoring an entire aspect of life which fell under the sign of the less beautiful and the irregular—an aspect which is no less essential towards the 'great synthesis'. The enormous vogue of neo-Platonism in Italy, a conciliatory philosophy which allowed a humanist to come to terms with theology, a scientist with metaphysics, a moralist with human weaknesses and men and women of the world with the 'things of the spirit', while it favoured that serene vision which stamped the Italian art of the great centuries, was also responsible for the diffusion of a culture whose pleasant but commonplace themes we come across in so many treatises of the Cinquecento, in numberless minor followers of Petrarch, and in academic art. With Foscolo, if we try to go beyond the exquisite ritual of images, we come across that Platonic undercurrent which, like the beautiful according to Winckelmann, reminds us of water 'which is better when its taste is least'. That is why Foscolo's poetry is appreciated only by his countrymen. His taste is too much tied to the taste of a period and of a language to be understood outside of Italy; the qualities of the cup in which that water is poured are likely to appeal only to Italians. The most recent English historian of Italian literature, Professor J. H. Whitfield[6] has wirtten: '*Le Grazie* remained a respectable monument, but not a vital sector of his *œuvre*. Recent Italian criticism has claimed it as the culminating point for Foscolo, and even as the highest point of lyric poetry in the Italian nineteenth century . . . Foscolo for the mere foreigner looms less large a figure than for the Italian critics.'

Byron's case is the exact opposite: both authors offer a good illustration of the truth that the touchstone for the universal validity of an author is his translatability. Foscolo and Puškin no doubt stand above Byron for craftsmanship, but they are untranslatable. When first reading Puškin, Gustave Flaubert exclaimed; '*Mais il est plat, votre poète!*', whereas anyone reading him in Russian will agree with Professor Ettore Lo Gatto when he speaks of 'the typical simplicity of his manner, capable of giving the most disturbing views of the unfathomable destiny of man by means of the most commonplace images'. When Alexandre Dumas in his *Voyage en Russie* wanted to give an example of Puškin's poetry, he heaped so many and such futile frills on the famous passage of *Eugene Onegin* on Petersburg, 'I love thee, Peter's creation', as to render it unrecognizable, because the bareness of the original did not appeal to him. A literal translation of Horace hardly appeals more to the general public. In short, the magic of such poets lies only in the language, and the only thing that may surprise us is that Foscolo, who possessed this requisite to a no lower degree than Puškin, failed to achieve an equal international reputation.

It is curious to notice that a German biographer of Byron, Helene Richter, in her book on the poet (1929), found the characteristics of the Empire style in his art.[7] Notwithstanding his admiration for classical models like Dryden and Pope, whose style he gawkily aped in *English Bards* and *Scotch Reviewers*, notwithstanding his professed devotion to Corneille's, Racine's, and Alfieri's tragedies, and his preference for such artists as Canova, Guido Reni and Guercino, and his aversion to Rubens, Byron lacked the eminently classical qualities of restraint,

---

[6] *A Short History of Italian Literature*, Penguin Books, 1960, pp. 219, 221.
[7] *Lord Byron, Persönlichkeit und Werk*, Halle, Saale, 1929.

economy, fastidiousness and the consciousness of limits. His careless treatment of language and metre caused an eclipse of his reputation as a poet in England during the nineteenth century. His dissatisfaction with the serene expression Thorvaldsen had given to his face in the bust inspired by the classical statue of Meleager is tell-tale enough: 'It is not at all like me; my expression is more unhappy'.

In a charming booklet on the art of arranging one's neck-tie in all the known and customary fashions (*L'Arte di mettere la propria cravatta in tutte le foggie conosciute e di uso*) published in France and Italy about 1830,[8] the seventh lesson is dedicated to the 'Byron tie', a kind of tie with a very slack and capricious bow. It is worth while to quote it, since it evokes the figure of the poet as his contemporaries saw him:

> As there was always something surprising in whatever sprung from Lord Byron's bizarre genius, one could not expect in the kind of tie which this prince of romantic poets had adopted either that painstaking elegance or that minute precision which generally characterize the ties of the fashionable in his country. One cannot deny that the least tightness, the slightest pressure exerted on the body cannot fail to act on the spirit. Who can maintian that a more or less starched, a more or less tight neck-tie, might not put a stop to the flights of fancy or stifle one's thoughts? Nevertheless there is reason to believe that the celebrated singer of the *Corsair* much feared the influence of the tie on his imagination, and that he only wore one when he was obliged to sacrifice himself to the ceremonies of practical life: and what seems to support this affirmation is that in the portraits of the noble lord, published in Italy and France also before his death, his neck is always seen as free from any constraint of a tie, like that of the unbridled steed mentioned in *The Corsair*.[9] The tie named after the most celebrated poet of our time presents a very marked difference from the majority of the other ties: this difference consists in its initial arrangement. Instead of placing it first against the front of the neck, one applies it on the contrary to its back, and then brings its ends forward below the chin and ties them into a wide knot or rosette, at least six inches long and four in circumference.

This bizarre knot of a tie could be taken as an emblem of the whole figure of the poet. Next to lines which are properly 'starched', i.e. that are properly constructed, those of Byron are slovenly, and he achieved

[8] The Italian version is attributed to a fictitious Conte Della Salda; I have a copy of the 1828 Naples edition, published by Porcelli.

[9] The Italian version of the Byron passage, runs: 'come quello dell'indomito corsiero sciolto da ogni sorta di freno (*Il Corsaro*)'. I could not trace the original in *The Corsair*, but in *Mazeppa* (ix) the steed is described as 'wild . . . and untaught/with spur and bridle undefiled'.

greatness only when he could pass slovenliness for deliberate *déshabillé*, that is in *Don Juan*, where he stressed the fluency of the colloquial style without losing the energy of the rhetorical. Byron's poetry as well as Byron's life belong to the category of things that must not be too closely looked into, things to which one must allow a certain latitude of motion, a certain irregularity: like, then, that rather bizarre tie which is exactly the opposite of the tie that has been given a proper finish with starch. Byron had rough manners with women as well as with the Muses; he was unable to keep a secret and to practise the art of wise aposiopesis; his very miserliness, in mature years, was the inevitable low-tide after a lavish generosity, and as for a consciousness of limits, it only existed in him as a spur to overcome them, since his vital sense was enhanced by transgression. He was an aristocrat, and yet he loved to show off like a *parvenu*, and this because after a childhood as an impoverished member of the aristocracy, he had suddenly found himself extolled to a peerage; he had a carriage made for him which was a copy of Napoleon's carriage, decorated his bed at Newstead Abbey with coronets and mottoes, and sported his motto also on the helmet worn on his Greek expedition. He was lazy and yet adored action, despised men and yearned for their applause. And the list of contraries might continue, a whole set of lights and shades: both generous and covetous, wanting in reverence and tender of heart, sceptical and superstitious, living in the moment and believing in eternity:

> But I have lived, and have not lived in vain:
> My mind may lose its force, my blood its fire,
> And my frame perish, even in conquering pain;
> But there is that within me which shall tire
> Torture and Time, and breathe when I expire.
>
> (*Childe Harold*, IV, cxxxvii)

It is curious to observe that similar characteristics are also found in Ugo Foscolo's life. It is enough to think of his self-portrait in a famous sonnet:

> Prodigo, sobrio, umano, ispido, schietto;
> Avverso al Mondo, avversi a me gli eventi.
>   Solo i più giorni e mesto e ognor pensoso.
> Alle speranze incredulo e al timore,
> Il pudor mi fa vile e prode l'ira.
>   Mi parla astuta la ragion; ma il core

111

Ricco di vizi e di virtù delira,
E sol da morte aspetterò riposo.[10]

This is a character which bears some resemblance to Byron's heroes, to the Corsair, whose name was linked with one virtue and a thousand crimes, to the gloomy Giaour, on whose forehead death was stamped. If, however, from the man we turn to the poet, we ought to say that Byron always expressed the whole of himself with his poses, his whims, his bizarrerie; Foscolo instead, as soon as he donned his singing robes, entered under the sign of Plato. One can certainly say that of that supreme harmony which is the essence of the highest kind of poetry, one hears the sound more distinctly in the few perfect compositions of Foscolo than in many ill-contrived poems of Byron: the latter displayed even too much in his work that volcanic turbulence that the Italian poet, with the exception of *Ortis*, knew how to contain within the limits of his private life. But when Foscolo, in his *Lettere scritte dall' Inghilterra*, tried to transfer the fluency and vivacity of his own epistolary style into a literary work he failed, and, although he went for help to Montaigne and Sterne, he produced a lifeless work, whereas Byron, when he started to talk in verse as in the letters to his friends, produced a model of *déshabillé* poetry from which Puškin had much to learn. Italian tradition was still influenced by the distinction between the written and the spoken language, and Foscolo, sheltered in Plato's laurel grove, did not find in himself the courage to abolish it. Surprisingly enough, Byron was actually helped in his major work, the creation of conversational verse, by two Italian poets: Pulci and Casti.

Apart from these differences, both Byron and Foscolo were sons of their age, not only thanks to the shadow of Werther which at the time fell almost everywhere, but also because of certain minor aspects which bear the stamp and the colour of a period. A few years ago Professor E. R. Vincent, in publishing an exchange of letters between J. C. Hobhouse and Foscolo apropos of the contributions of the latter to the commentary of the fourth canto of *Childe Harold*, opened his book (1) with an interesting parallel:

> Byron and Foscolo were not really alike either as poets or men. Yet there were curious similarities in their circumstances. Greece, Italy and England were written in their fates; one left England to live in Italy and die in Greece; the other, born in a Greek island, lived in Italy and came to stay

[10] 'Prodigal, thrifty, humane, rude, sincere; hostile to the world, the events hostile to me. Solitary most of the time and sad, and always absorbed in thought, incredulous to hopes as well as fears, shyness makes a coward of me, anger a brave man. Reason advises me cunningly; but my heart, rich in vices and virtues, raves, and only death will give me rest.'

and die in England. Their tracks crossed in Switzerland in 1816, but they did not meet then or at any other time. There was respect and a kind of fear on both sides; they knew of one another; they corresponded indirectly through others. They seem like two beasts of prey passing in a jungle, careful and polite, avoiding an unnecessary and probably hazardous proximity. Sometimes there is a growl and a flash of teeth.

But while a moment ago I said that Byron always mirrored himself in his work, both in his poses and his various moods, whereas Foscolo as a poet had a personality quite distinct from Foscolo the man, I do not wish to create the impression that I think Byron sincere and Foscolo insincere. Byron, who at bottom had much of the XVIIIth century rake, in his literary attitudes put to use the sinister sides of his soul, but Foscolo was an actor convinced of his romantic melodrama in his correspondence with Antonietta Fagnani Arese.

In 1824 Hobhouse wrote to Byron about Foscolo: 'I never heard him make a commonplace remark in my life.' I could not say that this is the impression of those who nowadays read Foscolo's letters to Antonietta Fagnani. The romantic lover according to conventional ideas is a fellow who gives himself up to despair, threatens to kill himself and soaks his letters to his beloved one with tears. Foscolo does all this, profusely and over and over again: 'When your sighs are transfused into my mouth, and I feel your arms hugging me . . . and your tears mix with mine . . . and . . . yes, I invoke death!'; 'You'll be the last eternal love of this unfortunate youth'; 'You'll be the last woman I shall love; and after you I'll have only solitude and a grave'; 'It is fit that I should take a decision, death; truly I cannot stand it any longer'; 'I'll carry away with me my terrible passion, your letters, all, all the sad and dear memories of your love; . . . either time and misfortunes will heal me, or I shall die far away from you, in order not to sadden you with the sight of my last misfortunes'; 'I enclose a letter you have written to me . . . which I have bathed and am bathing with my tears'; 'My fibres are like touched chords which trembling emit a sad, long, uncertain sound'; 'We'll share bread and tears'; 'Do you remember the day of my tears . . . the day in which I dissolved my whole soul on you, and bathed your breast and face with my tears'; 'I totter at every step, any food disgusts me, I lie awake at night like a hind, I moan for hours; or else I live in a deep stupor; and always with a fierce headache, a slow fever, and cold perspiration'; 'God Omnipotent, either quench in me this rage which consumes my heart, or else I will give myself up to all excesses'; 'What is left me but to cry, to cry for ever'; 'Only the grave is left me, the last refuge of unhappy men'; 'I'll shed my blood in order to make your life less sad'; 'I'll sit next to my fireplace, writing, crying, day-dreaming'. And so on; since almost every letter talks of gaping sepulchres, of adieus to the world, and of the end of one's days and sorrows, of loves ending in death, of life too much worn, and too early. 'Call me romantic', Foscolo writes once to his beloved, 'you'll be right, perhaps, but I shall not heal for this'. Romantic is the word: this is the time and the tone of *Ortis* whose accents we find in these letters destined to 'serve as raw material for a transfiguration into a romance', as the editor of the letters, Plinio Carli, has aptly remarked. There are however certain more intimate passages in those letters, about a 'little brother, who also cries, in his fashion, which were certainly not destined to this transfiguration, and we may feel surprised that both that melodrama of despair and this licentious farce were lived and experienced by the bard of the *Sepolcri* and *Le Grazie*. We find examples of the melodramatic as well as of the licentious manner also in Byron's love letters, as I shall say in a moment, but how should these astonish us from the mercurial, moody, dissolute author of *Don Juan*? Nowadays that the habit prevails for writers to lay bare even the most unmentionable corners of their private lives, and that Joyce, Henry Miller and Paul Léautaud have promoted to literary honours much more intimate confessions than the comparatively harmless ones of Foscolo's letters, we might rather admire the restraint of this latter which forbade the threshold of the sanctuary of Art to certain human passions and weaknesses; nevertheless to see the different aspects of Foscolo the man and Foscolo the poet causes a certain uneasiness, which may turn to a sneer in the less reverent. Thackeray might have reacted with a caricature, like that one of *le Roi Soleil* in his regalia next to the shrunken old man who hides behind the solemn mantle and wig. A certain uneasiness is caused also by his ceaseless looking at himself in a mirror for an eternal self-portrait, that portrait at which Foscolo worked with his own lines (the sonnet *'Solcata ho fronte . . .'*), and asked painters to work with their brushes. 'When I see myself importuned by a pack of dogs and foxes . . . in order to rout them I needs must roar like a lion': 'Alas, I roared that day like a tiger. . .'; 'When you'll know me better, you'll realize that I have not got a black soul; frequently swayed by anger, and nearly always by melancholy, I harm more myself than others'; 'Since nature has gifted me with a resentful soul . . . oppressed now by one, now by another passion . . . and my heart frequently causes tears in those who are dearest to me . . . why should this wretch live and torture himself; and never find rest; and always be at war with himself and others?'; 'No iniquitous or base action has ever contaminated my days'. We find the same posturing in his letters to Hobhouse *('Je ne vivrai jamais en lâche ni en ingrat')*, the same violent dramatization of an episode (the secret of Foscolo's collaboration to the commentary of *Childe Harold*) which left the Englishman comparatively calm, whereas Foscolo was talking of honour dragged to an abyss.

Pitiful letters those of Foscolo to Hobhouse, written in approximate and ungrammatical French. As for English, Foscolo never learned to write it decently, less pliant than Byron in this, whose love letters to Teresa Guiccioli are written in an Italian style which seems to be modelled on that of the libretti. Iris Origo who in *The Last Attachment*[11] edited those letters reproducing the originals faithfully, remarked that they light up an unfamiliar facet of Byron's character, a Byron under the influence of the Italian convention of the period: 'Passion, jealousy, storms, reconciliations, protestations of eternal fidelity . . . it is all, to English ears, curiously *formal*. What is odd in these earlier letters, too, is a total absence of his usual flippancy and irony—with which, however, he made sufficiently free in his letters *about* the affair, to his friends at home'. Byron used with Teresa the language an Italian lady of the period expected from her lover, and this language was more or less the same Foscolo used with Antonietta Fagnani. 'Sentiment, the most beautiful and fragile thing in all our existence'; 'You'll be my last Passion'; 'My soul is like the leaves which fall in the autumn: yellow throughout'; 'My life is now a perpetual agony'; 'It is impossible for me to live in this agitation for long—I am writing to you in tears—and I am not a man who cries readily—when I weep, my tears are from the heart, and are of blood'; 'As for my sadness . . . it is a real constitutional disease, which makes me sometimes fear a beginning of madness, and for this reason I keep myself in those moments aloof from everybody, as I don't want to make others unhappy'. Apparently there is no lack, in Byron's letters, of accents of that Priapean farce we have found, next to melodrama, in Foscolo's; but Marchesa Origo has not had the boldness of the editors of Foscolo, followers of Ham who 'saw the nakedness of his father, and told his two brethren'. There is no convention of the period of which the two poets are exempt, so true is it that in face of love and death all men

[11] *The Last Attachment*, The Story of Byron and Teresa Guiccioli as told in their unpublished Letters and other Family Papers, London, Cape and Murray, 1949.

behave in the same manner. The gift of a lock of hair, for instance: locks of hair in lockets or wrapped up in tissue paper among Byron's relics belonging to Teresa Guiccioli, locks of hair mentioned by Foscolo in his letters: 'The two locks of your hair . . . I'll have these sacred and precious souvenirs by me in all my wanderings; thus I'll comfort my unhappy days, and shall have them buried with me.'

Foscolo's love ideal, writes Professor Vincent, 'despite all the Isabella Teotochis and Antonietta Fagnanis [Foscolo called this latter a female Lovelace] of his career of gallantry, . . . was always and only to be found in a young, beautiful, intelligent and innocent girl.' And Professor Mario Fubini, another Foscolo scholar, says: 'The love the poet constantly idolized, even in the midst of very different passions, was for a wholly pure girl.' How pathetic, though, that last gesture of the poet, who, already forty-six years old and oppressed by debts and illness, proposed to Hobhouse's half-sister Matilda, twenty-three years old and one of the prettiest girls in England, as Hobhouse expressed himself, indignant at such boldness. Byron's Don Juan in the Greek island found Haidée:

> Round her she made an atmosphere of life,
> The very air seem'd lighter from her eyes,
> They were so soft and beautiful, and rife
> With all we can imagine of the skies,
> And pure as Psyche ere she grew a wife—
> Too pure even for the purest human ties;
> Her overpowering presence made you feel
> It would not be idolatry to kneel.

We are supposed to recognize in Haidée the portrait of Teresa Guiccioli, a woman, says Marchesa Origo, 'as silly as Augusta—and amoral too, in very much the same way'.[12]

Foscolo and Byron, then, in their behaviour showed affinities which one would vainly try to find in their very different artistic personalities. Their names can be linked together also as those of poets who believed in the future of Italy in an age full of darkness and depression for this country. It is worth noticing that in the Fourth Canto of *Childe Harold's Pilgrimage*, to whose commentary Foscolo was to contribute, helping Hobhouse with a brief survey of Italian literature, Byron celebrated Florence for that church which, as Foscolo had sung many

---

[12] A further proof of her amorality has come to light after I. Origo's book; see Raffaele Ciampini, *Il primo amante di Teresa Guiccioli* (con il carteggio inedito di Teresa Guiccioli e Cristoforo Ferri), Firenze, Barbera, 1963 (edition limited to two hundred copies).

years before, 'keeps the glories of Italy gathered together' (*accolte serba l'itale glorie*). An echo of Foscolo's hymn in praise of Florence (in *Dei Sepolcri*, 1806) with her 'hills rejoycing for the wine-harvest, and the valleys peopled with houses and olive groves' (*colli per vendemmia festanti e le convalli/popolate di case e d'oliveti*) we seem to catch in the far less inspired stanzas (xlviii f.) of Byron:

> Girt by her theatre of hills, she reaps
> Her corn, and wine, and oil, and Plenty leaps
> To laughing life, with her redundant horn.

But the echo becomes more distinct in the stanzas on Santa Croce (liv–lv):

> In Santa Croce's holy precincts lie
> Ashes which make it holier, dust which is
> Even in itself an immortality,
> Though there were nothing save the past, and this,
> The particle of those sublimities
> Which have relapsed to chaos: here repose
> Angelo's, Alfieri's bones, and his,
> The starry Galileo, with his woes;
> Here Machiavelli's earth return'd to whence it rose.
>
> These are four minds, which, like the elements,
> Might furnish forth creation:—Italy!
> Time, which has wrong'd thee with ten thousand rents
> Of thine imperial garment, shall deny,
> And hath denied, to every other sky,
> Spirits which soar from ruin: thy decay
> Is still impregnate with divinity,
> Which gilds it with revivifying ray.

The bodies of those great dead are enough, according to Byron, to confer immortality and glory on a country which seems to have lost everything, and Foscolo had written:

> Ma più beata che in un tempio accolte
> serbi l'itale glorie, uniche forse
> da che le mal vietate Alpi e l'alterna
> onnipotenza delle umane sorti
> armi e sostanze t'invadeano ed are
> e patria e, tranne la memoria, tutto.[13]

[13] 'But blessed the more as thou keepest gathered in one temple the glories of Italy, perhaps the only ones left since the ill guarded Alps and the overpowering vicissitudes of human destinies have swallowed thy arms and thy wealth, and altars, and fatherland, and everything, save memory.'

Our parallel between such different poets may stop here, while we feel them united in the same thought inspired by the mighty spirits whose mortal remains lie buried in Santa Croce, a thought which bears witness to their passioned concern for the destinies of Italy.

University of Rome

'The Author's own candles': The Significance of the Illustrations to *Vanity Fair*

DONALD HANNAH

THE nineteenth century was undoubtedly the great age of book illustration. The work of George Cruikshank or Edward Lear or Sir John Tenniel, to name only a few, indicates the diversity of the illustrations and shows how much they flourished. It is to this widely popular tradition that *Vanity Fair*, 'brilliantly illuminated with the Author's own candles', belongs. But the illustrations to *Vanity Fair* are not only of interest because of this, they can also contribute to a fuller understanding of the novel itself. It is the way in which they do this that I wish to consider here.

The function of the illustrations in *Pen and Pencil Sketches of English Society*, the sub-title of the monthly instalments, is to do precisely what Thackeray states: to illuminate the work of the pen. They do this in a way which is immediately apparent, and yet, because of this very fact, they can also be a distraction. The illustrations to *Vanity Fair* actually presents something of a paradox: they can illuminate, but they can also blur an essential characteristic of Thackeray the writer. When one reads the novel, the clarity and graphic quality with which the author has conceived many scenes is very noticeable, bearing witness to the possession of a vividly effective visual imagination. What illustration, for example, could equal the description, at the ball in Brussels, of George Osborne's note to Rebecca, placed in her bouquet, 'coiled like a snake among the flowers'?[1] Or could better the description of the relationship between Amelia and Dobbin suggested by the remark, 'Grow green again, tender little parasite, round the rugged old oak to which you cling'?[2] But the clearest example of this visual quality is given by the most famous scene of all, the death of George Osborne; and it so happens that one can measure very definitely the extent to which this particular scene is visualized by comparing it with its abstract equivalent. Thackeray's attitude to the war is implicit throughout the Waterloo part, but it is explicitly summed up in a comment, 'it taxes both alike, and takes the blood of the men, and the tears of the women'[3] A few pages later, this generalized comment is given particular concrete illustration: 'Darkness came down on the field and city: and Amelia was praying for George, who was lying on his face, dead, with a bullet through his heart.'[4]

The scope of *Vanity Fair* and its panoramic effect has often been remarked upon; but one can see that this effect is not primarily a result of the accumulation and amassing of details to fill in a broad canvas; it comes rather from the concretely visualized details unerringly selected and combined to give the most forceful and vivid impression. It is when Thackeray's visual imagination is most strikingly expressed verbally, in graphic terms, that the imaginative effect of the novel is greatest. In these passages we can see that the pen does not really need (and can even be hampered by) the pencil. The illustrations tend to present us with an all too explicit representation of the action; and in comparison with the richness of implication and complexity of attitude which lie behind Thackeray's most sharply imagined verbal pictures, the illustrations themselves seem lacking in depth and almost one-dimensional. Thackeray possesses a strong pictorial imagination, but it only functions with full effect in the context of the prose. The novel does not depend for its full communication of meaning and significance on the illustrations to it. Thackeray is not a prose Blake. The illustrations represent the simplest form of running commentary on the narrative; an accompaniment to the action rather than an integral part of it or an

---

[1] *Vanity Fair*, edited, with an introduction, by George Saintsbury, O.U.P., 1908, p. 357. This edition has been referred to throughout since it is the illustrated one which is most widely accessible.

[2] Ibid., p. 871.

[3] Ibid., p. 385.

[4] Ibid., p. 406.

amplification of it. The limited nature of this commentary is clear when one considers what is the central point in any discussion of *Vanity Fair* —the role of the commentator and the function of the prose comments. The argument is a complex one, but it can best be summarized by quoting from what is probably the most sharply critical and most subtly argued essay on Thackeray:

> Everything depends on the capacity of the novelist to encompass in his own personality an adequate attitude to what he is describing. . . . But constantly, throughout the whole novel, the effect produced by what the characters do is weakened or dissipated by the author's comments.[5]

The way in which the illustrations bear upon this point can be seen if those to *Vanity Fair* are compared with some of Thackeray's others. Thackeray, of course, illustrated many other works besides *Vanity Fair*, but of all these, the place where his pencil is given fullest play is in his letters. Reading through these in Professor Gordon N. Ray's splendid edition, one realizes the full extent of the attractiveness and charm of Thackeray's personality, qualities which made him such a popular figure among the various circles in which he moved from Grub Street to Grosvenor Square; and no small part of the attractiveness of this personality derives from his sketches. Two examples, trivial enough in themselves, must suffice. In a letter to Lady Molesworth dated 2 April 1848, he writes:

> Solomon in all his glory, I am sure, never had such a waistcoat as I shall have the honour of sporting at your party on Sunday 16. I imagine myself already attired in the brocade (see the next page): I will try, however, and not lose my head with vanity.[6]

and he includes a sketch of himself wearing the waistcoat. Similarly, in a letter to John Bell, the sculptor, apparently replying to a proposal to make a bust of him, he writes:

> You do me very much honour: and I already see myself in the Sculpture Room no 1556. Bust of a gentleman.[7]

and there is a sketch of the proposed bust of Thackeray in classical style, crowned with a laurel wreath.

Seeing sketches like these, commenting upon himself, one realizes

---

[5] Arnold Kettle, *An Introduction to the English Novel*, Hutchinson's University Library, 1951, Vol. I, pp. 158, 169.
[6] *Letters and Private Papers*, 1945, ed. G. N. Ray, Vol. II, p. 369.
[7] *Letters*, Vol. II, p. 519.

that there is, in fact, an essential element lacking in most of the illustrations to *Vanity Fair*—they comment upon the narrative, not upon the narrator. And this fact is thrown into even sharper relief if one compares them with the prose commentary, which both comments upon the narrative, and is used as the chief means of characterizing the narrator—indeed, to such an extent, according to hostile criticism, that the reader is never left unaware of the personality of the narrator 'intruding' between himself and the narrative. The illustrations, on the other hand, illuminate the narrative, but, except that they are recognizably Thackeray's own work, they do so without characterizing the narrator.

Are there, then, any illustrations to *Vanity Fair* which do more than simply this; which also characterize the narrator; and which, consequently, approximate more to the complex function of the author's commentary? There are, I think, three which can be singled out from the rest; three, which taken together, suggest one of the main aspects of the work; which illustrate graphically why Thackeray's narrative technique was not only deliberately chosen by him, but was one he was even forced to adopt by the nature of his subject and his awareness of this; and which, if they do not actually demonstrate 'the capacity of the novelist to encompass in his own personality an adequate attitude to what he is describing', do at least suggest where we should begin looking for it: in Thackeray's conception of his own relationship as narrator to the people of Vanity Fair.

One of these illustrations[8] is a small drawing of the puppet-master, attired in his livery, sitting cross-legged, with a puppet on a stick over one arm, and holding his mask in the other hand. The moony, bespectacled face, revealed from behind it, is, of course, Thackeray's. In *Vanity Fair* Thackeray is no longer working through an imaginary narrator: Michael Angelo Titmarsh is now replaced by William Make-

[8] *Vanity Fair*, p. 104.

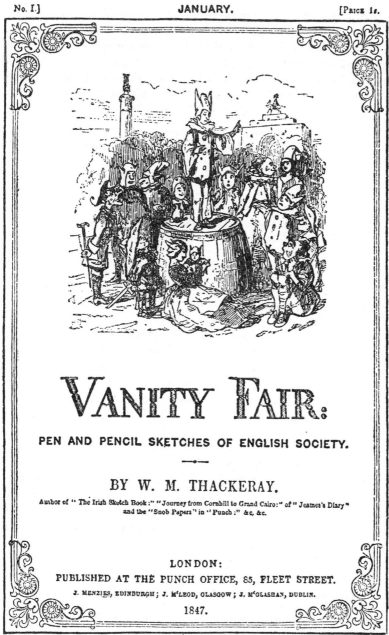

VANITY FAIR:

PEN AND PENCIL SKETCHES OF ENGLISH SOCIETY.

BY W. M. THACKERAY.

Author of " The Irish Sketch Book :" "Journey from Cornhill to Grand Cairo:" of " Jeames's Diary" and the "Snob Papers" in "Punch :" &c, &c.

LONDON:

PUBLISHED AT THE PUNCH OFFICE, 85, FLEET STREET.

J. MENZIES, EDINBURGH; J. M'LEOD, GLASGOW; J. M'GLASHAN, DUBLIN.

1847.

[Bradbury & Evans, Printers, Whitefriars.]

peace Thackeray; the Titmarsh signature, the pair of crossed spectacles, is now placed on Thackeray's face, and the author's own name appears on the cover or title-page. And the illustration found on the cover of the monthly instalments, and that used for the title-page of the first edition in 1848, are the two most revealing illustrations of all.

The one on the yellow cover of the monthly instalments depicts the narrator addressing his audience. Thackeray himself describes it best:

> But my kind reader will please to remember, that this history has[9] 'Vanity Fair' for a title, and that Vanity Fair is a very vain, wicked, foolish place, full of all sorts of humbugs and falsenesses and pretensions. And while the moralist, who is holding forth on the cover (an accurate portrait of your humble servant), professes to wear neither gown nor bands, but only the very same long-eared livery in which his congregation is arrayed: yet, look you, one is bound to speak the truth as far as one knows it. . . .
>
> And, as we bring our characters forward, I will ask leave, as a man and a brother, not only to introduce them, but occasionally to step down from the platform, and talk about them.[10]

For the first element, which makes this passage and its illustration of central importance to the novel, we must look to external evidence. As Professor Ray has pointed out in his essay, '*Vanity Fair*: One Version of the Novelist's Responsibility',[11] the last six paragraphs (now forming part of chapter 8) from which the passage quoted is taken, were not in that fragmentary draft which Thackeray began writing, and then laid aside: they were later inserted when he returned to it and started revising. These six paragraphs, Professor Ray says, 'sum up the serious and responsible view that he had come to take of novel-writing'.[12]

This is excellent—as far as it goes. For if these paragraphs grew out of this changed view of novel-writing, so also must the illustration to which they directly refer; and Thackeray used the illustration in the most prominent place possible in order to stress this view. A comparison of the variant readings of the manuscripts only confirms what literally confronted the contemporary reader denied the knowledge from this source. But this is not the only aspect which singles out this passage and illustration. In contrast, as we have seen, to the other illustrations, this is the only place where illustration and text are completely dependent

[9] The 1st edition reads 'these histories in their gaudy yellow covers have'.
[10] *Vanity Fair*, p. 95–6.
[11] Reprinted in *Victorian Literature. Modern Essays in Criticism*, ed. Austin Wright, 1961, pp. 342–57.
[12] Ibid., p. 347.

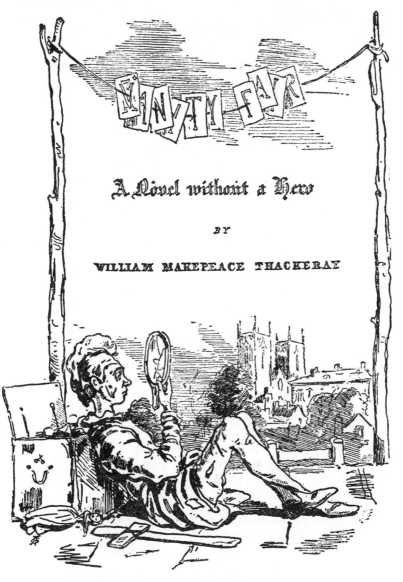

VANITY FAIR

A Novel without a Hero

BY

WILLIAM MAKEPEACE THACKERAY

LONDON.
BRADBURY & EVANS, BOUVERIE STREET.
1848.

upon each other for their full meaning; the sketch illustrates the text, and the text itself directly refers to the illustration. Moreover, it not only personifies the narrator; it also presents in pictorial terms the reason for the narrative method of *Vanity Fair*. In fact, all the main lines of the novel intersect at this point. The illustration and the text, taken together, demonstrate the attitude of the narrator to his audience: arrayed in 'the very same long-eared livery', a point which the illustration stresses; and, as a result of this, it also demonstrates his attitude to his characters: 'as a man and a brother', he will 'step down from the platform' and talk about them. Thackeray recognizes that as the moralist he is the connecting link between the two. But the moralist depicted on the cover is also the narrator of *Vanity Fair*; the narrative method of the novel is a result of Thackeray's awareness of the moral issue.

This awareness is given its fullest expression and significance in the illustration which was used on the title-page when *Vanity Fair* was published as a book. It is one which is clearly derived from the same theme expressed in the preface, 'Before the Curtain'. But in this case it is not the similarities between the text and the illustration which are of greatest importance, it is the differences. The preface begins:

> As the Manager of the Performance sits before the curtain on the boards, and looks into the Fair, a feeling of profound melancholy comes over him in his survey of the bustling place.

and goes on to describe the sights and scenes which he sees in the Fair. The illustration depicts the puppet-master sitting on the boards, leaning back against a box full of puppets; but the background is certainly not the scene of bustling activity described in the preface. Moreover, the puppet-master is not sitting and looking into the Fair; instead, he is holding up a mirror in which he is contemplating the reflection of his own face. Thackeray himself, in his letters, can supply the only comment necessary:

> Good God dont I see (in that may-be cracked and warped looking glass in which I am always looking) my own weaknesses wickednesses lusts follies shortcomings?[13]

The illustration of the puppet-master with his puppets contemplating his own image, is perhaps, the most apt and comprehensive example of the functioning of Thackeray's visual imagination. It is precisely right, and it illuminates the whole novel. For Thackeray in *Vanity Fair* is

[13] *Letters*, Vol. II, p. 423–4.

both puppet-master and one of his own puppets, pulled by the same strings, actuated by the same motives, which animate his own figures. It is his constant awareness of this fact, testified to by the illustration, substantiated by the novel itself, which gives that subtlety of treatment, that complexity of motive, and that adequacy of attitude which characterizes *Vanity Fair*. For it is here that the novel itself takes over from the illustration. And it faces the reader with another reflection; it is not only Thackeray who looks into the mirror.

University of Aarhus, Denmark

Anthony Trollope: The Novelist as Moralist

SHEILA M. SMITH

ANTHONY TROLLOPE is his own worst advocate. In *An Autobiography* (published posthumously 1883) he writes:

> ... I have ever thought of myself as a preacher of sermons, and my pulpit as one which I could make both salutary and agreeable to my audience. I do believe that no girl has risen from the reading of my pages less modest than she was before, and that some may have learned from them that modesty is a charm well worth preserving. I think that no youth has been taught that in falseness and flashness is to be found the road to manliness; but some may perhaps have learned from me that it is to be found in truth and a high but gentle spirit. Such are the lessons I have striven to teach; and I have thought that it might best be done by representing to my readers characters like themselves,—or to which they might liken themselves. (Ch. VIII)

These words suggest that Trollope has no conception of the novel as a work of art but regards it simply as jam in which the reader can swallow the moral lessons of mid-Victorian society. But it must be remembered that *An Autobiography* was written during the years 1875 and 1876. Like Ruskin[1] and Robert Buchanan,[2] Trollope feels that the artist and writer should defend the threatened structure of society by supporting its moral standards. So he stresses the novelist's moral preoccupations. However, the nature of these preoccupations requires further examination. His emphatic statement gives a very false idea of his concern with morality in his novels.

It is undeniable that Trollope is sometimes guilty of the kind of crude moralizing suggested by his own statement. For example, in *The Three Clerks* (1858) he preaches:

> Alaric Tudor was now a rogue; despite his high office, his grand ideas, his exalted ambition; despite his talent, zeal, and well-directed official labours, he was a rogue; a thief, a villain who had stolen the money of the orphan, who had undertaken a trust merely that he might break it; a robber, doubly disgraced by being a robber with an education, a Bill Sykes (*sic*) without any of those excuses which a philanthropist cannot but make for wretches brought up in infamy. (Ch. XXIX)

He gives his exemplum contemporary significance:

> Alas, alas! how is it that in these days such men become rogues? . . . Expediency is the dangerous wind by which so many of us have wrecked our little boats.

Then comes a rhetorical question:

> Who has given so great a blow to political honesty, has done so much to banish from men's minds the idea of a life-ruling principle, as Sir Robert Peel?

which introduces a virulent attack on Peel as a politician without principle.

Moreover, even when Trollope is not engaged in writing such obtrusive and over-emphatic sermons, his desire to teach can have a bad effect upon his technique, as in *Ayala's Angel* (1881). He wants to emphasize the folly of self-delusion, the danger of nourishing idealistic romantic dreams which blind the dreamer to love when it is offered her, so repeatedly he describes the ideal image of the Angel of Light, cherished by Ayala. Such repetition is tedious.

Yet it is not true that for Trollope moral preoccupations are simply sermonizing. In *An Autobiography*, Chapter XVIII, he discusses his novel *The Vicar of Bullhampton* (1869), 'written chiefly with the object

---

[1] In 'Fiction, Fair and Foul' (1880/1), [*Works of Ruskin*, ed. E. T. Cook and A. Wedderburn, London, 1908, (Vol. XXXIV)] Ruskin gathers together many of the ideas he expressed throughout the 'seventies in the letters of *Fors Clavigera*.

[2] Cf. 'The Fleshly School of Poetry', *Contemporary Review* 1871, written by Buchanan under the name 'Thomas Maitland'.

of exciting not only pity but sympathy for a fallen woman, and of raising a feeling of forgiveness for such in the minds of other women'. Discussing the character, Carry Brattle, he quotes from his original preface to the novel:

> She is introduced as a poor abased creature, who already knows how false were her dreams, with very little of the Magdalen about her— because though there may be Magdalens they are not often found—but with an intense horror of the sufferings of her position.

He then criticizes the double standard by which society condemns the woman for sexual immorality but excuses the man. He continues,

> And the punishment inflicted is of such a nature that it hardly allows room for repentance. How is the woman to return to decency to whom no decent door is opened? . . . To me the mistake which we too often make seems to be this,—that the girl who has gone astray is put out of sight, out of mind if possible, at any rate out of speech, as though she had never existed, and that this ferocity comes not only from hatred of the sin, but in part also from dread of the taint which the sin brings with it. Very low as is the degradation to which a girl is brought when she falls through love or vanity, or perhaps from a longing for luxurious ease, still much lower is that to which she must descend perforce when, through the hardness of the world around her, she converts her sin into a trade.

Trollope's criticism of public morality and his perception of the essential selfishness—'dread of the taint'—of this moral code which in fact increases the sinner's immorality, prove inadequate the notion that he is simply a purveyor of the moral clichés of his time, and reveal him as a man thoughtful of the nature of morality and concerned with the springs of human conduct.

Writing of the work of Jane Austen, Scott and Thackeray, and praising them for their moral effect, he remarks:

> It is not for the novelist to say, baldly and simply: 'Because you lied here, or were heartless there, because you Lydia Bennet forgot the lessons of your honest home, or you Earl Leicester were false through your ambition, or you Beatrix loved too well the glitter of the world, therefore you shall be scourged with scourges either in this world or in the next'; but it is for him to show, as he carries on his tale, that her Lydia, or his Leicester, or his Beatrix, will be dishonoured in the estimation of all readers by his or her vices.
>
> (*An Autobiography*, Ch. XII)

Here he denies that the novelist's business is to express 'bald' condemnations of immorality. Something more complex is required. Earlier in the same chapter Trollope suggests that the novelist is to 'make virtue alluring and vice ugly'. Part of the novelist's task is to represent moral goodness so that all shall desire it, a very subtle and very difficult thing to do. Dickens repeatedly failed to make virtue attractive, witness the Cheeryble brothers, Tom Pinch, Little Nell, Agnes Wickfield. His rare success in virtue is Pickwick. Trollope knew that he himself sometimes failed to make virtue interesting. In *An Autobiography* he says of *The Way We Live Now* (1875):

> The interest of the story lies among the wicked and foolish people,— with Melmotte and his daughter, with Dolly and his family, with the American woman, Mrs Hurtle, and with John Crumb and the girl of his heart. But Roger Carbury, Paul Montague, and Henrietta Carbury are uninteresting.

But Mr Harding of the Barchester novels is a rare example of a wholly successful good character in nineteenth-century fiction. Not only are his tenderness, generosity and unselfishness perfectly credible as they are revealed in his relationships with those about him; not only are his eccentricities endearing, consistent and presented with a sympathetic humour; but the reader is confronted with the man's moral nature, his steadfast belief in what is right and his refusal to subscribe to what is wrong, although this refusal brings him great discomfort and misery. Mr Harding's character indicates that Trollope, at his best, is concerned not so much with preaching sermons on his own or conventional themes, as with the reality of his characters' moral existence. The importance of the moral nature of a man or woman is one of the facts of the world which Trollope creates in his novels—and it is his strength to convince his reader that this is so, to make it impossible for Mr Harding to ignore his conscience and accept the comforts of the Wardenship. So that action springs from the character's moral nature, and one of Trollope's great themes is the way in which moral awareness—or lack of it—makes a character react to his circumstances. After her unfortunate passion for a scoundrel Lily Dale, in *The Small House at Allington* (1864), cannot love Johnny Eames as she feels a husband ought to be loved, so, for her, it is wrong to accept him as her husband. She persists in her refusal to the end of the book, despite the readers who wrote to Trollope and begged a happy ending.

Trollope is also interested in the differences between one man's moral nature and that of another. In this respect, his technique is expressive of his subject matter. For example, he often contrasts characters to emphasize a moral difference between them. The contrast between Mr Harding and his son-in-law Dr Grantly serves to define the precise moral character of each man. Dr Grantly is honourable and upright, he would never conspire to cheat anyone, but in the contrast between his reactions to the controversy concerning theWardenship of Hiram's Hospital—'The question is, whether this intruding fellow, and a lot of cheating attorneys and pestilent dissenters, are to interfere with an arrangement which every one knows is essentially just and serviceable to the church'—and those of Mr Harding—'he resolved in his misery and enthusiasm that he could with pleasure, if he were allowed, give up his place, abandon his pleasant home, leave the hospital, and live poorly, happily and with an unsullied name, on the small remainder of his means'—it is obvious that Mr Harding has the finer moral nature. Dr Grantly is a custodian of public morality, but Mr Harding suffers agonies of conscience which would never trouble the archdeacon, who has a hard shell bestowed by the grandeur and worldly importance of the Established Church.

In his magnificent portrait of the perpetual curate of Hogglestock, Mr Crawley, in *The Last Chronicle of Barset* (1867) Trollope examines the complexities of human conduct, the ambiguities of a moral position. Crawley is determined to do his duty and to act rightly, but in this determination is pride, resentment and a hardness which makes his wife suffer. His notion of what is morally right causes her great hardship, both material and spiritual, and excludes almost all tenderness from their relationship.

The portrait of Crawley exemplifies the idea that the state to which a man's character and actions (which are reactions of character to circumstance) bring him constitutes an implicit moral judgement on that man. Mr Crawley himself creates his own personal hell, which is itself a moral judgement on his conception of righteousness and duty, although contained in this judgement is admiration and compassion for the man who could hold so relentlessly to such beliefs. And the presentation of this judgement is sufficient. Occasionally Trollope comments on Crawley's situation, but he preaches no sermons on the character. Similarly, in *The Eustace Diamonds* (1873), Lizzie escapes all legal punishment, but Trollope shows that her misery brought upon herself by her lie about the diamonds and her marriage to Emilius (into which she is led by her admiration of the flashy and by her lack of moral strength to support her own life) are judgement enough. It is 'the punishment natural to the offence', as he writes of *The Claverings* (1867) in *An Autobiography* (Chapter XI), and that punishment is not a scourge from heaven but a state of mind which must be endured.

Occasionally in Trollope's novels the acute perception of man's moral nature and the impulse to preach exist side by side. For example, in *The Three Clerks*, some chapters after the sermon on Alaric Tudor's sins, there is a very perceptive description of his state of mind. Suddenly he realizes the nature of the hell he has been preparing for himself, and the state of moral degradation to which his actions have led.

A character's gradual moral degradation brought about by his choice of action is a subject which Trollope shares with George Eliot, whom he much admired. Like hers, his subject is not gods and demi-gods, but ordinary human beings, and like her he finds interest in 'that pleasureless yielding to the small solicitations of circumstance, which is a commoner history of perdition than any single momentous bar-gain' (*Middlemarch*, Chapter LXXIX). Carry Brattle is not a Magdalen —'though there may be Magdalens they are not often found'—but an honestly observed human being in circumstances partly of her own making.

This is the strength of Trollope's best novels, that he honestly observes human nature in everyday circumstances. They afford a legitimate pleasure of literature—the pleasure of recognition. In my first quotation from *An Autobiography* Trollope writes that he hopes to have a moral effect 'by representing to my readers characters like themselves,—or to which they might liken themselves', and later he demands 'Truth let there be,—truth of description, truth of character, human truth as to men and women'. (Ch. XII)

For Trollope this 'truth' includes the importance of moral choice as a shaping agent in men's lives, and it is this which gives a novel its organic unity. The organization of his novels is closely related to, and expressive of, their subject matter. In *An Autobiography* he criticizes the mechanically contrived novels which do not explore human living:

> The characters do not live and move, but are cut out of blocks and are propped against the wall. The incidents are arranged in certain lines— the arrangement being as palpable to the reader as it has been to the writer —but do not follow each other as results naturally demanded by previous action. The reader can never feel—as he ought to feel—that only for that flame of the eye, only for that angry word, only for that moment of weakness, all might have been different. The course of the tale is one piece of stiff mechanism, in which there is no room for a doubt. (Ch. XII)

Here, too, is a suggestion of life's infinite possibilities, which fascinate Trollope and which he conveys so well in his best writing.

He is particularly interested in examining his characters' states of mind at different periods of their lives, so indicating moral change. He seldom describes scenery, and he is not alive to the 'genius of place', as is Dickens, but in some of his novels, notably *Can You Forgive Her?* (1864) and *Phineas Finn* (1869), by retaining the physical framework for repeated scenes and manipulating the moral relationships expressed by them, he suggests increasing moral maturity or the increasing awareness of moral degradation. On the balcony of the hotel overlooking the Rhine at Basle Alice Vavasor decides to break her engagement with Mr Grey. She deludes herself into believing that she does this because he is too virtuous for her and succumbs to the sinister charms of her former lover, George Vavasor. Later, with Lady Glencora and Plantaganet Palliser, she visits the same hotel, and the view of the Rhine recalls the earlier scene and makes a stage in Alice's realization of her folly, false judgement and loss. Her growing awareness of Mr Grey's worth, and of her need of him, reaches its height when she is reunited with him on the same balcony. Similarly, Lady Laura, as she revisits with Phineas the waterfall where he once proposed marriage to her, realizes how wrong she was to choose Mr Kennedy and his wealth rather than Phineas and love. Phineas's memory of the earlier occasion has none of Lady Laura's tenderness and regret; in fact he wants to ask her advice about a new lover. He no longer cares for her, and her life is poisoned by the knowledge that she has irrevocably rejected something of great value which was once offered freely to her. Thus the constancy of the characters' surroundings is used to emphasize the changes in their moral existence.

In Trollope's novels a constant moral standard is implied. Sometimes his desire to strengthen and support the standards of Victorian society leads him to criticize newly-accepted false standards, for example the admiration given to successful dishonesty. He attacks this, not wholly successfully, in *The Three Clerks*. But *The Way We Live Now* (1875), describing the rise and eventual ruin of Melmotte the financier, is a much subtler study of lack of principle in public life.

At times Trollope's moral standards appear circumscribed by the age in which he lived. He liked order and system in his life, and he found that the accepted conventions supplied them. Marriage in his novels is a sacred institution. Lady Glencora is wrong to indulge her passion for the handsome wastrel Burgo Fitzgerald once she is married to

Plantaganet Palliser. She is wrong to make an exhibition of herself by waltzing with Burgo at Lady Monk's party. Yet although a strict moral standard is implied in his novels Trollope is well aware that life often falls short of this standard and—even more important—that it is intensely interesting when it does. He constantly surprises the reader by the complexity of his vision of ordinary life. His subject is the variety of human conduct and experience set against a stable moral standard. He represents not only Glencora's wrong conduct, but also the misery of the early period of her arranged marriage with the cold, if correct, Palliser. Emily Wharton in *The Prime Minister* will not desert her husband, Lopez, but the reader is fully aware of the hell she suffers married to such an adventurer. Trollope sometimes writes as though morality were in fact the conduct of a lady or a gentleman. But this is not crude snobbery or a short-sighted acceptance of the ideals of his day. His notion of a gentleman is not simply that of a man of high birth but embraces a man's moral nature. And, again, he is interested in the failures of human beings to achieve this standard—witness his intense interest in Lady Glencora who was no lady but all woman.

Trollope, like Jane Austen, ignored the heights and the depths of human nature. As Henry James said of him, 'His great, his inestimable merit was a complete appreciation of the usual'. In his novels he deliberately excludes the extremes of human conduct. But within the limits of his chosen subject he is often very perceptive of the facts of human experience as, for example, when he describes Phineas's reactions to his imprisonment for suspected murder; or the emptiness of the Duke of Omnium's life when he at last achieves his ambition and becomes Prime Minister.

Like George Eliot, Trollope took seriously the novelist's responsibility and saw it to consist in an exploration of man's moral nature. Read hastily *An Autobiography* represents the novelist as sermonizer, but read more carefully it points to his achievement in his best novels— a description of man's moral existence which includes compassion for his moral failings. There is, both in *An Autobiography* and in the novels, a desire to express moral precept, but there is also the more interesting, more artistically fruitful concern with the experience which produced the precept—man's moral nature itself.

University of Nottingham

James's Novel of 'Looming Possibilities'

IVO VIDAN

IN 1884, the year before the first instalments of *The Princess Casamassima* in the *Atlantic Monthly*, Henry James published an affectionate tribute to his late friend Ivan Turgenev,[1] who had, 'with that great tradition of ventilation of the Russian mind, windows open into distances which stretched beyond the *banlieue*'. Among other recollections James mentions an afternoon in 'the grey damp of a Parisian December' when 'Turgénieff talked almost exclusively about Russia, the nihilists, the remarkable figures that come to light among them, the curious visits he received, the dark prospects of his native land'.

When *The Princess Casamassima* appeared, reviewers found in it many 'reminders' of Turgenev's *Virgin Soil*,[2] and in more recent times it has been pointed out that practically every single character in one novel has his counterpart in the other.[3]

An additional, and more striking, echo of the Russian novel might be discerned in the apocalyptic note which is the distinguishing feature of the characteristic Jamesian atmosphere in *The Princess Casamassima*. In both novels the underground conspiracy, conducted by forces

[1] Reprinted in *Partial Portraits*, London, 1888.
[2] Gilbert Phelps, *The Russian Novel in English Fiction*, London, 1956, p. 85.
[3] Daniel Lerner, 'The Influence of Turgenev on Henry James', *The Slavonic Year-Book* (American Series I), Being Vol. XX of the *Slavonic and East European Review*, 1941, pp. 28–54.

K   137

outside the established order of things and beyond organized social control, has a peculiar emotional appeal. The reference is somehow 'beyond' the facts visualized and ascertainable by the author and his assumed audience. This creates an atmosphere of expected inevitability, an awareness of circumstances which are outside the familiar orbit, in fact an historical and ethical transcendence of reality.

In *Virgin Soil* the young Populists are all the time waiting for the 'moment' which is to arrive 'soon' but which they themselves have to bring about instead of expecting that things will be made ready for them. Their immense idealism is subjected to the superior will and pre-knowledge of the mysterious Vasily Nikolayevich who never actually appears in the book, but all the plotting, planning and decision-making can be implicitly traced back to him. As for the characters who can be met in the two novels, James, who unlike Turgenev had no direct contact with the democratic underground, presents his own as watching and looking for others who are directly engaged in action, rather than as active revolutionaries.

The one exception seems to be Paul Muniment, who is a parallel to Turgenev's self-assured, relaxed and clear-headed Solomin. His position in relation to the movement and to the Princess Casamassima has, however, a more fascinating analogy in another novel by Turgenev, *On the Eve*. Insarov, the uncommunicative Bulgarian, avenger of his people and his family, is a leader of the secret society to which he belongs. His people are the downtrodden proletarians of Slavo-Turkish politics, and like the Anarchists and Populists in the other novels, Insarov expects—and receives—a call which makes him depart into action. The attraction which Yelena feels for him is the profound excitement which an alien liberating force exercises upon a passionate female intuition hitherto confined by family and social propriety. Yelena's decision to set off at his side for the bracing yet merciless unknown, is also integrated into James's plot in the Princess's wholesale commitment to Muniment. Even the slight incident in which Yelena is noticed by her father's servant entering a house together with Insarov is used by James and transformed into a case for Hyacinth's ultimate inference that he had been abandoned and left out by the two people to whom he had given all his love and admiration.

Yet neither Insarov nor Solomin appear to have an inner world of their own, no existence beyond what they say or do. An English critic of Turgenev considers this to be a failure in characterization.[4] There-

---

[4] Richard Freeborn, *Turgenev, the Novelist's Novelist*, Oxford, 1960, p. 65.

fore one would like to point out that in the context of each novel there is an artistic reason for Turgenev's procedure. The two men mark the limit of the world which is presented, and the hidden aspect of their personality transcends the experience of both writer and reader.

The same is true of Muniment, but the opacity of his intimate character makes him unsympathetic, even repellent. Recent critics[5] have seen him as a self-preserving cynic, an incipient political bureaucrat of the modern age. The only thing he shares with Insarov, the self-sacrificing freedom-loving patriot, is his uncompromising adherence to his cause. Muniment's relationship to Christina, cold and calculating, is a frightening change from the fresh, warm youthfulness, the natural beauty of the sweeping, tragic enthusiasm which connects Yelena to Insarov. Christina, the Princess Casamassima, has the firmness and courage of Turgenev's women, but in the novel it is not she who, like Yelena, or like Isabel Archer of *The Portrait of the Lady*, gives the situation its emotional colouring and moral evaluation. Like Muniment, she is presented only from the outside, and is created for the reader mainly by her effect on a third, 'finely aware and richly responsible' character. For *The Princess Casamassima* is not the story of Christina as *On the Eve* is of Yelena, but of Hyacinth Robinson's awareness of his world. The other characters share his own search for an understanding of society and for the latent force which is doomed to subvert its apparent order, to destroy the norms which have been determining the life of all these individuals, and the roots of Hyacinth's own consciousness.

It is, therefore, not a novel about either Anarchism or Socialism, about radical thinking or revolutionary action. A study of *The Background of 'The Princess Casamassima'* by W. H. Tilley[6] in 1960 has amply corroborated Professor Trilling's[7] contention about 'the solid accuracy of James's political detail'. Yet James was probably sincere in saying that he recalled 'pulling no wires, knocking at no closed doors, applying for no "authentic" information'. His imaginative experience of the London scene was, as Mr Tilley shows, supplemented by the reports in *The Times* on assassinations, explosions, plots and secret societies, and on trials of members of terrorist organizations, ranging from Fenians to various international anarchist groups.

[5] Stephen Spencer in *The Destructive Element*, London, 1934; Lionel Trilling in *The Liberal Imagination*, New York, 1950; Irving Howe in *Politics and the Novel*, New York, 1957.
[6] University of Florida Monographs, Humanities, No. 5, Fall 1960, Gainesville, Florida. [7] *The Liberal Imagination*, New York, 1954, p. 79

According to Mr George Woodcock,[8] who is an authority on Anarchism, the conspiracy involving Hyacinth has features closer to those of the Blanquists than of Anarchists. James's novel, however, contains no direct image of the London political underground, nor does he claim to be referring to any particular group or organization. He never discusses any ideology or revolutionary programme.

> Vagueness of background and an abundance of detail combined to furnish James the opportunity to write a psychological study of revolutionists. . . . Since the *Times* did not clearly distinguish the several groups of revolutionists, and since it frequently suggested their common leadership and the international character of their operations, it may be said to have prepared its readers for the *Princess's* intimations of a great, organized, largely secret society—'an immense underworld, peopled with a thousand forms of revolutionary passion and devotion', which, being run by one or a few powerful men, threatens to rise up 'simultaneously in a dozen different countries', and will do so 'once the machinery is complete'.[9]

Yet in spite of Mr Tilley's most illuminative supply of source material, the novel can hardly satisfy as a 'psychological study of revolutionists' because of the very 'sketchiness and vagueness and dimness' of outline and the mutual position of the facts which it deals with. It is difficult to say whether James himself had at first hoped to write a novel about Hyacinth's 'subterraneous politics and occult affiliations', but in his Preface, written over twenty years after the novel, he playfully admits not to have not dealt with the 'positive quality for itself'.[10] Against a challenge by readers of a knowledge greater than his own he had in advance found what he calls 'the happy contention that the value I wished most to render and the effect I wished most to produce were precisely those of our not knowing, of society's not knowing, but only guessing and suspecting and trying to ignore, what "goes on" irreconcilably, subversively, beneath the vast smug surface'. This, indeed, seems to define the central image of the novel, the dominating theme which connects all the characters, the unifying pattern which enables us to see and appreciate the book as a whole.

It is most typical, for instance, that Diedrich Hoffendahl, who plays

[8] 'Henry James and the Conspirators', *The Sewanee Review*, 1952, pp. 219–29.
[9] Tilley, op. cit., pp. 24 and 29.
[10] All James's references to *The Princess Casamassima* come from his preface reprinted in *The Art of the Novel*, London and New York, 1953. The quotations from the novel itself are taken from the Harper Torchbooks edition which follows the text of the 'New York Edition'. The divergences between this and the original *Atlantic Monthly* version are so slight that they can be neglected for the purposes of this essay.

a central role in the subterranean movement, never appears on the scene. We know more biographical facts about him than Turgenev discloses about the ruthless Vasily Nikolayevich who, also from off stage, directs the Populists in *Virgin Soil*. But James deliberately does not tell us anything about his appearance, behaviour and personality, and it is interesting to note that in the definitive manuscript of *The Princess Casamassima* in the Houghton Library at Harvard the description of Hoffendahl as it appears in the novel has been subsequently inserted by James, whereas the page containing an earlier version has been torn out.[11] From his position outside the directly presented story Hoffendahl throws his shadow over the whole novel, producing an irresistible fascination upon the Princess, whose world he is threatening to destroy, giving a new direction to Hyacinth's sense of exclusion, and a new meaning to his disinheritance.

By insisting upon Hyacinth's origin James reverts from the suggestive indirections of most of his imagery to the biological determinism of Zola's Naturalist doctrine. Yet this motif is also incorporated into James's main theme. Millicent's question 'Who are you?' and Hyacinth's confessing to the Princess 'what he was' point to the deeper existential symbolism of Hyacinth's identity. Being a child of a dissipated English aristocrat and of a Frenchwoman of the people, a descendant both of irresponsible noblemen and of fighters in several bloody revolutions, contributes to his insecurity and his incapacity for adjustment. He sees a way out in an absolute irremediable commitment: his pledge to perform an act, undefined and unknown even to him, at an indefinite moment, which will probably cost him his life.

Hyacinth's oath reminds one strongly of Kirillov's decision in *The Possessed*, and it is interesting to speculate whether James could have been under the impact of Dostoyevsky while he was working on the *Princess*. It is likely, at least, that he was familiar with it through de Vogüë's studies on the Russian novel which had been appearing in *La Revue des Deux Mondes* since 1883.[12] Hyacinth's pledge is not, like

---

[11] The photocopied manuscript in James's handwriting is a very tidy copy of the *Atlantic Monthly* version of the novel. The original page 850 is missing and supplanted by a p. 850 and a p. 850 1/2 in James's handwriting, which on these pages is larger than in the rest of the manuscript. On the top of p. 851 a line and a half has been crossed out which does not appear in the published version ('any youth: he had begun to earn his living at the age of four'). The continuation is identical with the published version ('Muniment said that the affair . . .'—cf. p. 238 in the book).

[12] *The Possessed* appeared in French in 1886, the year in which the relevant instalments of *The Princess Casamassima* appeared in the *Atlantic Monthly* and in which it was published in book form.

Kirillov's suicide, the result of a metaphysical struggle, an eagerness to affirm a 'new and terrible freedom'. It is, on the contrary, a desperate attempt to have his beliefs implemented and ultimately justified by reality, at the expense of an independence which at that moment he has not yet learnt to value. As soon as he becomes aware of all 'the wonderful precious things, the fabric of beauty and power' his oath appears to him ill-advised and insubstantial; if he still feels committed to it, it is because it applies to a realm of values which he honours out of respect for his earlier human feelings, yet which is irrelevant to his new and more authentic choice. Suicide appears as the only solution of this conflict when even the last cord by which he has been tied to the ground of human loyalties, has snapped.

Many critics find *The Princess Casamassima* unsatisfactory because Hyacinth, with whom James seems to identify himself to an exceptionally high degree, is incapable of meeting the social reality implied in the novel on the terms which it imposes upon him. To F. W. Duppee he 'seems a case merely of unrequited sensibility',[13] and Irving Howe objects that 'Hyacinth thrives on renunciation the way heroes thrive on experience'.[14] According to D. W. Jefferson the novel fails to meet two possible requirements. Like *The Portrait of the Lady* it 'is sufficiently informative in its treatment of special social types to make the reader want more—unless he wants something quite different; that is, a closer registration of the central character's inner experience'.[15]

The substance of the novel lies, however, between an exploration of external, ascertainable relations and activities and the presentation of a central consciousness at work. It renders a universe of awareness of a subterranean potentiality, an effort to penetrate beyond the appearances of everyday routine into ultimate reality, an expectation of 'the day' of inevitable upsurge, of revolution in the etymological sense of the word, not of a social process or protracted struggle involving crises and sacrifices, but of an apocalyptic event to be expected with terror or with exultation. The selfless idealism of Turgenev's heroines—'When will the right day arrive?' is the title of Dobrolyubov's politically centred criticism of *On the Eve*—is heightened in the climax of Hyacinth's identification with the revolution. It comes, significantly, late in the book, among the very pages in which James describes Hyacinth's encounters with the poor in terms of acute repugnance.

[13] F. W. Dupee, *Henry James*, New York, 1956, p. 136.
[14] Irving Howe, *Politics and the Novel*, New York, 1957, p. 153.
[15] D. W. Jefferson, *Henry James*, Edinburgh and London, 1960, p. 64.

What was most in Hyacinth's mind was the idea, of which every pulsation of the general life of his time was a syllable, that the flood of democracy was rising over the world; that it would sweep all the traditions of the past before it; that, whatever it might fail to bring, it would at least carry in its bosom a magnificent energy; and that it might be trusted to look after its own. When this high, healing, uplifting tide should cover the world and float in the new era, it would be its own fault (whose else?) if want and suffering and crime should continue to be ingredients of the human lot.

It is true that 'with his mixed, divided nature, his conflicting sympathies, his eternal habit of swinging from one view to another, he regarded the prospect in different moods with different intensities'. But essentially, Hyacinth is ready to immerse himself 'in the destructive element', to relinquish his individuality as a 'mere particle . . . in the grey immensity of the people', as he told the Princess on their first meeting. He feels that his personal attitude ultimately does not matter, and actually looks forward to the coming flood:

> . . . there was joy and exultation in the thought of surrendering one's self to the wash of the wave, of being carried higher on the sun-touched crests of wild billows than one could ever be by a dry, lonely effort of one's own. That vision could deepen into ecstasy; make it indifferent if one's ultimate fate, in such a heaving sea, were not almost certainly to be submerged in bottomless depths or dashed to pieces on immovable rocks. . . .

There is an almost orgiastic abandon of the self in these images, conveying the rhythm of a libidinal release of pent-up energies. The drive of the flowing tide makes for the consummation and gratification of the instinctive urge towards total union, at the expense of individual consciousness. Yet occasionally, including the end of the passage, a rational qualification is introduced, an attempt at gaining a distance necessary for objective judgement:

> Hyacinth felt that whether his personal sympathy should rest finally with the victors or the vanquished, the victorious force was potentially infinite and would require no testimony from the irresolute.

An awareness of defeat undercuts the triumph of the uncheckable thrust beyond the solid boundaries of Hyacinth's fixed apartness— social, sexual, existential.

His final collapse is typified in the humiliating scene of his 'glaring through the fog', side by side with the Prince, spying on the Princess and Muniment, 'strange and detached because everything else of his past had been engulfed in the abyss that opened before him'. The vagueness of Hyacinth's hold on reality is irrevocably turned into nothingness and his experience of yet another personal betrayal—Millicent's—makes it pointless for him to stick to loyalties which had been formed on the basis of past beliefs. The end of the novel coincides with the disappearance of all conjecture, expectation, excitement, even of doubts, misgivings, apprehension.

'There are times when *The Princess Casamassima* seems almost designed to evade its own theme', says Irving Howe,[16] and accounts for this by James's uncertainty and lack of intimate knowledge of his political material. Yet is not James's feeling of his own situation, faced by the recalcitrant *source* of his material, in itself the theme of the novel? As he wrote himself, his scheme 'called for the suggested nearness to all our apparently ordered life of some sinister anarchic underworld', which was to be presented not in the shape of 'sharp particulars, but of loose appearances, vague motions and sounds and symptoms, just perceptible presences and general looming possibilities'.

It is customary to treat *The Princess Casamassima*, together with *The Bostonians*, and sometimes *The Tragic Muse*, as political novels or attempts at social realism. In these books James had indeed explored certain issues of public importance. But the real character of the two novels published in 1886 will be obscured if one fails to notice the differences in tone and method which relate each of them to very different groups of James's fiction. *The Bostonians*, with its essentially serene humour tinged with somewhat callow satire, shows but does not penetrate into the deeper issues, social and sexual, which are involved. It is reminiscent of *The Europeans* more than of any other novel, and by the harmony and simplicity of its outline it is also akin to *Washington Square*, another early, purely 'American' novel. *The Princess Casamassima* is less direct and more disquieting, and shares its theme of watching, prying, conjecturing, exploring and probing, with *The Aspern Papers*, *The Turn of the Screw*, *The Sacred Fount*—and beyond, with works of James's full maturity. In this book the novelist developed his theme in a study of a subject of infinitely wider scope than in any other of his works: the reaction of the society to which he belonged towards what it felt as a threat to its own foundation. Many features of *The Princess Casamassima*, like the social scene with which it is concerned, have dated by now and lost their immediate pertinence; and yet it

[16] op. cit., p. 146.

contains not only the disturbing and fascinating external analogies to the modern world, but is full of looming potentialities which the art of the novel, grappling with society, sex, self, with the theme of knowledge in relation to unalienable, hidden, suppressed yet subversive forces, has more fully discovered only in the twentieth century.

University of Zagreb

Corno Inglese: Notes on the texture of George Bernard Shaw's Musical Criticism

E. D. MACKERNESS

WITH the exception of some concert notices contributed on behalf of George Vandaleur Lee to a short-lived periodical called *The Hornet*, the greater part of George Bernard Shaw's significant musical journalism appeared in the pages of *The Star* and *The World* between 1888 and 1894.[1] Shaw's association with these papers is fully described in St John Ervine's *Bernard Shaw His Life, Work and Friends* (1956); and his progress as a music critic has recently been outlined by Dan H. Laurence in *How To Become a Musical Critic* (1960). From his miscellany, however, it is apparent that the well-known volumes of *London Music in 1888–89 . . .* and *Music in London 1890–94* by no means exhaust Shaw's best work in this field: and Mr Laurence's assemblage of fugitive pieces illustrates the wide range of the journals —from the *Pall Mall Gazette* to the *Magazine of Music*—which made use of Shaw's talents as a commentator on the musical scene. The extracts given in *How to Become A Musical Critic*, moreover, enable us to trace a distinct evolution in this branch of Shaw's *œuvre*. In the mid-seventies, for instance, he was producing rapportage of a comparatively conventional kind, enlivened by brief sallies of typically Shavian

---

[1] Shaw wrote many more articles on music, of course, right up to the end of his life.

humour. During the eighteen-eighties, though—in such periodicals as the *Musical Review* and the *Dramatic Review*—he begins to come into his own; and an essay in which he energetically disposes of Liszt's 'Dante' Symphony (and by implication condemns much other pro-gramme music) may be taken as representing his mature manner.[2] Many other examples could be quoted here. The prose style of 'Corno di Bassetto' is, fortunately, inimitable; as such it proved an asset to editors like T. P. O'Connor and Edmund Yates. In no other writing on music—in the English language, that is—are levity and seriousness of purpose so ingeniously intermingled. Yet Shaw's own contention that he 'vulgarized' music criticism must be taken with some reserve. For the very raciness and readability of his contributions to musicography frequently conceal the critic's ulterior objectives. It is the purpose of this essay to suggest the nature of these, and to examine some of the means by which they achieve expression.

I

At the time of Shaw's commencement as a music critic, the musical columns of leading daily and weekly papers were written by men whose enthusiasms for what was going on in the world of music were not invariably backed up by relevant knowledge or astute powers of discrimination. This could certainly not be said of old hands who, like H. F. Chorley, J. W. Davison and Francis Hueffer, were still surviving in Shaw's youth; but there were many others who, though competent enough as journalists, laid no special claim to profound musicianship.[3] Such individuals frequently traded on their connections with per-formers or cultivated the acquaintance of professors at the colleges of music. From the critical point of view there was nothing reprehensible about this; but in pursuance of their calling, writers of the last-named class tended to muffle the expression of forthright judgement so as to avoid giving offence. Shaw makes an amusing reference, in an essay on Mascagni, to those critics who 'keep only one quality of margarine, which they spread impartially over all composers of established reputa-tion; so that you shall not detect one hair's breadth of difference in their estimates of Beethoven and Meyerbeer, Wagner and Sir Arthur

---

[2] See *How to Become A Musical Critic*, 1960, p. 56 et seq.
[3] In this connection see Joseph Bennett, *Forty Years of Music 1865–1905*, 1908, p. 9: and the early chapters of Hermann Klein, *Thirty Years of Musical Life in London 1870–1900*, 1903.

Sullivan, John Sebastian Bach and the President of the Royal Academy of Music'.[4] But this phenomenon, as Shaw intimates, was merely symptomatic of something more serious—the anxiety to evade the necessity of eventual commitment. He regarded the whole business of analysis—the exhaustive discussion of musical procedures in terms of what he called the 'abracadabra of musical technology'—as one means of dodging the critic's true responsibilities. 'It is perhaps natural', he wrote in 1891, 'that gentlemen who are incapable of criticism should fall back on parsing; but, for my own part, I find it better to hold my tongue when I have nothing to say.'[5] And he looked with suppressed amusement on the discomfort frequently suffered by the compilers of programme notes—with their authoritative references to 'postludes brought to a close on the pedal of A, the cadence being retarded by four chords forming an arpeggio of a diminished seventh, each grade serving as tonic for a perfect chord', etc.—when faced with the disagreeable task of saying something pertinent about music they obviously found quite uncongenial.

But since the readers of *The Star* and *The World* were not aesthetically fastidious, it was essential that Shaw should discuss musical experiences in a way which would not scare or bore the layman. In carrying this ambition through, he occasionally saw fit to compare his own style with that of his colleagues on other journals; and to establish the appropriate tone he introduced diverting asides which only escape the charge of irrelevance by virtue of their uniquely informative qualities. Shaw's numerous impertinencies have a charm of their own, as in this comment on a performance in London by the French violinist César Thomson: '. . . I altogether decline to give an opinion on the strength of Paganini's contemptible variations on Non più mesta, to which I listened with the haughtiest indignation, though they of course produced the usual hysterical effect on those connoisseurs of the marvellous to whom great violinists are only side-shows in a world of fat ladies and children with two heads'.[6] But this sort of thing would hardly be acceptable if we were not made aware of the fact that Shaw's own command of the 'science' of music was far from negligible. His attitude towards it, as we soon discover, is informed by an intimate knowledge which earns him the right to speak slightingly of 'that

[4] *Music in London 1890–94* in the Standard Edition of the Works of Bernard Shaw, 1932, Vol. I, pp. 269–270.
[5] Ibid., Vol. I, p. 263.
[6] Ibid., Vol. III, p. 136.

dynasty of execrable impostors in tights and tunics, interpolating their loathsome B flats into the beautiful melodies they could not sing, and swelling with conceit when they were able to finish Di quella pira with a high C'.[7] For Shaw was the son of a fine mezzo-soprano vocalist, and had been 'steeped in romantic opera' from boyhood. And if his criticism consisted of nothing more than the varied remarks he makes on the mechanics of voice-production it would still be of the utmost value. Again and again he gives us illuminating comments on the vocal styles practised by various singers, famous and obscure; and this part of his writing shows a great awareness of the demands which different musical idioms make upon the singers' physical stamina and imaginative powers. This is brilliantly exemplified in an essay which appeared in the *Anglo-Saxon Review* (March 1901) on the occasion of Verdi's death. Here it is argued that whereas the music of Handel and Wagner is on the whole 'grateful' to the human voice, that of Verdi is less so because of the composer's tendency to pitch his melodies in the middle part of what Shaw calls the 'upper fifth of the voice'. And this in turn places a strain upon the singer which is unfavourable to true musicianship.

Not all lovers of opera would concur with Shaw's censure of Verdi's 'recklessness as to the effect of his works on their performers'. But in this instance he was not speaking without some authority. His know-ledge of such works as *Don Giovanni, Il Trovatore* and *Der Freischutz* was obtained at first-hand; and the home rendering of operatic selections such as he describes in his *Sixteen Self-Sketches* (1949) led him to place an over-riding importance on the dramatic as distinct from the 'abstract' potentialities of music in general. He even goes so far as to suggest that Meyerbeer's depiction of *Les Huguenots* in musical terms is more exciting than the prose fiction on which so much romantic opera is based: 'In the music you will find the body and reality of that feeling which the mere novelist could only describe to you. . . . As to (the) duels, what wretched printed list of the thrusts in *carte* and *tierce* delivered by D'Artagnan or Bussy d'Amboise can interest the man who knows Don Giovanni's duel in the dark with the Commandant, or Romeo's annihilation of Tybalt (not Shakespear's, but Gounod's Romeo), or Rauol's explosion of courage on the brink of the fight in the *Pré aux Clercs*.'[8] This (like much of the essay from which it is taken) is over-written; yet it testifies, despite the obvious special pleading, to

[7] Ibid., Vol. II, p. 179.
[8] *How to Become A Musical Critic*, pp. 216–17. The article in which this occurs ('The Religion of the Pianoforte') appeared in *The Fortnightly Review* for February 1894.

an inner possession of the music which is corroborated by later criticisms. On the subject of the relative merits of dramatic and absolute music, Shaw is often confused and inconsistent; and it will not do to turn a blind eye to certain shortcomings which will be mentioned presently. Yet with all his aberrations, Shaw was never guilty of the kind of unconscious obtuseness represented by the following extract from Ebenezer Prout's *Harmony: Its Theory and Practice* (1889). Speaking of a short quotation from *Parsifal*, Prout remarks that it involves 'a peculiarly harsh first inversion of the eleventh of C, the eleventh resolving on the third'. And he concludes (after reminding the reader that this particular harmonization breaks a rule he has enunciated earlier): 'This is not recommended for imitation; Wagner has no doubt introduced this very rough dissonance for the sake of the dramatic effect'![9]

It is, of course, easy enough to ridicule theorists like Prout and others among his contemporaries who wrote on the grammar of musical composition: if a heavily ironical handling of their customary mode of analysis is required it can be found in *The World* for 31 May 1893.[10] But Shaw's fulminations against the 'Mesopotamian' diction of formal musical disquisition must not be misunderstood, since they constitute something more than simple-minded outbursts of uncontrollable derision. Shaw knew well enough that the principles which dominated the academic study of music had long ago reduced the art to a complex system, and he took it upon himself to submit the deficiencies of this—when considered in its extreme form—to forensic examination. He mistrusted the zeal with which teachers of harmony and counterpoint insisted on adhering to established dogmas, and held the view that allegiance to strict orthodoxy in such matters was damaging to any adventurous composer's integrity. 'It may be true', he wrote in 1885, 'that the best contrapuntists were also the most skilful composers; but their good counterpoint was the result of their skill, and not their skill the result of their counterpoint.'[11] Unhappily, the deliberate 'attempt to pass off the forms of music for music itself' had become an accepted convention in some quarters, with the result that turgid insipidities were habitually regarded as above reproach, while the work of composers who showed unorthodox tendencies (like Hermann Goetz, for example) was politely elbowed aside. 'The fact is', wrote

[9] Prout, *Harmony: Its Theory and Practice*, 1889, p. 170.
[10] *Music in London 1890–94*, Vol. II, p. 321.
[11] *How To Become A Musical Critic*, p. 104.

Shaw, 'there are no rules, and there never were any rules, and there never will be any rules of musical composition except rules of thumb; and thumbs vary in length, like ears.' He goes on; 'Doubtless it is bold of me to differ from such great musicians as Albrechtsberger, Marpurg, Kiel, Richter, Ouseley and Macfarren as against such notoriously licentious musical anarchists as Bach, Handel, Haydn, Mozart, Beethoven and Wagner; but the fact is, I prefer the music of these insubordinate persons.'[12] The supreme instance of music itself triumphing over the mere *forms* of music was, of course, Wagner, whose persistent violation of established canons, though startling enough, had a distinct rationale. 'There is not a single bar of "classical music" in The Ring', Shaw tells us in *The Perfect Wagnerite*, '—not a note in it that has any other point than the single direct point of giving musical expression to the drama. In classical music there are, as the analytical programs tell us, first subjects and second subjects, free fantasias, recapitulations, and codas. . . . Wagner is never driving at anything of this sort. . . . And this is why he is so easy for the natural musician who has had no academic teaching.'[13] In this case, we must admit (after taking into account the implications of Shaw's pronouncement) that the difficulties which do actually confront us in Wagner's works are brushed aside a little too confidently; yet we must remember that *The Perfect Wagnerite* is an essay in partisanship, not a carefully documented piece of musicological research.

Shaw's remarks on non-dramatic vocal music were often unusually caustic; and much of his sarcasm was directed towards that well-established nineteenth-century institution, the choral festival. The custom, on festival occasions, was to produce one or two well-known works from the standard repertory together with some specially commissioned novelties by contemporary composers. This practice, as Shaw was quick to perceive, gave rise to a minor tradition of tediously fabricated odes, oratorios and cantatas which were hardly likely to stand the test of time. His notice of Hubert Parry's *Judith, or the Regeneration of Manasseh* (1888) is a locus classicus in this connection. 'Judith', he writes, 'consists of a sort of musical fabric that any gentleman of Mr Parry's general culture, with a turn for music and the requisite technical training, can turn out to any extent needful for the purposes of a Festival Committee. There is not a rhythm in it, not a progression, not a modulation that brings a breath of freshness with it. . . . The

[12] *Music in London 1890–94*, Vol. III, p. 163.
[13] *The Perfect Wagnerite* in *Major Critical Essays*, Standard Edition, 1932, p. 168.

instrumentation is conventional to the sleepiest degree.'[14] With this judgement the Special Correspondent of the *Musical Times* was half inclined to agree. Reporting the first performance at Birmingham Town Hall (in October 1888) he was so bold as to maintain that 'the set airs, perhaps, are open to the general criticism of lacking in some measure a striking distinctiveness of melody' and that 'in performance a sense of dulness was decidedly felt'. But on reading this account, one detects in it an unmistakable compliance with the views expressed in an article on 'New Works at Birmingham' published in the *Musical Times* a month beforehand. This stubbornly pedestrian analysis of *Judith* (by the same author?) reaches a curious level of equivocation in the following observation: 'It may be urged that the melodies (of the second scene), if not absolutely commonplace, lack special distinctiveness, *but they have an effect of truth to the situation and circumstances such as is, perhaps, better than originality.*' There could hardly be a more patent example of abject ineffectiveness than this laboured write-up, which in style and outlook runs entirely counter to all that Shaw was trying to do in musical criticism.

As for the more familiar items which figured in the festival programmes, Shaw regarded such things as Gounod's *Redemption*, Brahms's *Requiem* and Mendelssohn's *St Paul* with unconcealed distaste; they presented themselves to his mind as instances of ardent religiosity doing duty for genuine inspiration. Modern oratorio was 'mostly a combination of frivolity and sensuality with hypocrisy and the most oppressive dullness'.[15] In order to discover true religious feeling expressed in music which could hold the listener's attention *as music*, one had to turn to Beethoven's Choral Symphony or to Mozart's *Requiem*: and Shaw's scathing comments on the 'oratorio system' stand as both a condemnation of evident fatuity in musical art and a unique placing of the kind of sensibility which treated massive performances of sacred music under concert conditions as a respectable substitute for devotional exercise.

II

To some of his fellow practitioners in the sphere of musical criticism, Shaw's efforts must have seemed ill-mannered, eccentric and unnecessarily mischievous.[16] But very few of his contemporaries shared

[14] *London Music in 1888–89 . . .*, 1937, p. 43.
[15] *Music in London 1890–94*, Vol. III, p. 200.
[16] Shaw was, in fact, threatened with libel actions during his career as a music critic.

his gift for piercing through apparently promising exteriors and distinguishing the dead from the living in musical composition. It is true that he had his moments of wrong-headedness: too often if a work showed signs of 'dullness' it was casually written off. It is surely a little wide of the mark, for instance, to suggest that *Elijah* is utterly 'thoughtless', that Schubert's Great C Major Symphony is 'exasperatingly brainless', or that Hermann Goetz's Symphony in F is 'the only real symphony that has been composed since Beethoven died'.[17] All the same, Shaw's judgements were the product of an active intelligence working its way through a substantial body of musical compositions uninhibited by damaging *a priori* considerations. Corno di Bassetto's weekly chronicle of musical events brought forth many spirited reassessments; moreover, his partiality for dramatic music and his respect for 'organic form' was compatible with a sixth sense that although music is in an obvious way non-moral, the listener's musical susceptibilities need constantly to be checked against the promptings of non-musical experience.

This accounts, among other things, for the unusually apt analogies which are found everywhere throughout Shaw's musical writings. To take a few samples at random. In August 1889 Shaw congratulated the *Musical Times* for reprinting some of Edward Fitzgerald's notes on music (extracted from his letters) and wrote: 'On the whole, Fitz was a sound critic; ... he knew one sort of music from another, and was incapable of speaking of the overtures to Mozart's Zauberflöte, Beethoven's Leonora and Rossini's William Tell *as if they were merely three pieces cut off the same roll of stuff by three different tailors.*'[18] His antipathy to Brahms led to many sly comments: 'Mind, I do not deny that the Requiem is a solid piece of music manufacture. *You feel at once that it could only have come from the establishment of a first-class undertaker.*'[19] Unlike Henry Chorley, Shaw regarded Wagner as a good conductor—provided that the orchestra made allowance for his unusual mannerisms and his 'tense neuralgic glare'—and in 1890 blamed the Philharmonic Society for not engaging him over a longer period: 'but instead of having the sense to hold on to him ... they dropped him *like a hot potato* after one year, and clung to Mr Cusins ... from 1867 until it became evident, a few years ago, that *decomposition had set in*'.[20]

---

[17] *Music in London 1890–94*, Vol. III, p. 94.
[18] *London Music in 1888–89 ...*, pp. 189–90.
[19] Ibid., p. 376.
[20] *Music in London 1890–94*, Vol. I, p. 32.

Dozens of comparable examples could be cited. But when Shaw claims that 'perspective' occasionally comes into his writings on music, he means that in general he is not disposed to discuss opera, concertos, symphonies and so forth in terms which are calculated to exclude the uninitiated. In all this he is deeply indebted to the vividly illuminating figures which crowd into his prose. And this section of his work has a decided kinship with that of another great master of analogy, Dickens.

Shaw used to quote Dickens with great frequency, and fell into the habit of appropriating Dickensian turns of phrase for his own purposes. And the force of Dickensian analogy—the product of a mind which, as Shaw remarks, is constantly 'taking life with intense interest, and observing, analysing, remembering with amazing scientific power'— finds a counterpart in many passages from Shaw's writings on music. Thus he concludes a paragraph about the Birmingham Festival of 1891: 'On the Passion Music day I escaped the corner (of the hall), and shared a knifeboard at the back of the gallery with a steward who kept Bach off by reading the Birmingham *Daily Post*, and breathed so hard when he came to the bankruptcy list that it was plain that every firm mentioned in it was heavily in his debt.'[21] That does not, perhaps, achieve the full piquancy of Dickens at his liveliest—though there is a certain affinity between it and the kind of thing represented by the description of Wemmick in *Great Expectations* despatching morsels of food into his mouth 'as if he were posting them'. A later account (1892) of the annual competition between the Board School choirs at Exeter Hall is closer in effect to Dickens's own style: 'Some young ladies behind me were eagerly scanning the choristers to find "the angel". . . . There were dreamy, poetic, delicate-featured boys and girls; docile, passively receptive ones . . .; little duchesses whom I should have liked to adopt, little dukes who would have been considerably enriched if anyone had cut them off with a shilling. . . . But angel there was none, except all our good and bad angels, who, being two to each member of a crowded audience, must have been kept pretty constantly on the wing to avoid being crushed.'[22] And a report on a Historical Recital at which Edgar Jacques gave a running commentary has an engaging near-Dickensian whimsicality: 'when Jacques pleaded that the American (organ) was "something between" the organ in the Albert Hall and the portable organs of Palestrina's day, and frankly gave up the harpsichord as a bad job after the audience had listened to it for half an hour with unsuspicious awe, the twinkling of his eye

[21] Ibid., Vol. I, p. 256.   [22] Ibid., Vol. II, p. 199.

betrayed the suppressed convulsions within.'[23] Had Dickens taken on
the task of regular music critic, one feels, this is what his criticism might
have been like. But the point of these quotations is not merely to under-
line an obvious indebtedness; it is rather to mark off Shaw's kind of
sensibility from that of the critic whose response to music causes him to
become wrapped up in the elaborate solemnity of what is to him a construction of subjects, counter-subjects and expositions. The latter class
of individual, it need hardly be pointed out, seldom rises to the level of
literary accomplishment achieved in the musical writings of George
Bernard Shaw. These are not only brilliant contributions to the
periodical criticism of a specific period: they also have a vigour and
incisiveness which transcends the particular requirements of time and
place.

III

Shaw's place in the tradition of 'radical' journalism to which Dickens
—and before him Leigh Hunt—contributed, is established by reason
of the stand he took on the 'music for the people' issue, which occupied
the minds of many liberally inclined music-lovers during the later
nineteenth century.[24] An ardent supporter of the proposal that the local
rates should be drawn upon to help finance municipal bands and other
musical entertainments, Shaw was in sympathy with John Ruskin's
view that 'the people (should be) permitted daily audience of faithful
and gentle orchestral rendering of the work of the highest classical
masters'.[25] Despite the fact that so much of his noteworthy criticism
concerns itself with performances at which the 'shilling public' was not
the most influential part of the audience, Shaw persisted in propagating
the notion that the best music is not to be regarded as a monopoly of
privileged cliques: it is something which belongs, or ought to belong, to
all. And freedom of access to it is distinctly in the public interest. 'Just
as the river is useful to men who do not row', he wrote in 1890, 'the
bridges to West Enders who never cross them, and the railways to the
bedridden, so the provision of good music and plenty of it smooths life
as much for those who do not know the National Anthem from Rule
Britannia, as for those who can whistle all the themes in the Ninth

[23] Ibid., Vol. II, p. 100.
[24] See E. D. Mackerness, *A Social History of English Music*, 1964, p. 200.
[25] *Music in London 1890–94*, Vol. III, p. 205. Shaw is here quoting a passage from
Ariadne Florentina reproduced on page 56 of A. M. Wakefield's *Ruskin on Music*, 1894.

Symphony'.[26] But the business of advancing the musical education of the masses could not be contemplated in this 'age of general insensibility to music' until the militant complacency of the Philistine had been freely rebuked. In an essay published on the occasion of Shaw's ninetieth birthday Professor E. J. Dent observed that G.B.S. was never, in his capacity as a music critic, 'systematically truculent' like his colleague John F. Runciman.[27] Yet he *was* systematically trenchant because he clung to his conviction that the critic must perpetually be denouncing charlatanry, favouritism and polite imposture. The liberties he took when discussing the public appearances of famous conductors and performers would not be tolerated today. But there is more to Corno di Bassetto's facetiousness than the element of spiteful irreverence which at first sight seems to have prompted many of his more strenuous tirades. For Shaw the act of writing music criticism was a public duty in which his responsibilities towards those who bought *The Star* and *The World* took precedence over whatever respect he might have for the controlling interest of those papers. And the idiosyncrasies of his musical journalism are never at enmity with the intention which animates so much of his best creative work—the intention, that is, to vindicate with fearless provocativeness the enduring and undeniable Sanity of Art.

University of Sheffield

---

[26] Ibid., Vol. I, p. 26.

[27] J. F. Runciman was music critic of the *Saturday Review* at a time when Shaw was contributing theatrical notices to that paper. A gifted and perceptive writer, he was also something of a poseur. His 'impetuous frankness', as he called it in a dedicatory letter in his book *Old Scores and New Readings, 1894*, cost Frank Harris some heavy lawyers' bills.

The Rhetoric of Sincerity: *The Autobiography of Mark Rutherford* as Fiction

GAMINI SALGADO

'We ought to endeavour to give our dreams reality, but in reality we should preserve the dream.' (William Hale White: *More Pages from a Journal*. O.U.P. 1910)

WHAT does it mean to say that a book should be read as a novel? With most books of course, the question does not arise. They are, fairly recognizably, either novels or not. But there are always marginal cases, as there may be in the other arts. (Is it a sculpture or a mobile?). Some travel books, dramatized tracts, romances—*Sea and Sardinia* for instance, or *Candide* or *Rasselas*. Curiously enough, autobiographies are rarely problematic in this respect—John Stuart Mills's, or Edmund Gosse's or Collingwood's is, what it purports to be, the record of the historical development of a single living personage, or a phase of that development. At first glance this would seem to be quite as adequate as a description of *The Autobiography of Mark Rutherford*, but the similarity is superficial and deceptive.

The first expectation we give up when we begin a novel is that of literal truth:

An autobiographical novel may well have not only the same formal characteristics as an autobiography but also much the same degree of

GAMINI SALGADO

factuality (and the same applies in principle to the history and the historical novel). Nevertheless, the matter of factuality seems to be crucial. All works of literary art may be imaginative and inventive, but the distinguishing characteristic of works of creative literature is that they are imaginative, inventive and *fictional*. . . . The point is that the book purports to be life-like but not to be factual while an autobiography or history purports to be factual—and in the last analysis stands or falls by its factuality.[1]

The question 'Did this really happen?' becomes meaningless in reading a novel, except for the most simple-minded reader (or the most super-sophisticated, like Miss Mary Macarthy). Instead, we begin to be concerned with questions like: 'In what sense is this true? What is this particular scene, dialogue, description, doing here? Why do these people behave like this?—and finally, How does this concern me?' We do not think of the ideas and opinions expressed by the characters as in themselves the most important part of the book, nor do we regard the author's summing-up as the distilled essence of the whole, as the concluding sections of autobiographies often implicitly invite us to do. Rather, the novelist holds with 'Mark Rutherford' that 'what we believe is not of so much importance as the path by which we travel to it' (p. 126). Character, setting, action, dialogue—in a word, *form*, begins to impose itself on our attention. The reading of a novel becomes a continuing experience, instead of a necessary preliminary to the acquisition of information. The distinction is a rough and ready one, but it will serve for the examination of a single book. *The Autobiography of Mark Rutherford* demands that we bring to it the framework of expectation that we ordinarily bring to a novel. Only then does its full richness reveal itself.

Two preliminary points need making. The first is that though *Mark Rutherford's Deliverance* was intended as a sequel to the Autobiography, it has none of the coherence and compactness of the earlier book; any pretensions which it has to formal organization have disappeared by the time we reach the Notes to the Book of Job. The Autobiography is a novel by itself, with its own shape and structure.

The second point is that in many places the Autobiography is not literally faithful to the facts of Hale White's life.[2] Hale White was an efficient and successful civil servant, both as subordinate and as superior; Mark and Ellen in the book are separated for many years, while

[1] Allan Rodway, *Science & Modern Writing*, Sheed & Ward, 1964.
[2] See Chs. II–IV of Irving Stock's study or C. M. Maclean's *Mark Rutherford: A Biography of William Hale White*, MacDonald, 1955.

160

Hale White married his fiancée; unlike the hero of the Autobiography, Hale White did not complete his theological training; as far as is known, no character corresponding to the Mardon of the book existed. These are a few of the many discrepancies between the facts of the book and the facts of the author's biography. The book may be accurate in a general sense, but as a detailed factual record of one man's life *Mark Rutherford's Autobiography* is not 'true'. Hale White himself tells us elsewhere that 'there is much added which is entirely fictitious'.[3]

In the most obvious sense, the shape of the book is somewhat different from that of many autobiographies. It begins with childhood, as autobiographies commonly do, but it does not conclude with some momentous climactic event, such as the author's marriage, or his winning a seat in Parliament, or the making of his first million pounds. The conclusion is more like that of a novel in that it relates to the theme, which is indicated in the quotation from Hale White's Journal which I have used as an epigraph. It is the classic theme of the contrast and conflict between the objective and the subjective view of self: the self's sense of being a free agent in a world of infinite freedom and possibility (the dream) and the self externally viewed as utterly constricted by heredity, temperament, tradition and circumstance (reality). And as the dream of intellectual and spiritual freedom comes up against the reality of the parched and shrivelled doctrinal system of the Dissenters and undergoes the 'death' of disillusion, so in the larger world the hero's desire to translate the dream into reality must confront the inexorable fact of death—not his own death which 'is not an event of (his) life' because 'it is not lived through', but the death of two others—one who embodied the goal of the dream of love and the other the dream of true spiritual freedom. And in spite of the impulse to moralize death and thus in effect to diminish its inexorability (exemplified here, in appropriate fictional form, in the Unitarian preacher's sermon at Mardon's funeral), the hero remains faithful to the truth of feeling. The preacher points out that—

> Mardon would live as every force in Nature lives—for ever; transmuted into a thousand different forms; the original form utterly forgotten, but never perishing.

on which the hero mournfully reflects:

> This may be true, but, after all, I can only accept the fact of death in silence, as we accept the loss of youth and all other calamities. (p. 136)

[3] *The Early Life of Mark Rutherford by Himself*, O.U.P., 1913, p. 5.

Just as the ending of the book avoids the note of complacent sum-
mary which occurs in many autobiographies, so its opening resolutely
refuses the kind of justification often pleaded by writers of autobiography. ('At the request of many friends. . . .', 'A record of modest
success over four decades in the world's largest plastic toothpick
factory may not be wholly devoid of interest', etc.) The problem that
Rutherford raises is in fact the imaginative writer's central problem,
the problem Strindberg focused on in his attack on naturalistic drama:

> Here we have the ordinary case which is so much in demand these days,
> the *rule*, the human norm, which is so banal, so insignificant, so dull that
> after four hours of suffering you ask yourself the old question: how does
> this concern me?[4]

Strindberg puts the matter from the spectator's or reader's point of
view, Rutherford from the writer's:

> Of what use is it, many persons will say, to present to the world what is
> mainly a record of weaknesses and failures? If I had any triumphs to tell;
> if I could show how I had risen superior to poverty and suffering; if, in
> short, I were a hero of any kind whatsoever, I might perhaps be justified in
> communicating my success to mankind, and stimulating them to do as I
> have done. But mine is the tale of a commonplace life, perplexed by many
> problems I have never solved; disturbed by many difficulties I have never
> surmounted; and blotted by ignoble concessions which are a constant
> regret. (p. 1)

The 'writer' feels the manuscript may be worth preserving for two
reasons (though he will not undertake the responsibility of publishing
it). The first is that it may be of social and historical interest, recording
as it does a neglected phase of provincial English religious life; and it is
as such that the book has been considered, if at all. The other is the
novelist's reason, the appeal to what is common in our common
humanity:

> In the next place, I have observed that the mere knowing that other people
> have been tried as we have been tried is a consolation to us, and that we
> are relieved by the assurance that our sufferings are not special and peculiar,
> but common to us with many others. (p. 2)

Although this second apology has been almost completely ignored, the
book as a whole is written very much in its spirit. It is identical with
the apology of many seventeenth-century spiritual autobiographies,

---

[4] August Strindberg, 'On Modern Drama and Modern Theatre', 1889. Reprinted in
Playwrights on Playwriting ed. Toby Cole, MacGibbon & Kee, 1960.

which were one factor in the rise of the novel; but here it functions not at its face value but as itself a novelistic device.

There is a point at which the novelist and the chronicler of religious dissent meet. As Irving Stock has pointed out, Rutherford's quarrel against Calvinism was precisely that it betrayed the best insights of its founders in not matching precept with practice. And the form best suited for demonstrating this (as opposed to merely asserting it) is the novel, whose staple is just this incongruity between inner life and outward behaviour. Thus a scene like that of the 'Dorcas meeting' described in Chapter III is a small triumph of the novelist's art of selection and presentation. The four pictures on the wall, the two dominant ones being those of Mr and Mrs Snale, the others of the Holy Ghost's descent and the Last Judgement, with the irony of the contrast between those represented in the picture as receiving the blessing of the Holy Spirit ('a number of persons sitting in a chamber, and each one with the flame of a candle on his head') and those assembled at the meeting in the complacent confidence of having already received that blessing; the 'fineness of tact' which issued in the reading of births, marriages and deaths from the dissenting journal, where it would not have been proper to read them from any other; and above all, the very accent of simpering hypocrisy in Mr Snale's objections to readings from *The Vicar of Wakefield* (the choice of this book, the story of a happy clergyman, has its own charge of irony):

'Because you know Mr Rutherford' he said with his smirk, 'the company is mixed; there are young leedies present, and *perhaps*, a book with a more requisite tone might be more suitable on such an occasion'. (p. 31)

—these are products of the novelist's distinctive insight and achieve their effect in terms of the novel's internal economy, whatever their value as evidence to the social historian.

The outstanding example in the book of the use of straightforward documentary material for imaginative purposes is the first sermon preached by the young Mark Rutherford (Ch. III). Taken in isolation, the content of the sermon has a representative quality which has often been noticed. It is in its own way as classical an instance of the mid-Victorian response to the crisis in faith as Tennyson's *In Memoriam* or Arnold's great essay on Literature and Dogma. But thus to isolate it is to lose a great deal of its power. To feel its full impact, the sermon should be read in the context of poignant irony prepared for it by such things as the young Rutherford's buoyant optimism at the prospect of making his mark as a preacher ('The congregation had increased a good deal during the past four weeks, and I was stimulated by the prospect of the new life before me'); the contrast between the speaker's theme of the vital *necessity* behind all true religious seeking and the all-too-evident absence of any such necessity in the religious life of the community; the idea of Christianity as 'essentially the religion of the unknown and of the lonely; of those who are not a success'; most of all by the soul-chilling failure to make any kind of human contact with his flock. This failure becomes explicit in the hero's reflective consciousness later, but is presented when it occurs through two austere vignettes, each of which takes up no more than a sentence:

> Nobody came near me but my landlord, the chapel-keeper, who said it was raining, and immediately went away to put out the lights and shut up the building.

And:

> When I got home I found that my supper, consisting of bread and cheese with a pint of beer, was on the table, but apparently it had been thought unnecessary to light the fire again at that time of night. (p. 36)

—'apparently it had been thought unnecessary . . .'—the very impersonality of the syntax heightens the speaker's sense of utter estrangement, while the putting out of the lights and the absence of a fire have a vividness and force which has nothing to do with whether or not these things really happened.

Mark Rutherford's Autobiography is a kind of *Pilgrim's Progress* in reverse, with all the joy of the journey at the beginning and the burden to be shouldered at the end. (Hale White was born in the same town and into the same religious tradition as Bunyan). The book's force and poignancy spring, as I have said, from the sense of tension between actuality and possibility, between the straightforward, often pedestrian history that is recounted and the constant sense of other and immensely richer possibilities of action and development. Amidst all the disenchantments of the world, the dream remains haunting and alluring to the end. Compare for instance, the hero's early vision of ideal friendship (Ch. II) with the series of more or less stultifying relationships in which he is actually involved. This tension between the actual and the possible (surely one of the chief sources of the novelist's strength) acquires an ironic cutting edge in the book's viewpoint—in the fact that it is written in distant retrospect, several years after the events which it depicts are supposed to have taken place. The hero and the narrator are in effect two different personages. The 'I' who suffers is removed in time from the 'I' who creates. The danger here is that the later, sadder and wiser 'I' might begin to patronize the younger and more ardent self and if Hale White's interest in his own life had been predominantly that of the moralizing biographer, this might well have happened. The inevitable result would have been the diminished reality and authenticity, in the fictional sense, of the younger 'I', the book's hero. In fact, it is the solidity of this younger self, its hopes, confusions and anxieties to which we respond most deeply in the book. Doubtless Mr Stock is right in calling this device 'the backward glance of a philosophic mind, concerned to present not a mere collection of personal anecdotes but a ripened insight into the quality and meaning of a life's experience'.[5] My point here is that the insight and the experience are delicately balanced, so that one does not diminish the vividness of the other.

The note of patronage which does occur in the book is not found in the attitude of the writer to the hero, but rather in the attitude of the 'editor' Reuben Shapcott towards the work which he introduces. Hale White's chief reason for using the elaborate fiction of an editor may well have been his natural shyness and his desire to maintain anonymity within his domestic and social circle. But this is an explanation of origin, not of function. The actual effect of the device is curiously double-edged. On the one hand, the solemn and sententious editorial preface is obviously intended to 'place' the life-story in its proper Victorian context—drawing out, in suitably ponderous terms, the moral of the story. But returning to it, or recalling it as we read the rest of the book, we see that it is not the editor who delivers a judgement on the book; rather it is the book, with its freshness and vitality, its poignant sense of time passsing and its intense awareness of the precariousness of human relationships, which 'judges' the measured, temperate, but somehow shallow and self-approving attitude of 'Reuben Shapcott'. Another implicit judgement on the prefatory moralizing is the final editorial note with its feeling of human warmth and its sense of having been the editor's immediate reaction ('A more perfect friend I never knew'). There is something—something of generosity, of openness to experience and real compassion—in Mark Rutherford which is beyond the reach of Shapcott's cautious hindsight. The effect is in some respects like that of Conrad's use of the

[5] Irving Stock, *William Hale White*, p. 91.

middle-aged English teacher as chronicler of the tempestuous events and personalities of *Under Western Eyes*. But it is an effect which we can only feel if we are prepared to take the fiction seriously *as* fiction.

Just as the novelist's interest in the reality of his hero prevents the younger Mark Rutherford from being swamped by his older self, so we have a novelist's concern with character and motivation ensuring the fullness of existence of other characters. As in many novels, these characters are static in relation to the hero, in that what is problematic to him is to them a matter of past history. (Miss Arbour typifies a choice in love, Mardon in intellectual life and so on). But they do not exist solely in order to portray a facet of the author's consciousness or to provide convenient illustration of this or that point. They do enrich and intensify the development of the theme, but this is a by-product of their full and rich presentation within the whole story. Before they do anything else, these characters take hold of our imagination, and they do this pre-eminently through the novelist's art. That art works equally effectively in miniature, as in the presentation of brother Holderness, the travelling draper who confesses:

> crimes which, to say the truth, although they were many according to his own account, were never given in that detail which would have made his confession of some value. He never prayed without telling all of us that there was no health in him, and that his soul was a mass of putrefying sores; but everybody thought the better of him for his self-humiliation. (p. 11)

—or on a more extended scale, as in Edward Mardon (whose middle name of Gibson, given in expectation of plenty from an aunt of the same name, was changed to Gibbon by its owner out of admiration for the historian).

As with character, so with incident and description. Consider the placing of the two main 'inset' stories, that of Miss Arbour and that of the butterfly collector. Both occur at points where their relevance to the development of the theme is immediately obvious. Less obvious perhaps, but equally effective in guiding our response are such details as Mr Hexton's wishing to substitute a stuffed dog for the books which his bride has put on the shelves (Ch. v), the 'diagram representing a globe, on which an immense amount of wasted ingenuity had been spent to provide the illusion of solidity' (p. 112), and Theresa's breaking of the flower vase when she reaches the end of her recital (Ch. ix). All these have the untidiness and materiality of fiction together with its capacity to widen and illuminate the theme.

But Hale White's chief novelistic device is pervasive rather than local in its operation. It is the one to which my title refers, the rhetoric of no rhetoric. If rhetoric is the art of persuasion, then no one persuades us more effectively than the man who succeeds in convincing us that he is inept or uninterested in the rhetorical arts. This is exactly what the narrator of the Autobiography contrives to do. It is as much a rhetorical device as the invention of an 'editor', but far more difficult to employ successfully, and correspondingly more effective when successfully employed. 'It may be ignominious to confess it' Rutherford writes of his divided emotional loyalty, 'but so it was; I simply record the fact'. This note is sounded consistently throughout the book. It is the voice of a man scrupulously concerned to speak the whole truth as far as he sees it, no more and no less. Very early in the book we are told that one of the things the narrator absorbed from his family background was 'a rigid regard for truthfulness', and this facet of the narrator's character blends perfectly with the tone of plain sincerity. It is the quality which above all attracted André Gide:

> The very style of William Hale White (Mark Rutherford) is exquisitely transparent, scintillatingly pure. He develops to perfection qualities that I wish were mine. His art is made of the renunciation of all false riches.[6]

Part of the false riches is the novelist's often-evident inventiveness. At least twice Mark Rutherford refers to the novelist's freedom as something denied him. In a letter to his father, Hale White himself put the point like this:

> No literary world here [he writes, speaking of the Gospels] no writing for the sake of writing, no thought of publishing here, no vain empty cleverness, attempted merely for the purpose of glorifying the writer in the reader's eyes.

and a little later:

> In nine-tenths of the books I read, I feel just as a magnet I should think feels when there is a card put between it and a piece of steel, as if it would long to pierce through the covering and get at the real true metal. So in books you feel as if a film were between you and the author which you could not pierce, as if you would give anything to get really at the heart-felt thinkings of the man.[7]

In her brilliant, if finally perverse essay 'The Fact in Fiction', Mary

---

[6] André Gide, *Journals*, Vol. III, pp. 337–8. Quoted in Irving Stock, op. cit., p. 5.
[7] Quoted in Irving Stock, op. cit., p. 43.

Macarthy lists as the distinguishing features of the novel, the absence of the supernatural, factual accuracy, 'the breath of scandal', and a clear locative sense. All these are present in *Mark Rutherford's Autobiography*. Miss Macarthy also comments on the role of the narrator in guaranteeing veracity, and of the 'editor' in 'authenticating the manuscript' (apropos of *Lolita*)—remarks which are relevant and helpful in a reading of Hale White's novel. But the most important guarantee of veracity is the sincerity of the style, which is the most difficult and rewarding kind of rhetoric. There may appear to be a certain gracelessness in talking of sincerity as an attribute of the work instead of the man, but it is the only sense with which the critic can properly concern himself. The demand that sincerity should be more than an effect of the completed work, should be in fact the description of the mental state of a person unknown to us at the time he composed the work, is not only unverifiable—it is, in the strictest sense, impertinent.

University of Sussex

Arthur Graeme West: A Messenger to Job

DENNIS WELLAND

THE distinction which no student of the literature of the First World War has yet drawn with complete satisfaction is between its literary and its documentary value, nor perhaps can such a distinction now be firmly drawn. Continuing to seek in that literature a record of 'how they felt about the war', we shall single out names like Wilfred Owen, Isaac Rosenberg, Siegfried Sassoon and Edmund Blunden whose reputations are established, but the danger is that, probably more and more, we shall speak collectively even of these and certainly of others. Edith Sitwell in conversation once referred to the frontispiece of Owen's *Poems* (1920), as 'the photograph of any young officer killed in the war'. The remark does less than justice to the dignified sensibility of his features, and yet it is symptomatic of the ease with which we use phrases like 'the lost generation', facilely imputing an identity of response that blurs their individuality. Most of this literature may be subsumed under the title of one of Blunden's poems, 'Report on Experience', but these reports are almost always delivered in the spirit of the messenger to Job: 'I only am escaped alone to tell thee'. This is especially true of Arthur Graeme West, to whom very little attention has been paid, beyond an occasional passing reference in surveys of war literature. His *Diary of a Dead Officer* was published posthumously in 1918, and only one of his poems had by 1964 appeared, to the best of my knowledge, in one anthology.[1] The *Diary* has never been reprinted and perhaps does not need to be, yet it ought not to be allowed to escape unhonoured into oblivion, if only because it is as near as we can come to the authentic contemporaneous voice of any dead officer of the First World War. Unlike most other war writers, even those published after their deaths, West was not writing for publication; the extracts from his diary that, with two letters and nine poems, make up the book, were written with no reader over his shoulder and with no opportunity to focus into art the experiences and emotions he describes. Typical of his generation in some respects, the personality that emerges from the diary is of greater interest for its isolated individuality.

Born in September 1891, he moved before he was ten from the country to London, his family making their new home in Highgate. From Highgate School he won, at the age of fourteen, a scholarship to Blundell's School, Tiverton. Another pupil who must have been admitted at the same time, for he was only a month older than West, was C. E. M. Joad, and in 1910 the two went up to Balliol together. Although the introduction to the *Diary* bears only the initials 'C. J.' and makes no reference to the circumstances in which the writer knew West, we have it on Blunden's authority that Joad was the editor of this volume.[2] The self-effacing note of this introduction, so utterly uncharacteristic of the later Joad, may have seemed to him consistent with his position as a Civil Servant (he was with the Board of Trade and the Ministry of Labour from 1914 until returning to academic life in 1930) or it may have been dictated by a desire to let West speak for himself. In *Who Was Who 1951–1960*, however, the *Diary* is not listed among Joad's publications, nor does he mention it in his autobiography, although he might well have drawn on it at several points in the chapter 'How I Became a Pacifist: the Last War and the Next'.[3] That West and his diary should have disappeared from Joad's memory as completely

[1] *The Diary of a Dead Officer; being the posthumous papers of Arthur Graeme West* (London, George Allen & Unwin, n.d.) pp. xv, 96. British Museum Catalogue gives [1918] as date of publication; accession stamp in B.M. copy dated 14 January 1919. *The Athenaeum*, however, in a brief notice (No. 4639, March 1919, p. 119) gives the publication date as [1919]. 'The Night Patrol' appeared in Frederick Brereton, *An Anthology of War Poems*, London, Collins, 1930, pp. 161–3.

[2] Edmund Blunden, *War Poets 1914–1918*, London, Longman's, Green for the British Council and the National Book League, 1958, p. 23.

[3] C. E. M. Joad, *Under the Fifth Rib: A Belligerent Autobiography*, London, Faber & Faber, 1932, Ch. III, pp. 63–97. (Republished 1935 as *The Book of Joad*.)

as they have from so many other records of the period is explained by
Joad's candid admission 'I cannot say that at this time I placed much
value upon friendship, or took trouble to cultivate my friends or to
keep them';[4] this attitude is apparent in the introduction to the *Diary*
despite the intimacy with which he speaks of West both as boy and
undergraduate. There is even a hint of jealousy in the comment that
'In July 1910, somewhat to the general surprise, West obtained the
School Scholarship to Balliol College' (p. x). Joad presents him as 'a
quiet effaced sort of individual, alternately bullied by big boys when
they wanted to evince their superiority to "worms", and cajoled when
they wanted their exercises done, but on the whole too obscure to be
actively disliked' (pp. ix–x). His enthusiasm for reading and for ento-
mology 'combined to damn him as a public schoolboy' (p. ix). But at
Oxford 'his personality expanded and developed in a remarkable way'
and he became 'extraordinarily well-educated' and widely read, even
though, as Joad records in a somewhat condescending parenthesis, 'he
took only a third in Mods. and a second in Greats, and worked hard for
them too' (p. x). Unathletic but fond of walking and of the country-
side, a lover of beauty in pictures, furniture and china but with little of
an ear for music, a man whose charm of manner defied definition
because of his 'quiet, tranquil, and unassuming' nature: West as Joad
paints him has a sort of typicalness, and Joad was obviously attracted
to him primarily because he was 'so eminently companionable, and
above all, such a good listener' (p. xi).

Yet they had much in common beyond the love of walking and the
hatred of war. Their literary tastes were similar: the Joad who in his
own diary of 1946 asks testily 'Why does nobody read Meredith now?'[5]
had praised in West the ability to catch 'at once the style and spirit of
the writer he reverenced at the moment, and in his conversation could
not help unconsciously reflecting it. I never met a man who could talk
"Meredith" conversation so well as he could' (p. x). In one of the letters
in the *Diary* (presumably the 'Dear Lad' to whom it is addressed was
Joad) West refers to himself 'chanting verses of "Love in the Valley" '
in a rest camp in France in February 1916 and adds 'Yes, by all means
send me "Tom Jones": those long things I can manage very well here,

[4] Ibid., p. 23
[5] C. E. M. Joad, *A Year More or Less*, London, Victor Gollancz, 1948, p. 51. In fact
there was a revival of interest in Meredith about this time, especially among men of Joad's
generation. Sassoon's *Meredith* was published in the same year and Sir Osbert Sitwell in
1947 had chosen 'The Novels of George Meredith' as the subject of his Presidential
address to the English Association.

when we are back from the hellish trenches' (p. 12); in September 1939 Joad describes himself as 'sitting in the garden of an Amberley cottage reading *Tom Jones*—I wanted something to take my mind off the contemporary scene'.[6] Early in his career as a private in the army West expressed the fear that some of the more lumpish of his companions would 'rise, like H. G. Wells's Morlocks in the "Time Machine", from their position of excluded ugliness and possess the house' (p. 3); thirty-two years later Joad records that he has always 'thought of those who tended [machines] very much as Wells caused us to think of the Morlocks in *The Time Machine*'.[7] West's war-time reading also included Wells's *Boon* (p. 49), the *Odyssey* (p. 5), medieval ballads (p. 95) and, in the trenches, *The Faerie Queen* (p. 12), ' "Tristram Shandy" with much pleasure' (p. 72) and 'Thyrsis' and 'The Scholar Gipsy' (p. 71). He alludes also to Mark Rutherford (p. 6) and Rupert Brooke's 'The Great Lover' (p. 10), while a reference (p. 73) to *Tess of the d'Urbervilles* suggests he was more sympathetic to Hardy than was Wilfred Owen. (An unpublished letter of Owen's observes with sturdy independence 'Sassoon admires Thos. Hardy more than anybody living. I don't think much of what I've read. Quite potatoey . . .')[8]

West had remained at Oxford until the Christmas vacation of 1914 when his patriotic application for a commission was rejected because of his eyesight and he immediately enlisted as a private in the Public Schools Battalion. Joad does not identify any of the other units to which West was to belong, and with excessive caution uses only the initial letter and dots for the names of places and people, but it is clear that West remained in the infantry. After basic training he went to France as a private in November 1915, returning four months later for officer training in Scotland (references to 'South Beach Hotel in T . . .' (p. 27) and a Sunday afternoon visit to Glasgow Art Gallery (p. 36) suggest that it may well have been in the vicinity of Troon, an area also used for training in the Second World War). His training completed in August 1916, he spent some weeks on leave at Box Hill in Surrey and returned in September as an officer to France where he remained until he was killed in April 1917. Of this event Joad comments 'Even his death was irrelevant. He died, it seems, in no blaze of glory, he died

---

[6] C. E. M. Joad, *Journey through the War Mind*. London, Faber & Faber, 1940, p. 37.

[7] *A Year More or Less*, p. 177. In *Under the Fifth Rib* Joad frequently acknowledges the influence of Wells on his own thinking (see note 10 below); the Morlocks also occur in this book at p. 175.

[8] Wilfred Owen to E. Leslie Gunston, 22 August 1917. Printed by kind permission of Harold Owen and E. Leslie Gunston.

leading no forlorn hope, but struck by a chance sniper's bullet as he was leaving his trench' (p. xiv).

The diary extracts occupy sixty-seven octavo pages and are divided into four sections; the first (pp. 1–13) deals with his career in the ranks, the second (pp. 17–43) with his officer training, the third (pp. 47–61) with his last leave, and the fourth (pp. 65–76) with his final tour of duty in France. The letter from the front (pp. 11–13) which concludes Part One anticipates Owen in such passages as:

> The spring is manifest here in young corn, and the very air and strong winds: and even here I react to it. . . . How bloody people seem to be in England about peace and peace meetings. I suppose they are getting rather Prussian in the country. . . . I have contracted hatred and enmity for nobody over here, save soldiers generally and a few N.C.O.'s in particular. For the Hun I feel nothing but a spirit of amiable fraternity that the poor man has to sit just like us and do all the horrible and useless things that we do, when he might be at home with his wife or his books, as he preferred. Well, well; who is going to have the sense to begin talking of peace? We're stuck here until our respective Governments have the sense to do it. (pp. 12–13)

Officer training served only to intensify his hatred of N.C.O.'s, and indeed the unit seems to have had more than its fair share of the unintelligent, bullying and brutal martinets, commissioned and non-commissioned, towards whom West trained himself to adopt an attitude of Stoic resignation. It is an attitude, he recognizes, 'of Nihilism rather than Stoicism. For Stoicism's fundamental assumption was the positive one that only the good is good, and for that we should live; whereas I sometimes think rather that nothing is good or has any permanent value whatever' (p. 34). Against this he can set only the belief in the reality of 'the feeling of pain or pleasure, together with thought. To bring happiness into the world is the only aim of action. . . . It is true that I get happiness from being with my friends, from reading and writing, therefore I do it and can justify myself in doing it; it is true that I bring happiness to my parents by doing and suffering things which, while they do me no harm, please them. But all other creations that are supposed to have a claim on my time and life I spurn' (p. 35). This loyalty to his parents was later to be a determining factor in a spiritual crisis. His emphasis on the supremacy of personal relations and the prevailing liberal humanism in his writings recall E. M. Forster, but his zest for the exquisitely experienced sensation owes something too to Walter Pater who figures in one of West's poems and whose influence may also be seen in the next entry, the visit to Glasgow Art Gallery. Emerging from the Gallery, West feels that he is confronting not an actual landscape but a work of art:

> There seemed a kind of film in the air which gave to the scene the semblance of a painting, already feeling the hand of Time, and separating it, as by a pane of glass, from the beholder, rendering it remote and not a creation of the passing day. In the background were high piled grey-white clouds, above which an indeterminate milky blue intensified into a deep azure: spires and towers sprang up behind the large solid blocks of building, very Dutch in character, that skirted the confines of the park. (pp. 36–7)

But the scene dissolves, life ceases to imitate Art, and West is left with his pressing ethical problems.

The most interesting statement of these is developed in Part Three, while he is on his last leave. Among the other claims upon his time and life which, in the passage already quoted, he had spurned, were the consolations of belief in a benevolent deity: 'If there is a God at all responsible for governing the earth, I hate and abominate Him—I rather despise Him' (pp. 35–6). By August 1916 he had rejected not only 'the conventional religion that once bound me' but also any belief 'even in Christ as an actual figure' (p. 47). In this, of course, he differs from Owen, Sassoon and others who, as I have argued elsewhere, differentiated between an Old Testament God whom they abjured and an historical Christ whom they respected.[9] West's approach to pacifism was more intellectually rationalistic than Owen's: Owen could never have written 'I loathe and scorn all emotionalism and religious feeling' (p. 47) and he is the greater poet for it, yet the West who did write it was partially deceiving himself and was to become, just as much as Owen, 'a conscientious objector with a very seared conscience'.

This is why the *Diary* is so interesting and so moving: West, formulating his position for himself and not to persuade others, is released from the necessity of dialectical consistency and we have instead the naked grappling of a man with his own soul. Later in the trenches he was to try to explain his position to others, only to be met

[9] D. S. R. Welland, *Wilfred Owen: a Critical Study*, London, Chatto & Windus, 1960, pp. 84–8. Joad (*Under the Fifth Rib*, pp. 70–1) records a Welsh minister writing to a conscientious objector in prison 'The Sermon on the Mount was for the new kingdom, but since the world has rejected that kingdom, God has been obliged to go back to Old Testament methods'.

with 'a few of the usual jabs at Balliol' or, when his sincerity was recognized, 'the idea that intellectual convictions of this sort must of necessity imply some fearful moral laxity' (p. 71). Sadly but with justice he was to conclude 'The most religious men are really the extreme Christians or mystics, and the atheists—nobody can understand this. These two classes have really occupied their minds with religion' (p. 71). (Somebody who could have understood this and whose work exemplifies its truth was, of course, Bernard Shaw.[10]). On leave at Box Hill, happy among his family and friends, and confirmed in his atheism, West found himself suffering 'a violent revulsion from my old imagined glories and delights of the Army (such as I had had)—its companionship, suffering courageously and of noble necessity undergone—to intense hatred of the war spirit and the country generally. . . . Never was the desire to desert and to commit suicide so overwhelming' (p. 50). He had been brought to this by having 'read a good deal of liberal literature', especially Bertrand Russell's *Justice in War-Time* which had recently appeared. This collection of essays had argued the case against war with a cool rationalism that was even prepared to justify some wars, but not the present one, which it attacked on grounds of economics, political morality, ethics and common sense. What must have spoken with eloquent directness to West was the opening 'Appeal to the Intellectuals of Europe' and the essay entitled 'The Danger to Civilization' in which Russell described with devastating accuracy the psychological effect of modern war on the participants: in addition to physical and mental damage and mutilation there is another danger. 'Familiarity with horrors makes war seem natural, not the abomination which it is seen to be at first. Humane feeling decays, since, if it survived no man could endure the daily shocks. . . . Will even the most hardened moralist dare to say that such men are morally the better for their experience of war?'[11] Foreseeing the virtual obliteration of a complete generation and the consequent debilitating effect on culture and civilization, he predicts also that recovery will be further delayed by economic exhaustion. The impact of this on West made him compose a letter to his Adjutant 'telling him I would not rejoin the Army nor accept any form of alternative service, that I would rather be shot than

[10] Joad 'discovered' Shaw at Balliol and must have discussed him with West. ('Shaw, and in a lesser degree Wells, came so to dominate my mind that they may be said to have formed it': *Under the Fifth Rib*, p. 19). The preface to *Androcles and the Lion* (1914) might have come to West's mind in this connection.

[11] Bertrand Russell, *Justice in War-Time*, Chicago and London, the Open Court Publishing Co., 1916, p. 111.

do so, and that I left my name and address with him to act as he pleased'
(p. 51). Had the letter been sent, West might have preceded Siegfried
Sassoon to Craiglockhart Military Hospital by some twelve months and
perhaps even survived to write his own *Sherston's Progress*. Instead he
rejoined his unit and returned to France, not in the spirit of altruistic
responsibility to his comrades that took Owen and Sassoon back, but
because of an understandable reluctance to give pain and distress to his
family. The passage in which he describes his vacillation first at the
pillar box and next day at the telegraph office is written with an honesty
and an insight into human frailty that needs no adventitious drama or
embellishment to make it memorable: this is how we have all behaved
at some time or other, and the unheroic anti-climax is conveyed with a
wryness that combines self-knowledge, self-amusement and self-
contempt. The emotionalism which he 'loathed and scorned' had
defeated the rationalism that had brought him to this position, and the
recognition of this only increased his unhappiness. In this mood he
wrote the second letter to (presumably) Joad and went back to his
regiment on 21 August 1916.

At this point in the *Diary* Joad departs from the chronological
sequence.[12] The letter of 21 August follows an entry dated 24th; two
entries dated 11 September are separated by others of 24 September and
6 September in that order; and the one dated 24 September should really
be the third entry in Part Four. This is presumably why Edmund
Blunden suggests that the book 'was edited too much according to
Joad's pacifism',[13] for in his Introduction Joad seems to forestall this
criticism in other respects by the assertion that he has omitted 'only
names and a few details that were too painful or too private for publication' (p. xiv) and a footnote (p. 42) carefully qualifies West's strictures
on hospitals by insisting that they 'are not applicable to the majority of
military hospitals, or to the more modern establishments'. The entry
of 24 September might have been used to conclude Part Three, for it
summarizes West's agonized hostility to war and asks passionately
'Then why, in God's name, go on?' (p. 58). To follow it with the more
detached and lyrical passage of 6 September written on a short London

[12] He appears to do so at one other place: the last diary entry (p. 75) which follows one
of 3 November 1916 is dated 'Saturday Feb. 10th 1916'. This, however, is a slip either of
the pen or the printer and should read '1917'; the letter at p. 11 is dated 'Saturday, Feb.
12th 1916' which would make 10 February fall on a Saturday in 1917, and it is clear from
this letter that West had just emerged from a spell of trench duty, not from the more
pleasant course of special training which the final entry describes.

[13] Blunden, loc. cit. (Note 2).

leave and the extract of 11 September on 'the supreme value of human love' (p. 61) is pointless. It would, however, have been best to adhere to the chronological sequence, for the indignation of 24 September is not the product of abstract argument as it is made to appear by its re-positioning. It asks specifically 'What *good*, what *happiness* can be produced by some of the scenes I have had to witness in the last few days?' (p. 57). These included, on 20 September, a bombardment which prompts some of West's most graphic writings:

> The trench was a mere undulation of newly-turned earth, under it some-where lay two men or more. You dug furiously. No sign. Perhaps you were standing on a couple of men now, pressing the life out of them, on their faces or chests. A boot, a steel helmet—and you dig and scratch and uncover a grey, dirty face, pitifully drab and ugly, the eyes closed, the whole thing limp and mean-looking; this is the devil of it, that a man is not only killed, but made to look so vile and filthy in death, so futile and meaningless that you hate the sight of him. (p. 67)

The relentless candour of this exemplifies excellently the atrophying of humane feeling which Russell had seen as necessary if the daily shocks were to be endured. 'I can only force myself to continue in a kind of dream-state; I hypnotize myself to undergo it' is how West puts it (p. 57). The brutality of the scene brutalizes the beholder and his record of it (which, I repeat, is not being written to shock those who have not seen these things). Yet if pity for the dead seems pointless, pity for the living is not possible either: the men in their funkholes in the side of the trench 'sit like animals for market, like hens in cages (p. 67). . . . Of course, when a shell falls on to the parapet and bores down into the earth and explodes, they are covered over like so many pota-toes. It is with the greatest difficulty that we can shift the men into another bit of trench and make them stand up' (p. 68).

In his best poem, 'The Night Patrol', written in France, in March 1916, the dead are de-humanized into merely revolting landmarks to guide the party back:

> Only the dead were always present—present
> As a vile sickly smell of rottenness;
> The rustling stubble and the early grass,
> The slimy pools—the dead men stank through all,
> Pungent and sharp, as bodies loomed before,
> And as we passed, they stank: then dulled away
> To that vague foetor, all encompassing,
> Infecting earth and air. (p. 82)

One corpse

> lay on his back and crossed
> His legs Crusader-wise; I smiled at that,
> And thought on Elia and his Temple Church. (p. 82)

The poem ends on a similar note of detached understatement:

> We turned and crawled past the remembered dead:
> Past him and him, and them and him, until,
> For he lay some way apart, we caught the scent
> Of the Crusader and slid past his legs,
> And through the wire and home, and got our rum. (p. 83)

Others of his poems lack this control: one attacking the 'happy warrior' type of poetry opens promisingly:

> God! How I hate you, you young cheerful men,
> Whose pious poetry blossoms on your graves
> As soon as you are in them (p. 79)

but it dissipates its energy in invective and becomes too localized a satire on one particular poem by an Oxford undergraduate; again, however, there is some vigorous description of death in the trenches. Another, 'The Last God', also begins well:

> All Gods are dead, even the great God Pan
> Is dead at length; the lone inhabitant
> Of my ever-dwindling Pantheon (p. 88)

but this degenerates into an unexpectedly sentimental and emotional preciousness. The subject is more felicitously treated with a jaunty irony in 'The Traveller':

> Oh, I came singing down the road
>   Whereon was nought perplext me,
> And Pan with Art before me strode,
>   And Walter Pater next me.
>
> I garnered my 'impressions' up,
>   Lived in each lovely feature,
> 'I burned with a hard gem-like flame'
>   And sensitized my nature. (pp. 91–2)

The four are suddenly joined by 'the maid Bellona':

> My three companions coughed and blushed,
>   And as the time waxed later,
> One murmured, pulling out his watch,
>   That he must go—'twas Pater.

> And very soon Art turned away
>   Huffed at Bellona's strictures,
> Who hurried us past dome and spire
>   And wouldn't stay for pictures.
>
> But old Pan with his satyr legs
>   Trotted beside us gamely,
> Till quickening pace and rougher road
>   Made him go somewhat lamely. (p. 92)

Eventually in kindness of heart the poet dismisses Pan and goes on alone with Bellona:

> And still we fare her road alone
>   In foul or sunny weather:
> Bare is that road of man or god
>   Which we run on to-gether. (p. 92)

Using a similar image ('This is the track my life is setting on') Wilfred Owen was to find in a sense of spiritual companionship a comfort that West denied himself. The dominant note of the *Diary* is of loneliness: a man talking to himself because he can no longer be sure others understand him. West is not a major writer. His prose is enlivened only by occasional imaginative touches as when he describes a railway journey: 'you lean out of the window and look up the long vertebrate rod of carriages, watch them turn and tail round the curves' (p. 60). In verse, as even the best passages quoted will show, his grasp on the iambic pentameter is unsure, his control of his material uncertain. Much of what he has to say has been said and said better by others, but what is important is his honesty. Though intellectually inclined, he is not an original thinker nor a powerful one, but he tries to achieve independence: 'I am very unhappy. I wish to make clear to myself why, and to thrash out what my desires really tend to' (p. 56). Above all, he is aware of man's capacity for change and for development: 'The tendency to seek for finality, to look for some resting place in development, some road offering shelter more permanent than nightly inns is a delusion, and not to be acquiesced in. Still the change goes on and still I travel forward' (p. 53) (this immediately after his decision to return to the army instead of making a separate peace). In the confusion and contradictions that the process involves we can hear an authentic voice and one that in its agonized solitude is less isolated and less negative than it believed itself to be.

University of Manchester

America, My America

BRIAN LEE

... the sense of doom deepens inside me, at the thought of the old world which I loved—and the new world means nothing to me.[1]

WHILE it is not possible to say exactly when it was that Lawrence finally abandoned his long, personal struggle against the decadence of white civilization, a handful of letters which he wrote in the summer of 1923 to John Middleton Murry and others, show him to have arrived just then at a crucial turning point in his continuing search for 'that living something that stirs way down in the blood, and *creates* consciousness'.[2]

He had decided reluctantly and pessimistically to return once again to Europe to give it one more try; to see whether the kind of life he dreamed about could yet be realized in England. Even before he reached New York though, on his long journey eastwards, the dream had fallen through and he had forced himself to recognize that he was still at war with that 'world', and what it stood for, whether American or European. New York itself and the sight of 'Liberty clenching her fist in the harbour' finally sent him hurrying West again, back to the mountains and deserts of Mexico, leaving Frieda, who, he said, had Devonshire on her mind, to sail to England alone. Of course, Lawrence did eventually

[1] *The Letters of D. H. Lawrence*, ed. Aldous Huxley, 1932, p. 575.
[2] *Letters*, p. 635.

follow her in the winter of that same year, but only to have all his earlier fears confirmed:

> Oh, London is awful: so dark, so damp, so yellow-grey, so mouldering piece-meal. With crowds of people going about in a mouldering, damp, half-visible sort of way, as if they were all mouldering bits of rag that had fallen from an old garment. . . . How awful it would be, if at this present moment I sat in the yellow mummy-swathings of London atmosphere— the snow here is melting—inside the dreadful mummy sarcophagus of Europe, and didn't know that the blue horse was still kicking his heels and making a few sparks fly, across the tops of the Rockies. It would be a truly sad case for me. . . . It's no good. I've GOT to ride on a laughing horse. The forked radish has ceased to perambulate. I've *got* to ride a laughing horse. And I whistle for him, call him, spread corn for him, and hold out an apple to him, here in England. No go! No good! No answer![3]

Lawrence was to ride his laughing horse in books like *St Mawr* and *The Plumed Serpent*, and in his last years search older cultures than our own for new gods to worship. More interesting though than his celebration of Mexican or Mediterranean cultures is his analysis of the death of European and American civilization both in his fiction of the early nineteen twenties and in his *Studies in Classic American Literature*, which was first published in book form in 1923.

Most of the essays which make up this latter book—Lawrence's most sustained piece of literary criticism—were originally written in 1917 and published in the *English Review* between November, 1918 and June, 1919. When he came to revise them four years later he brought to the work an important new qualification, a first hand knowledge of America; and this knowledge forced him into a number of radical revaluations. Comparison of the early and late versions of these essays —facilitated by the recent republication of the uncollected versions[4]— should help to throw light on a decisive period in Lawrence's development and also may tell us something about his critical assumptions and procedures.

Perhaps the most marked difference between the two versions is one of tone. In the first Lawrence attempts to woo the mind of the reader with what looks like cool logical demonstration and impeccable deductive reasoning. The opening essay which sets out his thesis and explains his method provides a good example of this. It is called 'The Spirit of Place'. From a few overlapping axioms he sets out to derive a theory of

---

[3] *Letters*, p. 593.
[4] D. H. Lawrence, *The Symbolic Meaning*, ed. Armin Arnold, 1962.

art which will allow him to explain the development of nineteenth-century American literature in terms of its geographical origins. All art, he says, partakes of the spirit of place in which it is produced. But most works, he goes on, and particularly American ones, are characterized by a duplicity, a contradiction between the artist's overt, didactic import and a profound, symbolic import which expresses his unconscious soul, and it is, of course, this latter, symbolic meaning of works of art which interests Lawrence. In order to discover it, however, he goes first, not to the works themselves, but to the history of the colonization of America. Carrying over his concept of duplicity from art to life he finds that the original Puritan settlers of New England were motivated not by what they professed—a desire for religious liberty—but rather by its opposite, a lust for repression. This seeming paradox is explained by another law: that of the dual motion of all passions, towards, on the one hand, liberation, and on the other, 'the utter subjection of the living, spontaneous being to the fixed, mechanical, ultimately insane *will*'.[5] The history of American life, and by extension, American art, is that of the steady growth of this negative, repressive lust for control, which has resulted in a monstrous, mechanical democracy. Eventually, however, America itself, the land, will insist on expressing itself and inaugurate a new way of living. This 'mystic transubstantiation' Lawrence evokes for us at the very end of his essay:

> At present there is a vast myriad-branched human engine, the very thought of which is death. But in the winter even a tree looks like iron. Seeing the great trunk of dark iron and the swaying steel flails of boughs, we cannot help being afraid. What we see of buds looks like sharp bronze stud-points. The whole thing hums elastic and sinister and fatally metallic, like some confused scourge of swinging steel throngs [*sic*]. Yet the lovely cloud of green and summer lustre is within it.[6]

In paraphrase, the logical hiatuses and *non sequiturs* in Lawrence's argument are baldly evident. In his own exposition they are disguised to some extent by a variety of devices which help to bolster the impression of scientific explanation. On closer examination, though, these analogies, illustrations and historical generalizations can be seen for what they are, unrestrained metaphysical flights dressed up as rigorous philosophical demonstrations. For example, writing about the subject of 'vital magnetism' he says:

[5] *Symbolic Meaning*, p. 26.   [6] *Symbolic Meaning*, p. 30.

It follows, also, that if the Atlantic sea-board of Europe lies under the spell of the far-off American vital magnetism, the Atlantic sea-board of America must lie under the spell of Europe.

And developing this line of thought in the same paragraph, he goes on:

If we can understand the sending of wireless messages from continent to continent, can we not much more readily understand that the unthinkably sensitive substance of the human intelligence could receive the fine waves of vital effluence transmitted across the intervening space, could receive, and, as in a dream, plainly comprehend?[7]

More damaging though to his argument than these specious analogies and false inferences, is his account of the European migrations to America in the early seventeenth century. For the sake of his thesis he must maintain that the continent was peopled by men whose basic aim was the establishment of a religious tyranny, a 'lust to destroy or mutilate life at its very quick'. But in support of this contention Lawrence can only offer a view that the Massachusetts Bay Colony rivalled the Spanish-American Inquisition in its religious cruelty, and an undeveloped hint about the physiological changes wrought upon the ruddy, English yeoman stock by life in these inhospitable surroundings. If we leave aside this idea about physical change, which does not seem to lead him anywhere, and ignoring the fact that his account of Puritan Orthodoxy is an obvious distortion of a complex historical situation, Lawrence does not even hold consistently to these views anyway, but by appealing to his own law about the duality of all passions, is able to assert finally that the force which compelled millions of men to cross the ocean could not be merely the negative lust to destroy life after all, and that we have only to wait patiently for the true spirit of America to declare itself.

As an essay in speculative philosophy, 'The Spirit of Place' is in every way unsatisfactory, yet in condemning it one is at the same time aware that it contains some of the most original and important truths about American art and society that we have. Might it be that Lawrence's revisions succeeded in revealing these insights more clearly by separating them from a pretentious and unnecessary ratiocinative framework? Certainly the later version is much more economically organized, and the criticisms he makes acquire a new force in his terse aphoristic style. For example, his somewhat laboured distinction in the

[7] *Symbolic Meaning*, p. 23.

184

first essay, between the symbolic and didactic meanings of literary works is reformulated in what was to become his most memorable and controversial dictum, 'Never trust the artist. Trust the tale'. And even though he has to elaborate on this piece of cryptic wisdom, he does so with a metaphoric vigour beyond anything in the earlier version:

> You have got to pull the democratic and idealistic clothes off American utterance, and see what you can of the dusky body of IT [the whole soul of America] underneath.[8]

Armin Arnold, in differing from this view, says in his Introduction to 'The Spirit of Place' that Lawrence is thrown into fits of hysterical shrieking by such words as 'democracy', 'liberty', 'Whitman' and 'idealist'. This seems to be a quite inaccurate description of Lawrence's tone in the 1923 essay. I can find no sign of hysteria in Lawrence's remarks, nor for that matter any sign of Walt Whitman either.

It is true that Lawrence does not make any really new points in the later work, and that the exigencies of his style occasionally force him into minor obscurities, but he does manage to convey a powerful feeling of involvement even though he is most often writing in disappointed recoil from the discovered reality of American society. If it is the case, as Arnold claims, that the piece was composed 'in the white heat of anger and excitement',[9] this is anyway preferable to the affected academicism of his first attempt. The real measure of Lawrence's criticism, though, is its adequacy in coping with individual works, and at this point it will be useful to look more closely at one or other of his essays on the classic American writers, to discover whether there is any truth at all in the view that his growing sense of despair and disillusion in fact impaired his critical abilities.

Lawrence's ecstatic praise of James Fenimore Cooper is well known. In a letter to Catherine Carswell, written in 1916 he maintained that beside the 'lovely, mature and sensitive art' of Fenimore Cooper, the 'journalistic bludgeonings of Turgenev, Tolstoi, Dostoevsky, Maupassant, Flaubert' all appear 'so very obvious and coarse'.[10] While Lawrence at no time repudiated his views about the beauty of the American myth created by Fenimore Cooper in the Leatherstocking Tales, what strikes one most forcibly in reading side by side the two versions of his essay, is the way in which his experience of American

---

[8] D. H. Lawrence, *Studies in Classic American Literature* (n.d.), p. 14.
[9] *Symbolic Meaning*, p. 15.
[10] *The Collected Letters of D. H. Lawrence*, ed. Harry T. Moore, 1962, p. 488.

life moves him to a reconsideration of the relation between this myth and the actualities he observed there.

Lawrence's critics have not usually understood the true significance of these revisions. Martin Green cites Lawrence's estimate of *The Deerslayer* as 'one of the most beautiful and most perfect books in the world: flawless as a jewel and of gem-like concentration',[11] and contrasts this with his subsequent remark, 'It is a gem of a book. Or a bit of perfect paste in a perfect setting, so long as I am not fooled by pretence of reality'.[12] This reversed evaluation, based upon identical analyses of the novel, proves, says Mr Green, that Lawrence was not really concerned to write literary criticism at all, but to define America as a mode of being.[13] Only if we accept the principle of realism as a criterion of value can Lawrence be said to have reversed his original evaluation of the book. What has changed is his perception of what *The Deerslayer* is about, and all literary criticism, however formal, must eventually come to terms with the presented experiences of the work.

Armin Arnold similarly fails to realize that the derision and disrespect expressed by Lawrence in the later essay is directed, not at the Leatherstocking Tales, but at Cooper himself, whose divided and deracinated state is seen to mirror accurately Lawrence's own:

> As I say, it is perhaps easier to love America passionately, when you look at it through the wrong end of the telescope, across all the Atlantic water, as Cooper did so often, than when you are right there. When you are actually in America, America hurts, because it has a powerful disintegrative influence upon the white psyche.[14]

Lawrence continued for a time to cling to a tenuous belief in the eventual fulfilment of the Leatherstocking myth, to hold a faint hope for a future opening out into the new areas of consciousness predicated in the loveless, sexless, wordless relationship of Natty Bumppo and the Indian Chingachgook, but finally he was forced to acknowledge that the collapse of the inorganic and mechanical democracy—imaged in the sloughing off of the old psyche and the falling down of the American factories—was not going to be realized in any foreseeable future. There was nothing left for him then but to pack up and give way to what he called his 'bit of a *Heimweh* for Europe'.[15]

[11] *Symbolic Meaning*, p. 106.
[12] *Studies*, p. 63.
[13] Martin Green, *Re-appraisals: Some Commonsense Readings in American Literature*, 1963, pp. 232–3.
[14] *Studies*, p. 54.   [15] *Letters*, p. 656.

As for the literary or critical implications of Lawrence's fresh insights, these can perhaps be best approached by way of his own development as a novelist. One of the commonplaces of modern criticism has it that something went wrong with his artistic growth after the completion of *Women in Love* in 1916, and the degree of failure in his later novels is seen to be directly proportionate to the amount of overt philosophizing in them. According to such criticism, *Aaron's Rod*, *Kangaroo*, *The Plumed Serpent* and *Lady Chatterley's Lover* in particular, exhibit Lawrence's growing inability to integrate structure and texture, form and substance, or symbolic and didactic meanings. J. I. M. Stewart, for example, writing about *Kangaroo*, finds that the 'transcendental ecology' in it—the symbolic description of the ancient Australian landscape—'conflicts almost absurdly with elements in Lawrence's political fable',[16] and attributes the seemingly arbitrary structuring of the novels of this period to the continuous pressure of having to earn a living as a novelist, and use whatever incidental materials were to hand. And Ian Gregor, discussing *Lady Chatterley's Lover* concludes that 'the polemical drive has not been adequately countered by the fable. The book is challenging not as a work of art ought to be, by being disturbing, but rather by demanding agreement'.[17] In essence both these writers are adapting the criticism that Lawrence himself made when writing about Hardy as early as 1914, when he said:

> Because a novel is a microcosm, and because man in viewing the universe must view it in the light of a theory, therefore every novel must have the background or the structural skeleton of some theory of being, some metaphysic. But the metaphysic must always subserve the artistic purpose beyond the artist's conscious aim. Otherwise the novel becomes a treatise.[18]

And in Lawrence's best work this is just what we find; a respect for the sanctity and mystery of character and situation and a refusal to compromise his sense of felt life in the interests of a meaning or a morality. But as he progressively discarded his interest and belief in the reality of man in society, so he lost his ability to write in the old way, and in his later fiction poetry gives way to prophecy and symbolism to sermonizing. The large, sweeping rhythms of life which subtly control the organization of incident in *The Rainbow* are replaced by the ragged

[16] J. I. M. Stewart, *Eight Modern Writers*, Oxford, 1963, p. 544.
[17] Ian Gregor and Brian Nicholas, *The Moral and the Story*, 1962, p. 245.
[18] D. H. Lawrence, *Phoenix*, 1955, p. 219.

discursiveness of *Kangaroo*. And as with large things, so too with small. Even the hens, which in *Sons and Lovers* peck at the food on Miriam's trembling hand, and delicately delineate without superfluous comment an aspect of her growing love for Paul Morel, only serve in *Lady Chatterley's Lover* as crude prologue and illustration to the first erotic encounter between Connie and Mellors.

This divorce between image and idea in Lawrence's later work—so deep that it manifests itself not only in radical compositional faults, but also in minor failures of detail—stems from his utter rejection of that 'world' which for the true novelist is the only possible ground of moral value. And in the classic American writers of the nineteenth century he saw reflected the same doubts about the validity of human societies that had been besetting him. One of the reiterated complaints of American novelists in this period—it is repeated in almost identical language by Fenimore Cooper, Hawthorne and Henry James—was that the New World could not provide a dense enough medium for the working of their talents; and their typical solution to this problem, when they did not, like James, seek out a new milieu altogether, was to create a myth of American life in extreme symbolic situations, quite remote in place or time from the world they actually inhabited. There were other, minor novelists, like Dreiser and Howells, who did persevere in an attempt to create realistic fiction out of indigenous materials, and significantly Lawrence completely ignores them. He also, inexplicably, chose not to write about Mark Twain, a novelist whose duplicity was surely equal to that of Fenimore Cooper, Hawthorne or Melville. Lawrence did, however, write about one American poet: Whitman, inevitably. But here, the very singleness of Whitman's vision appears to have baffled Lawrence, and though he makes a half-hearted attempt to produce a *true* interpretation of the poet's work, most of the essay merely oscillates between the poles of uncontrolled rage and indiscriminate sympathy.

But emphasis ought to be laid finally on Lawrence's major positive achievement, and this surely was to recognize and explain, as no English critic before him had succeeded in doing, the uniqueness of American literature; to reveal behind the face of the transplanted European, 'the very intrinsic-most American', under the innocence of the well known children's tales the profoundly alien American art-speech.

University of Nottingham

Satire as a form of Sympathy:
D. H. Lawrence as a Satirist

R. P. DRAPER

IN Chapter 9 of *Lady Chatterley's Lover* Connie Chatterley, who has been listening to Mrs Bolton's Tevershall gossip, reflects that 'one may hear the most private affairs of other people, but only in a spirit of respect for the struggling, battered thing which any human soul is, and in a spirit of fine, discriminative sympathy. For even satire is a form of sympathy. It is the way our sympathy flows and recoils that really determines our lives'. Such a view would seem to contradict all received notions of satire. Antipathy rather than sympathy is for Pope the foundation of satire:

> Ask you what provocation I have had?
> The strong antipathy of good to bad.

And James Sutherland in his recent study of *English Satire* insists that the satirist must judge and punish unsympathetically—'if he makes too many allowances he will end by writing something quite other than pure satire'. One could immediately concede that Lawrence writes impure satire; indeed, the main purpose of this essay is to examine the nature of that impurity. But first it must be said that Lawrence's conception of satire, though it does not belong to the main stream, is not so radically different as this opposition between sympathy and antipathy suggests. Connie Chatterley's reflections go on from the passage already quoted to what is now a famous assertion about the novel: 'And here lies the vast importance of the novel, properly handled. It can inform and lead into new places the flow of our sympathetic consciousness, and it can lead our sympathy away in recoil from things gone dead.' This shift from satire to the novel is a little confusing, but the thought is not discontinuous. Sympathy for Lawrence clearly has both positive and negative forms which he calls 'flow' and 'recoil', and satire—when, like the novel, it is 'properly handled'—is one of the means by which the negative form of sympathy can be stimulated. The distance from Pope's 'strong antipathy' is thus not so great as it first appeared to be.

There is, however, still a very important distinction to be made, one which explains why Lawrence should choose to speak of two forms of sympathy rather than to adhere to the more familiar contrast between sympathy and antipathy. For him flow and recoil are intimately related. The satirical recoil is that which clears the way for the more positive flow. There is a parallel to this in the way Lawrence presents the relationship between life and death as at once opposite and complementary. Whatever has the odour of death upon it is anathema, yet the dying off of the exhausted and outworn is a necessary condition of the preservation and strengthening of life. Death can thus, as in 'The Ship of Death', merge imperceptibly into life: the Popeian antithesis dissolves. Nothing quite so mysterious can be said of Lawrencean satire, but the similarly close relationship between recoil and flow makes pure satire a comparatively rare thing in his work. His satire also dissolves, sometimes into comedy, sometimes into tragedy, with a slightly disconcerting, oscillatory effect.

In *England, My England* this type of satire can be seen at work. The object of attack is a marriage of spurious vitality the decay of which becomes a symbol for the general sapping of English vitality associated in Lawrence's mind with the First World War. The opening pages are the best. By a poetically suggestive use of repetition Lawrence creates the impression that 'savage' and 'primeval' forces, closely linked with strong 'sunlight' and the 'vividness of flamy vegetation', linger on in the corner of Hampshire where the tale is set. This creates a positive flow of sympathy; but already a satirical recoil accompanies it, provoked by the 'high, childish, girlish voices, slightly didactic and tinged with domineering' crying out: 'If you don't come quick, nurse, I shall run out there to where there are snakes.'

The snake-symbol, as so often in Lawrence, emphasizes the Janus quality of the writing, its combination of flow and recoil. The snake belongs with the primitive vitality of Saxon England, but is an un-pleasant threat to the human beings who are encroaching upon it; yet the spoilt offspring of the human beings are satirized by virtue of their attitude towards the snake. Later, when Winifred discovers a snake with a frog in its mouth, Lawrence's prose suggests both the human revulsion which it excites and a justified resentment on the part of the snake at human interference which turns recoil into flow. As the snake slides 'angrily away', Lawrence comments: 'That was Crockham. The spear of modern invention had not passed through it. . . .'

By oscillating between his poetic and satirical styles Lawrence brings the primitive, non-human world of Crockham and the snake into a relationship with the modern, human world which underlines the decadence of the latter. The oldness of Egbert and Winifred's house forms a link with the primitive, but for them it is reduced to the picturesque; and there is a parallel to this decline into the picturesque in Lawrence's language which first evokes Winifred as 'young and beautiful and strong with life, like a flame in sunshine', then becomes self-consciously 'poetic' in the image of Egbert as 'tall and slim and agile, like an English archer', and finally reaches the clipped, deflation-ary last sentence of the paragraph: 'They were a beautiful couple.' This contracting movement is followed by one that is expansive. The next paragraph opens with a second laconic sentence, and after giving some hard facts about Winifred's father, who provides the financial basis for her and Egbert's idyllic existence, again passes through somewhat picturesque writing to reach its conclusion in 'Winifred's cottage crouching unexpectedly in front, so much alone, and so primitive'. After more such expansion and contraction the tale comes to rest in a mingled style, syntactically informal and casual in tone, which conveys the decline of the primitive forces through a relaxed mockery of the cult of spontaneity and passion which it has now become: 'And Egbert was a born rose. The age-long breeding had left him with a delightful spontaneous passion. . . .'

Lawrence does not, unfortunately, maintain this poise for very long. He wishes to show the cracks in this balanced situation becoming crevasses. With the injury of Egbert's daughter—she cuts herself on a sickle which he has carelessly left in the grass, and is crippled—satire is virtually abandoned for tragedy. Egbert himself becomes a stranger in his own family, and then, as a private soldier, a victim of the war machine. He is no longer seen in the satirical guise of an 'epicurean hermit', but as a last representative of the primitive English vitality being reduced to 'pure mechanical action'. His death, like the death of Gerald in *Women in Love*, is an 'extremity of dissolution' suggesting, though with none of the power of *Women in Love*, the end of a phase of human civilization.

The close relationship between recoil and flow poses a problem in the handling of form which *England, My England* with its awkward mid-stream change from satire to tragedy fails to solve. *The Captain's Doll*, a comedy streaked with satire in the Beatrice and Benedick tradition, is much more successful in maintaining its formal unity; but it is, nevertheless, threatened at one point with a similar diversion into tragedy. Mrs Hepburn's arrival in Germany to put a stop to her husband's affair with a woman of aristocratic descent is treated in a brilliantly satirical manner. She appears as a typical member of the pre-war English middle class, absolutely certain of her right to be deferred to on every occasion. Beneath her façade of politeness she is thoroughly ill-mannered, and her pretended concern for her husband, Captain Hepburn, covers a ruthless determination to get her own way. The rapid patter of her banal conversation puts the finishing touch to her as a woman for whom selfishness and social position are identical. But after her death (which is itself an odd, semi-satirical Forsterian accident) Hepburn's statement that she was 'Like some sort of delicate creature you take out of a tropical forest the moment it is born, and from the first moment teach it to perform tricks' gives her a totally unexpected dimension. The Mrs Hepburn we have seen suddenly becomes a shell hiding a warm life which we now glimpse for the first time. Or, rather, we now look at her from two points of view instead of one. Satirically, she is a dry, brittle creature from which we instinctively recoil; but from the new point of view her brittleness is the result of a denial of which she is the tragic victim. Lawrence, a little arbitrarily perhaps, refuses to allow this new perception to alter the nature of his story, as had happened in *England, My England*. He keeps to the central comedy of Hepburn and Hannele's struggle for the *maistrie*; but the sense of other possibilities evoked by the transformation of our view of Mrs Hepburn is kept alive and helps to give *The Captain's Doll* a fluid, uncommitted quality which prevents its satire from hardening into cocksureness.

Lawrence's satire is at its finest, as far as the tales are concerned, in *The Man Who Loved Islands*. This is not to deny the virtue of *Things*, a brilliant sketch in which several aspects of his satirical technique are cleverly combined—the off-hand colloquial style; the semi-dramatic narrative which simultaneously mimics and criticizes the victims of the satire; the mocking repetition of key words ('free', 'beauty', 'full and beautiful life'); and the sardonic conclusion which brings to the surface an underlying vulgarity. But the satire of *Things* is on one level only, and this has a limiting effect not to be found in *The Man Who Loved Islands*. The two tales share certain features, and this gives them a superficial similarity, but in essentials *The Man Who Loved Islands* belongs with *England, My England* and *The Captain's Doll*. Its tragic implications release the sympathetic flow absent from *Things*, making it a tale of more genuinely Lawrencean satire. At the same time it is more of an artistic whole than *England, My England* and more willing to develop its tragic implications than *The Captain's Doll*.

The Master of *The Man Who Loved Islands*, like Egbert, is an 'epicurean hermit'. He seeks aesthetic retreat on a comfortably provided pastoral island, but finds himself exposed to disturbing influences from a primitive and violent past. Egbert and the Master also have in common the search for happiness through the picturesque, though with the Master marriage is not part of this ideal, his sexual experience on the second island being perfunctory and disenchanted. His illusions are to do with himself as a benevolent despot, 'a delicate, sensitive, handsome Master, who wanted everything perfect and everybody happy. Himself, of course, to be the fount of this happiness and perfection'. His relationship with his 'people' is described in language that is sharply satirical, but not without feeling for the man's point of view, as Lawrence's use of the bird image in the following passage suggests:

> So, in fine weather, the bailiff would see the elegant tall figure in creamy-white serge coming like some bird over the fallow, to look at the weeding of the turnips. Then there would be a doffing of hats, and a few minutes of whimsical, shrewd, wise talk, to which the bailiff answered admiringly, and the farm-hands listened in silent wonder, leaning on their hoes.

This benevolent relationship is founded, however, on a 'general goodwill' that lacks the sustaining warmth of real likes and dislikes, and on the Master's money. When he finds that the island is eating away his capital he has to sell out to a honeymoon hotel, and in the process discovers that his 'people' have been swindling him. Money thus mocks general goodwill. But the mockery also seems to come from the island itself. A cow falls over a cliff, and when its dead carcass is found the 'beautiful, expensive creature' is already 'looking swollen'. This suggestion of corruption (reminiscent of the sickly-smelling death of Bill Cooley in *Kangaroo*) is a sardonic comment on the idealism of the Master and the first hint of a kind of satirical retributive force aimed at the Master from the island's outraged primitive past. As this grows stronger the Master becomes afraid of the island and of the repressed life within himself that it evokes:

> ... He felt here strange violent feelings he had never felt before, and lustful desires that he had been quite free from. He knew quite well now that his people didn't love him at all. He knew that their spirits were secretly against him, malicious, jeering, envious, and lurking to down him.

The tone of the story is here becoming more tragic, but not to the exclusion of satire; and as yet the dominant tone remains that of dry mockery. It is on this lighter note that the history of the first island ends. The Master gibes at his own pastoral retreat with the words: 'There, take that, island which didn't know when it was well off. Now be a honeymoon-and-golf island!'

The second island, a mere 'hump of rock', offering the Master no more than a 'commonplace six-roomed house', denies him the luxury of such benevolent illusions as he had entertained on the first. He continues to work on his book about flowers, but the publication no longer bothers him, and he drifts away from contact with life. Again, Lawrence's feeling for the Master's point of view is evident in the evocativeness and sympathetic flow of the language:

> ... He no longer fretted whether it were good or not, what he produced. He slowly, softly spun it like gossamer, and if it were to melt away as gossamer in autumn melts, he would not mind. It was only the soft evanescence of gossamy things which now seemed to him permanent. The very mist of eternity was in them. Whereas stone buildings, cathedrals for example, seemed to him to howl with temporary resistance, knowing they must fall at last; the tension of their long endurance seemed to howl forth from them all the time.

Something of Lawrence's own dislike of the massively permanent enters into this passage: it echoes the conflict in *The Rainbow* between Will's ecstasy over Lincoln cathedral and Anna's rejection. Yet 'mist of eternity' is still tinged with satire, and the whole passage sounds what is intended as a slightly false note. Although the Master has grown impatient with the assertiveness of stone buildings, he is drifting into illusion of another kind by attributing a spurious permanence to shadowily impermanent things, and in the language of the passage, beautiful as it is, there is a correspondingly pseudo-poetic quality which gives a delicately satiric expression to the Master's progress from illusion, through disillusion, to yet further illusion.

The third island is even smaller and barer than the second: '. . . never a tree, not even a bit of heather to guard. Only the turf, and tiny turf-plants, and the sedge by the pool, the seaweed in the ocean'. This Wordsworthian 'visionary dreariness' could almost be taken as a symbol for the bedrock of reality on to which experience has at last forced the Master. But the truth is that the Master has experienced nothing. He is a figure both terrible and absurd, a diminutive Timon, lurching from an unreal benevolence to an equally unreal hatred, not only of mankind, but of all forms of life. The sheep have to be removed from the island because to the Master 'There was a suggestion of cold indecency about them'; even the sight of his own name on a letter offends him; and at last he wants 'Only space, damp, twilit, sea-washed space!' In keeping with the Master's warped subjectivity the snow that now begins to fall is presented as a ghastly parody of life, a 'new, white brute force' which drops 'panther-like'. And it is by means of the snow and the isolating sea that Lawrence offers the last, silent and most intensely satiric comment, which is also a poignantly tragic one, on the Master's career:

> How long it went on, he never knew. Once, like a wraith, he got out, and climbed to the top of a white hill on his unrecognizable island. The sun was hot. 'It is summer,' he said to himself, 'and the time of leaves.' He looked stupidly over the whiteness of his foreign island, over the waste of the lifeless sea. He pretended to imagine he saw the wink of a sail. Because he knew too well there would never again be a sail on that stark sea.

The Man Who Loved Islands, brief as it is compared with the novels, is for Lawrence an unusually long piece of sustained satire. It might be argued that his typically satirical utterance is to be found in the short bursts of fire which make up the verse of *Pansies* and *Nettles*, some of which, in Professor Pinto's words, are 'brilliant and incisive satiric commentaries on western civilization'. Examples are 'Wages', 'Modern Prayer' (the two singled out by Professor Pinto), 'Willy Wet-Leg' and 'Don'ts'. There is, however, a sharpness of definition in these verses— often accompanied by a caustic effect in the rhymes—which represents something more like the one-sided exaggeration of traditional satire than the flow and recoil most characteristic of Lawrencean satire. In verse, as in prose, he is more himself when he is stepping aside from platitudes, or undermining a stock response, rather than slamming a door in one's face.

On a minor level this is the quality to be found in 'The Oxford Voice', 'To Women, As Far As I'm Concerned' and 'In A Spanish Tram-Car'. The major poems of this kind of satire—and they include some of Lawrence's most original work—are to be found in the *Birds, Beasts and Flowers* volume and *Last Poems*. In 'The Evangelistic Beasts', for example, the poem on 'St Matthew' checks the conventional Christian notion of spiritual 'uplifting' by its insistence on the fact of man's being a man:

> So I will be lifted up, Saviour,
> But put me down again in time, Master.

And the witty presentation of the converted lion in 'St Mark'—

> There is a new sweetness in his voluptuously licking his paw
> Now that it is a weapon of heaven.
> There is a new ecstasy in his roar of desirous love
> Now that it sounds self-conscious through the unlimited sky—

is a nicely controlled comment on the persistence of unregeneracy in supposedly regenerate man. In 'Red Geranium and Godly Mignonette' it is the cliché reverence for 'the Most High' which is undermined, at the same time as a subtler and more deeply religious conception of godhead and creation is finding expression.

Recoil and flow in such a poem as 'Red Geranium and Godly Mignonette' are inseparable. Satire dissolves into a strange, new, evocative world; one almost steps over into the mythopoeic territory of 'For The Heroes Are Dipped In Scarlet' and 'Bavarian Gentians'. The poem which poises most ambiguously on this dividing line—just, and only just, retaining the title of satire, but for that reason being almost the quintessence of Lawrencean satire—is 'Fish'. This is one of the most remarkable instances of Lawrence's uncanny ability to feel himself into forms of life that are fascinatingly alien to human life, and through this very emphasis on difference make an oblique reflection on us (and on the domesticated animals that can be approximated to us). Negatives which explore the very fishiness of the fish quietly mock the physical intimacies that are familiar to us:

> But oh, fish, that rock in water,
> You lie only with the waters;

One touch.
No fingers, no hands and feet, no lips;
No tender muzzles,
No wistful bellies,
No loins of desire,
None.

Occasionally, a stray phrase of the colloquial-satirical style breaks the surface, such as 'What price *his* bread upon the waters?' Occasionally, the poem moves towards the self-consciously prophetic, as when Lawrence dwells on the theme that 'His God stands outside my God'. But for the most part it is neither overtly satiric nor prophetic. It is a poem of wonderfully alive shifts of tone. In its language and rhythms it creates a sliding, elusive form of life that at once communicates directly, without the interposition of the explaining mind, the graceful freedom of 'otherness', and obliquely criticizes the messiness of human emotions. Here, if anywhere, the paradox of Lawrencean satire is justified. 'Recoil from things gone dead' in human existence is so closely related to 'the flow of our sympathetic consciousness' towards the fish that the satire is felt only as the negative complement to a marvellously positive flow towards life.

University of Leicester

E. M. Forster and D. H. Lawrence: Their Views on Education

GEORGE A. PANICHAS

'There is a teacher for boys at school, but we, the poets, are teachers of men.'—Aristophanes

IN his admirable study, *Freedom and Authority in Education*, G. H. Bantock reminds us that 'artists are so much better guides than the professional educators'.[1] Two artists who testify eloquently to the truth of this observation are E. M. Forster and D. H. Lawrence. Although no high-sounding titles of treatises on educational topics appear among the works of either writer, both disclose an intense and steadfast concern with the meaning, the needs, and the trends of education in the twentieth century. Poetic insights, not scientific statements, give expression to their attitudes. If Forster and Lawrence do not diagnose educational issues in strictly academic or scientific terms, they nevertheless dramatize in their writings the tensions emanating from an educational technocracy that inevitably emerges in a universe that Lawrence describes as:

The world of reason and science, the moon, a dead lump of earth, the sun,

[1] G. H. Bantock, *Freedom and Authority in Education*, London, 1952, p. 162.

199

so much gas with spots: this is the dry and sterile little world the abstracted mind inhabits.[2]

Forster's educational aims might best be termed corrective; that is, his main aspiration is to correct a bad condition, a 'muddle', and to emphasize 'the belief that man is, or rather can be, rational, and that the mind can and should guide the passions towards civilization'. Accordingly, Forster feels, education should serve as a kind of antidote against the realization that 'all life is perhaps a knot, a tangle, a blemish in the eternal smoothness'. At the same time it should assist human beings, who are 'fighting to reach one another', to ameliorate the human condition by cultivating the 'generous impulses'—'tolerance, good temper and sympathy'. In this respect, Forster's educational thinking, echoing Cardinal Newman's concept of a humane and liberal education enhanced by 'freedom, equitableness, moderation and wisdom', focuses on the idea of enlightening a world grown 'uncomfortable', 'miserable and indignant', 'disordered'—a world in which violence 'is, alas! the ultimate reality on this earth, but it does not always get to the front'. His total vision is rooted in his recognition of the periods in life when a goblin walks 'quietly over the universe from end to end' and the intervals when force and violence are absent. It is these intervals which produce 'civilization.' In the effort to preserve this civilization and to resist and to contain 'the armies of darkness', Forster sees in education perhaps his most effective instrument.

When we turn to Lawrence's educational preoccupations, on the other hand, we shift from a lyrical orientation to a prophetic awareness. Not only is there a difference of vision but also a difference of energy in Lawrence's response: the reticent strain is replaced by the passional; the controlled tone gives way to prophetic song, which, as Forster tells us in *Aspects of the Novel*, 'is bound to give us a shock'. This shock is endemic to the sense of mission in the prophet's desire 'to root out, and to pull down, and to destroy, and to throw down, to build and to plant'.[3] The fact is that Lawrence seeks not to change a particular condition but to cure it. *'Cure the pain, don't give the poetry'*.[4] This is Lawrence's advice to Forster, and no words better indicate his variance from Forster in their approaches to education. To the question 'What has gone wrong?' Lawrence replies:

[2] 'A Propos of *Lady Chatterley's Lover*', *Sex, Literature, and Censorship*, edited and with an Introduction by Harry T. Moore, New York, 1959, p. 107.
[3] Jeremiah i. 10.
[4] *The Collected Letters of D. H. Lawrence*, edited and with an Introduction by Harry T. Moore, New York, 1962, Vol. I, p. 318. My italics.

Our education from the start has *taught* us a certain range of emotions, what to feel and what not to feel, and how to feel the feelings we allow ourselves to feel.[5]

Hence to solve the problems of education, of civilization, really, it is first necessary, he insists, to re-define concepts, to achieve new meaning:

> Education means leading out the individual nature in each man and woman to its true fullness. You can't do that by stimulating the mind. To pump education into the mind is fatal. That which sublimates from the dynamic consciousness into the mental consciousness has alone any value.[6]

Strongly autobiographical factors pervading and influencing Forster's and Lawrence's treatment of education cannot go unnoticed. Forster's dislike of the public school system, for instance, goes back to his own years as a day boy at Tonbridge School (1893–7). The unhappiness that he associates with public school life is reflected in *The Longest Journey*, mainly in the character of Rickie Elliot, who 'crept cold and friendless and ignorant out of a great school, and praying as a highest favour that he might be left alone'. Sawston School, as depicted in this novel, epitomizes Forster's explicit criticisms of a 'beneficent machine' which inflicts physical pain ('We can just bear it when it comes by accident or for our good . . . except at school')[7] and which shouts, 'Organize', 'Systematize', 'Fill up every minute', 'Induce *esprit de corps*'. Its loneliness and its bullying are especially intolerable:

> An apple-pie bed is nothing; pinches, kicks, boxed ears, twisted arms, pulled hair, ghosts at night, inky books, befouled photographs, amount to very little by themselves. But let them be united and continuous, and you have a hell that no grown-up devil can devise.[8]

In particular the unkind treatment of day boys is poignantly rendered in an episode in which Mr Pembroke ends an assembly of students with the singing of the recently composed school anthem (the words of which Forster appropriated from his own school song, *Carmen Tonbridgiense*). Having given the 'right intonation' to the lines 'Perish each sluggard! Let it not be said/That Sawston such within her halls hath bred', he notes sarcastically to his young audience: 'You're as tuneful as—as day boys!'

[5] 'A Propos of *Lady Chatterley's Lover*', *Sex, Literature, and Censorship*, p. 88.
[6] *Fantasia of the Unconscious*, with an Introduction by Philip Rieff, New York, 1960, pp. 112–13. This edition also contains *Psychoanalysis and the Unconscious*.
[7] *Where Angels Fear to Tread*, 1905, Ch. IX.
[8] *The Longest Journey*, 1907, Pt. I.

Upon the death of his great-aunt, Marianne Thornton, in 1887, Forster received a legacy of £8,000, which later enabled him to study at Cambridge and thereafter to travel for a few years. In 1897 he entered King's College, where he took Second Class Honours in the Classical Tripos in 1900, Second Class Honours in the History Tripos in 1901, and an M.A. in 1910. He was elected a Fellow in 1927, during which year he was Clark Lecturer at Trinity College. Cambridge, Frank Swinnerton has remarked, was 'the most wonderful thing that ever happened to him'.[9] Forster leaves no doubt concerning the veracity of this statement. Somehow his vision of education always reverts to the 'magic years' re-created in the first part of *The Longest Journey*: to the Cambridge which 'had taken and soothed him, and warmed him, and had laughed at him a little, saying that he must not be so tragic yet awhile, for his boyhood had been but a dusty corridor that led to the spacious halls of youth'; which had taught him 'that the public school is not infinite and eternal'. Above all, it brought him into contact with tutors and with resident fellows 'who treated with rare dexterity the products that came up from the public schools', teaching them to respect a man's efforts 'not so much to acquire knowledge as to dispel a little of the darkness by which we and all our acquisitions are surrounded'.

Studying classics under the tutelage of Nathaniel Wedd, Forster, like Mr Lucas in his short story 'The Road from Colonus', 'caught the fever of Hellenism'. In its beginnings his Hellenism must likewise be linked with that of his close friend, the don G. Lowes Dickinson. To understand the following passage from Dickinson's *The Greek View of Life* (first published in 1896) is to become aware of the impact that the ideas of this book had on the Forster of the 1890s and that helped eventually to shape a generous part of his educational outlook as well as even the idiom of his art:

> Harmony, in a word, was the end they [the Greeks] pursued, harmony of the soul with the body and of the body with its environment; and it is this that distinguishes their ethical ideal from that which in later times has insisted on the fundamental antagonism of the inner to the outer life, and made the perfection of the spirit depend on the mortification of the flesh.[10]

Doubtless, Hellenism of this kind inheres in Forster's belief that we

[9] Frank Swinnerton, *The Georgian Scene*, New York, 1934, p. 391.
[10] G. Lowes Dickinson, *The Greek View of Life*, London, 1957, pp. 253–4.

must sustain at all costs those values in education which he objectifies in generosity and kindness; in warmth, 'without which all education is senseless'; in respect for the 'delicate imaginings' and the 'relaxed will'. However, it must be emphasized that Forster's early Hellenism—the simple and idealizing sort as embodied in the Pan-like figure of a Stephen Wonham—changed through the years, so that when we move from *Howards End* (1910) to *Pharos and Pharillon* (1923), we become increasingly aware of a Hellenism that 'implies a recognition and acceptance of complexity', as one critic puts it.[11] In some ways Forster's recent Introduction to William Golding's *Lord of the Flies* underscores the evolvement of this less romantic and less idealized Hellenism as it reacts against the Hellenism 'so drubbed into us at school' and 'against the tyranny of Classicism—Pericles and Aspasia and Themistocles and all those bores', to quote from his essay on C. P. Cavafy.[12] Thus Forster's admiration of Piggy, though it evokes the Hellenism preached by Dickinson, cannot fail to show a demanding sense of historical reality:

> He knows that nothing is safe, nothing is neatly ticketed. He is the human spirit, aware that the universe has not been created for his convenience, and doing the best he can. And as long as he survives there is some semblance of intelligence.[13]

As is well known, Lawrence did not attend a famous public school. A 'scholarship boy' with a County Council stipend of £15 a year, he studied at Nottingham High School (1898–1901), a 'purely bourgeois school', he later observed. In his early work he does not say very much about the school; and, unlike Forster, he re-creates no memorable schoolboy experiences.

It is evident that although Lawrence received excellent instruction at the High School, he was unhappy there. With the exception of George H. Neville, a close friend during the Eastwood and the Croydon years, he was not intimate with the other students. Besides, the daily trips from Eastwood to Nottingham must have proved exhausting for a frail youth. Neville recalls this period in these words:

> Then followed our High School days together, starting from home shortly after seven o'clock in the morning and returning just before

[11] See G. D. Klingopulos, 'E. M. Forster's Sense of History: and Cavafy', *Essays in Criticism*, Vol. VIII (April, 1958), pp. 156–65.
[12] See 'The Poetry of C. P. Cavafy', *Pharos and Pharillon*, 1923.
[13] See Forster's Introduction to William Golding's *Lord of the Flies*, New York, 1962, p. x.

seven at night with always a pile of lessons to do later. . . . Even in those days, Lawrence had that little, troublesome, hacking cough that used to bring his left hand so sharply to his mouth—a cough and an action that he never lost.[14]

Lawrence was not destined to attend Cambridge and 'to see up there', in Forster's phraseology, 'what you couldn't see before and mayn't ever see again'. After his graduation from Nottingham High School, he served for a few years as a pupil-teacher and as an uncertificated teacher in Ilkeston and in Eastwood. In 1906 he enrolled in the 'normal course' at Nottingham University College, obtaining a 'teacher's certificate' in 1908. For Lawrence these were not 'magic years':

> College gave me nothing, even nothing to do—I had a damnable time there, bitter so deep with disappointment that I have lost forever my sincere boyish reverence for men in position.[15]

If Cambridge constituted for Forster a recovery of values, Nottingham University College led to Lawrence's loss of reverence. Chapter xv in *The Rainbow*, 'The Bitterness of Ecstasy', crystallizes this bleak fact. Yet his disillusionment, be it noted, must not be construed as a criticism of the standard of instruction he received. We need only read Jessie Chambers's memoir to appreciate both the intellectual depth and the cultural vitality of Lawrence's educational background.

At first Lawrence was enthusiastic about his studies. In *The Rainbow* the early response of Ursula Brangwen to Nottingham University College (a re-creation of Lawrence's own) is of the same quality as Forster's response to Cambridge: 'She scribbled her notes with joy, almost with ecstasy'; the black-gowned lecturer was a 'priest'; the college was 'holy ground':

> Her soul flew straight back to the medieval times, when the monks of God held the learning of men and imparted it within the shadow of religion. In this spirit she entered college. . . . Here, within the great, whispering sea-shell, that whispered all the while with reminiscence of all the centuries, time faded away, and the echo of knowledge filled the timeless silence.[16]

But perhaps because Ursula had too much reverence did 'a harsh and ugly disillusion' overcome her as she gradually became aware that college was

[14] *D. H. Lawrence: A Composite Biography*, edited by Edward Nehls, The University of Wisconsin Press, 1957, Vol. I, p. 34.
[15] *The Collected Letters of D. H. Lawrence*, Vol. I, pp. 8–9.
[16] *The Rainbow*, Ch. xv.

a second-hand dealer's shop, and one bought an equipment for an examination. This was only a little side-show to the factories of the town. . . . This was no religious retreat, no perception of pure learning . . . it was a sham store, a sham warehouse, with a single motive of material gain, and no productivity. . . . And barrenly, the professors in their gowns offered commercial commodity that could be turned to good account in the examination room; ready-made stuff too, and not really worth the money it was intended to fetch; which they all knew.[17]

Lawrence's words in 'Education of the People' (1918) that 'The choice is between system and system, mechanical or organic',[18] return us to their dramatic context in *The Rainbow*, to the laboratory scene that finds the physics instructor, Dr Frankstone, talking to Ursula. That we should not find a special mystery in life, that life should consist in merely a complexity of physical and chemical activities already known to science—these are the bare facts of existence which the good instructor imparts to a dismayed Ursula! Is it any wonder, then, that Lawrence condemns an educational system for surrendering to a 'process of derangement' and 'sheer mechanical materialism' which force 'all human energy into a competition of mere acquisition'?

Whereas Lawrence's reactions to education developed in the midst of working-class life in the English Midlands, with its great nonconformist tradition, Forster's reactions were shaped by the gentlemanly middle class, with its public schools and its ancient universities:

> I belong to the fag-end of Victorian liberalism [Forster writes], and can look back to an age whose challenges were moderate in their tone, and the cloud on whose horizon was no bigger than a man's hands. In many ways it was an admirable age. It practised benevolence and philanthropy, was humane and intellectually curious, upheld free speech, had little colour-prejudice, believed that individuals are and should be different, and entertained a sincere faith in the progress of society.[19]

Forster's bent, furthermore, belongs to the Cambridge-Bloomsbury *ethos*: the Cambridge which produced Rupert Brooke, a Kingsman and a 'golden young Apollo', pitiably unready for the crisis of 1914, and as Lawrence wrote, 'a Greek god under a Japanese sunshade, reading poetry in his pyjamas, at Grantchester—at Grantchester upon the lawn where the river goes';[20] the Bloomsbury which in time of crisis, as

[17] Ibid.
[18] *Phoenix: The Posthumous Papers of D. H. Lawrence*, edited and with an Introduction by Edward D. McDonald, London, 1936, p. 611.
[19] 'The Challenge of Our Time', *Two Cheers for Democracy*, New York, 1951, p. 56.
[20] *The Collected Letters of D. H. Lawrence*, Vol. I, p. 337.

Professor Johnstone has commented, 'remembered boating parties and summer days when all the good things of life seemed to have co-alesced'.[21] Forster's attitude was shaped by a 'civilization' typified by intelligence and by humane liberalism, but also by a softness that, to be properly understood, is best defined by Lionel Trilling's statement that Forster 'is content with the human possibility and content with its limitations'.[22] Forster says of himself:

> The education I received in those far-off and fantastic days made me soft and I am very glad it did, for I have seen plenty of hardness since, and I know it does not even pay.[23]

Again and again he returns to these Cambridge years to re-experience that exhilaration which in *Howards End* touches even the harried and squalid life of Leonard Bast:

> Perhaps the keenest happiness he had ever known was during a railway-journey to Cambridge, where a decent-mannered undergraduate had spoken to him.[24]

It is this Cambridge which Forster wants to be preserved:

> Cambridge still keeps her antique shape. No idealistic millionaire has yet raped her. . . . O leave her where she is and as she is, leave her to her peculiar destiny.[25]

In all likelihood Lawrence's criticisms of Forster, who spent a few days with the Lawrences in Greatham, Sussex, in February of 1915, could be interpreted as an arraignment of the Cambridge *ethos*, of Cambridge education, of the Cambridge 'type' ('Through good report and ill such men work on, following the light of truth as they see it; able to be sceptical without being paralysed', etc., if one wants to persevere with Dickinson's sonorous description).[26] 'There is something real in him', Lawrence wrote of Forster, but 'the grip has gone out of him', 'the man is dying of inanition'; 'he tries to dodge himself—the sight is pitiful':

> Forster is not poor, but he is bound hand and foot bodily. Why? *Because he does not believe that any beauty or any divine utterance is any good*

[21] J. K. Johnstone, *The Bloomsbury Group*, New York, 1963, p. 18.
[22] Lionel Trilling, *E. M. Forster*, Norfolk, Connecticut, 1943, p. 22.
[23] 'The Challenge of Our Time', *Two Cheers for Democracy*, p. 56.
[24] *Howards End*, 1910, Ch. xiv.
[25] 'Cambridge', *Two Cheers for Democracy*, p. 350. Cf. 'A Letter [from] E. M. Forster,' *The Twentieth Century*, Vol. CLVII (February 1955), p. 99.
[26] Quoted by Noel Gilroy Annan, *Leslie Stephen*, London, 1951, p. 286.

any more. Why? Because the world is suffering from bonds, and birds of foul desire which gnaw its liver. Forster knows, as every thinking man now knows, that all his thinking and his passion for humanity amounts to no more than trying to soothe with poetry a man raging with pain which can be cured. . . . Will all the poetry in the world satisfy the manhood of Forster, when Forster knows that his implicit manhood is to be satisfied by nothing but immediate physical action.[27]

('Perhaps my character did not pass the test of the Sussex Downs. . .', Forster ruefully observed fifteen years later in the *Nation and Athenaeum*.)[28] What must remain obvious is that Forster's views of education are anchored in the pre-1914 Cambridge, when, to quote John Maynard Keynes, 'We were living in the specious present, nor had begun to play the game of consequences'.[29] Indeed, Forster's peculiar shying away from 'the game of consequences', so clearly detected by Lawrence, is visible in his fictional characters like Philip Herriton and Rickie Elliot. Always, then, Forster speaks for the survival of institutions, for a leisurely process of education, for a Cambridge that moulded his humanity and his fairmindedness (he was one of the very few back in 1930 to defend Lawrence's artistic genius against the 'obituary-mongers', as H. J. Massingham aptly termed them),[30] but that in other ways contributed to his 'general lack of vitality':

> But surely [Dr Leavis demurs], what a critic who takes Forster seriously must be very largely concerned with nowadays is how that university didn't equip him to deal with the milieu into which it sent him—the milieu, so closely connected with Cambridge, that became Bloomsbury?. . . How can so sensitive, decent and generous a mind have allowed itself to be so much *of* a milieu so inferior?—so provincially complacent and petty?[31]

Still, the frequently cited 'perils' to and 'limitations' of Forster's liberalism and humanism cannot enfeeble either the integrity or the maturity of his vision.[32] The so-called softness of his attitude, further-more, should not be confused with the decomposition portrayed in the character of Sir Michael in the story 'The Point of It', who, having

[27] *The Collected Letters of D. H. Lawrence*, Vol. I, pp. 317–18. Lawrence's italics.
[28] *The Nation and Athenaeum*, 29 March 1930, p. 888.
[29] John Maynard Keynes, *Two Memoirs*, London, 1949, p. 95.
[30] *The Nation and Athenaeum*, 5 April 1930, p. 12.
[31] See 'Meet Mr Forster', *Scrutiny*, Vol. XII (Autumn 1944), pp. 308–9.
[32] See, for example, Frederick C. Crews, *E. M. Forster: The Perils of Humanism*, Princeton, New Jersey, 1962; Donald Hannah, 'The Limitations of Liberalism in E. M. Forster's Work', *English Miscellany*, Vol. XIII (Rome, 1962), pp. 165–78; Alan Wilde, *Art and Order: A Study of E. M. Forster*, New York, 1964.

'mistaken self-criticism for self-discipline . . . had muffled in himself and others the keen, heroic edge'. Education can produce persons like Mr Pembroke, the organizer whose 'plump finger was in every pie'; Cecil Vyse, who plays 'tricks on people, on the most sacred form of life that he can find'; and even Tibby Schlegel, who though 'he had lost his peevishness [and] . . . hid his indifference to people . . . had not grown more human'. These characters stand for the shabbiest aspects of education, in which a public-school accent remains constant, and remind us of what can go wrong. These, Forster is saying, represent tendencies and dangers which to ignore is to surrender to a debility synonymous with irresponsibility—a 'sign of decay', so to speak. But that a choice is possible; that there are positive values of education which can sustain life against the Pembrokes and the Vyses; that there exist persons like Stewart Ansell, who has a 'glimpse of comradeship', and a humane schoolmaster like Mr Jackson, with whom students 'remained friends . . . throughout their lives': these are redeeming alternatives which need to be affirmed.

Cantabrigian society was revealed to Lawrence during a visit arranged by Bertrand Russell, 6–7 March 1915. But Lawrence's reaction, particularly to the Cambridge 'type', was far from agreeable. He felt that 'Fabianism, Socialism, Cambridgism and advancedism of all sorts' were 'like poison', 'a nasty form of dry rot on the human species'.[33] When we remember the Cambridge of this period—and the constellation formed by Russell, Keynes, Lytton Strachey, Leonard Woolf, G. E. Moore, J. M. E. McTaggart and Dickinson—when, as Keynes declares, 'Cambridge rationalism and cynicism [were] . . . at their height', with victory resting exclusively

> with those who could speak with the greatest appearance of clear, un-doubting conviction and could best use the accents of infallibility,[34]

it is not in the least difficult to understand why Lawrence could not approve of Cambridge 'civilization'. To Lawrence Cambridge constituted 'one of the crises of my life':

> It . . . made me very black and down. I cannot bear its smell of rottenness, marsh-stagnancy. I get a melancholic malaria. How can so sick people rise up? They must die first.[35]

His words underscore an intuitive response to and rejection of a

[33] *D. H. Lawrence: A Composite Biography*, Vol. I, p. 407.
[34] Keynes, *Two Memoirs*, p. 85.
[35] *The Collected Letters of D. H. Lawrence*, Vol. I, p. 330.

'civilization', of an education (with its 'accents of infallibility'), which Lawrence equated with a temper devoid of reverence and with a cast of mind that Keynes himself, on later reflection, censured for its thinness and superficiality:

> I can see us as water-spiders, gracefully skimming, as light and reasonable as air, the surface of the stream without any contact at all with the eddies and currents underneath.[36]

It is clear, moreover, that Lawrence's reactions to the social order of his time resulted from intense personal involvement. 'For him . . . the *whole* process had been lived', Raymond Williams rightly insists, 'and he was the more conscious of the general failure, and thus of the general character of the system'.[37] Indeed the Lawrence of 1915 had already served as a schoolmaster at the Davidson Road School at Croydon (1908–11); had, as is re-created in Ursula Brangwen's teaching experiences, come face to face with 'the man's world'; had suffered the weariness, the grim realities of a 'hard, malevolent system' —the days of 'battle and hate and violence', 'the sums, the grammar, the quarterly examinations, the registers'. That he had been a teacher who had also experienced 'the passion of instruction' is apparent to anyone who reads the school chapters in *The Rainbow* and in *Women in Love* or ponders lines like the following from one of Lawrence's school poems, 'The Best of School':

> This morning, sweet it is
> To feel the lads' looks light on me,
> Then back in a swift, bright flutter to work:
> Each one darting away with his
> Discovery, like birds that steal and flee.
> Touch after touch I feel on me
> As their eyes glance at me for the grain
> Of rigour they taste delightedly.
> ....
> I feel them cling and cleave to me
> As vines going eagerly up; they twine
> My life with other leaves, my time
> Is hidden in theirs, their thrills are mine.[38]

To repeat: 'The *whole* process had been lived.' Surely it is in the

[36] Keynes, *Two Memoirs*, p. 103.
[37] Raymond Williams, *Culture and Society 1780–1950*, Penguin Books, 1961, p. 202.
[38] *The Complete Poems of D. H. Lawrence*, edited and with an Introduction and Notes by Vivian de Sola Pinto and Warren Roberts, New York, 1964, Vol. I, pp. 51–2.

GEORGE A. PANICHAS

pain and in the truth of these words that we find Lawrence's remarkable grasp of the innermost issues of education, of a system in which

> The first great task was to reduce sixty children to one state of mind, or being. This state must be produced automatically, through the will of the teacher, and the will of the whole school authority, imposed upon the will of the children—

as well as a system in which the teacher was often

> liable to attack from either side at any minute, or from both at once, for the authorities would listen to the complaints of parents, and both would turn round on the mongrel authority, the teacher.[39]

It was precisely with such intelligence and with such experience that Lawrence, in March of 1915, confronted Cambridge 'civilization'. Yet Russell and Keynes deliberately aimed their conversation 'at Lawrence', and Professor G. E. Moore, who sat next to Lawrence in Hall, 'found nothing to say to him'![40]

Unfortunately, the lie that Lawrence was 'an ignorant man in the sense that he was unaware of how much he did not know', as T. S. Eliot believed,[41] and as the literary establishment has maintained for years and years, still gains in circulation. Recently, for example, J. I. M. Stewart in his *Eight Modern Writers* perpetuates the same old dreary lie, the same misrepresentation concerning Lawrence's working-class background, with this assertion: 'But humble birth, plebeian manners, and irregular education can never be other than disadvantageous circumstances, and Lawrence seldom forgot that they had been his'.[42] (Mr Stewart, no doubt, feels it his task here to remind his readers that Lawrence had not seen 'the light of Cambridge'—or, worse, had never been in attendance at Christ Church!)

Any comparison of the educational views of these two writers cannot avoid the fact that in Forster the vision is mediate, which is to say, the result of delicate interweavings of and tensions between 'actions and meditations'. In shunning the extremes of 'contending assertions', Forster allows a necessary place for the mind. Indeed, the habit of intellect and a predisposition towards introspection are basic elements of his art. He could not repudiate them without seriously menacing his regard for the continuity of life:

[39] *The Rainbow*, Ch. XIII.
[40] *D. H. Lawrence: A Composite Biography*, Vol. I, pp. 286, 574 note 103.
[41] See T. S. Eliot's Foreword to Father William Tiverton's [the Rev. Martin Jarrett-Kerr's] *D. H. Lawrence and Human Existence*, London, 1951.
[42] J. I. M. Stewart, *Eight Modern Writers*, Oxford University Press, 1963, p. 484.

I am speaking like an intellectual, but the intellectual . . . is more in touch with humanity than is the cultural scientist. . . .[43]

He considers the intellect useful, for it can become a light penetrating the emotions. Ultimately, therefore, Forster salutes the intellect because of its potentialities in the scheme of things. It is with especial approbation that he quotes from his Cambridge teacher Oscar Browning, whose words at the same time define an important aspect of Forster's own attitude:

> I have been drawn to think rather of the tens who have failed than of the units who have succeeded, and of the ore that lies buried in our social strata rather than of the bright coins that circulate from hand to hand. If a field of coal or of some other material lies unworked and unused, yet it is always there. It may be kept for some future age when its wealth will be more needed, and posterity will bless the prescience and parsimony of their ancestors who refrained from using it. But the human mind is born and lives and perishes. If it is unenlightened, it passes away into its native darkness. [44]

Indeed, the endurance of 'belief in the human race', Forster says, is directly related to the need for exploring and cultivating available human resources before they pass into extinction.

Lawrence's vision, in contrast, is immediate: there can be neither respect for nor compromise with a way of life in a 'state of funk': 'For all strife between things old is pure death'.[45] Tensions in Lawrence are not relieved in a perilous balance between action and meditation, between the passion and the prose. 'The last three thousand years of mankind', he declares, 'have been an excursion into ideals, bodiless-ness, and tragedy, and now the excursion is over'.[46] To Lawrence the problems of education require instant, total action, inasmuch as man has fallen 'from spontaneous reality into dead or material reality': 'All our education should be a guarding against this fall.'[47] The re-orientation of education, he says, must begin with the premise that 'mental consciousness' in not a goal but a cul-de-sac. By no means, however, does Lawrence discredit the use of the mind, for it can be 'a great indicator and instrument': But 'the mind as author and director of life is anathema'. Conventional learning *per se* for Lawrence becomes

[43] 'The Challenge of Our Time', *Two Cheers for Democracy*, p. 60.
[44] Quoted in 'Cambridge', *Two Cheers for Democracy*, p. 352.
[45] *Phoenix*, p. 675.
[46] 'A Propos of *Lady Chatterley's Lover*', *Sex, Literature, and Censorship*, p. 106.
[47] *Phoenix*, p. 714.

'intellectual understanding' rather than 'living understanding', and it is too often attached to some imposed '*standard* of instruction', to 'regulation patterns', to 'moral bullying':

> There should be no effort made to teach children to think, to have ideas. Only to lift them and urge them into dynamic activity. The voice of dynamic sound, not the words of understanding. Damn understanding. Gestures, and touch, and expression of the face, not theory. Never have ideas about children—and never have ideas *for* them.[48]

Again and again he exposes the inconsistencies of educators who 'talk of free-expression, and . . . proceed to force all natures into ideal and aesthetic expression'. Hence, he feels that a disbalance has led to children's degenerating 'into physical cloddishness or mechanical affectation or fluttered nervousness', into 'the nervous, twisting, wistful, pathetic, centreless children we are cursed with'. The cure, as Lawrence envisions it, must entail a severe de-intellectualization, so to speak, the restoration of a 'non-ideal, passional' element to human relations, and the sparking of an 'emotional *rapport*', a certain fearlessness and openness in dealing with the young: a display of 'clean, fierce rage' co-existent with 'all love and tenderness'; a willingness, as well, to '*leave the child alone*, in his own soul'. Were one to choose an epigraph for Lawrence's educational views, these words from William Blake's 'The Proverbs of Hell' would be appropriate: 'The tigers of wrath are wiser than the horses of instruction'—a sentiment, by the way, which finds its parallel in Lawrence's declaration in *Etruscan Places* that 'what one wants is the actual vital touch. I don't want to be "instructed"; nor do many other people'.[49]

As critics of education, Forster and Lawrence together yield a completeness and a sympathy of vision arising from a direct concern with the tasks and the responsibilities of the system. A primary impulse behind their reactions is a distress with increasing mechanization in the educational process, epitomized by a belief that 'school is [or should be] the world in miniature'. But that education can be something more than the external world, that it is, in fact, 'a sacred business': these, Forster and Lawrence agree, are irrevocable truths. Indeed, it is their belief that education has a greater destiny than is generally allowed it which unites them. 'Educators . . . will be the priests of life', writes Lawrence, 'deep in the wisdom of life. They will be the life-priests of the new

---

[48] *Fantasia of the Unconscious*, pp. 114–15.
[49] *Etruscan Places*, 1932, Ch. VI.

era'.[50] For Forster education means 'the help of good will plus culture and intelligence' and 'the good sense that persists in the human organism even when it is heated by passion'. For Lawrence education means the attainment of 'a perfect correspondence between the spontaneous, yearning, impulsive-desirous soul and the automatic *mind* which runs on little wheels of ideas'. Forster protests against a system leading to unhappiness; Lawrence protests against a system leading to 'the tragedy of ugliness'. Forster speaks to the heart; Lawrence speaks to the 'man alive'. Both voice warnings that cannot be ignored, except at our peril.

Although they approach educational problems from often opposing positions, they stand together in their reverence for an underlying mystery in human life that defies what Forster speaks of as the 'implacable offensive of Science' and what Lawrence terms 'an outward system of nullity', when,

> Living as we do entirely in the light of the mental consciousness, we think everything is as we see it and as we think it.[51]

It is awareness of the need to renew contact with the values beneath standardized instruction that is an impelling force in the educational attitudes of these two writers. In order to renew this contact Forster and Lawrence do not flinch from asking basic questions of our civilization: 'What is education all about? What is it doing? Does anybody know?'[52] If not always or not fully satisfactory, their answers are indispensable to the debate that still continues, and must continue, if modern education is to mean more than just enabling us to get jam today and—yes, more jam tomorrow.

University of Maryland

---

[50] *Phoenix*, pp. 606–7.
[51] *Phoenix*, p. 634.
[52] *Phoenix*, p. 587.

Alan Sillitoe's *Saturday Night and Sunday Morning*

J. R. OSGERBY

ON the whole, Sillitoe's critics have regarded him either as a sensationalistic writer exploiting, if not actually encouraging, promiscuity and violence,[1] or as a 'social realist' making vivid use of autobiographical material but lacking the artist's capacity to elicit significant order from this material.[2] This study seeks to show not only that both these views are mistaken, but also that Sillitoe deserves to be treated seriously, as one of the most important of our contemporary writers.

An *Evening Standard* reporter, describing his interview with Sillitoe after the popular success of the novel *Saturday Night and Sunday Morning*, said, 'Anyone who thought he was advocating the Arthur Seaton way of life (booze, sex and money) was mistaken. What he was doing was deploring the state of society that forces an Arthur Seaton

---

[1] The cover of the paperback version, published in 1960 by Pan Books Ltd. (to which version page numbers of extracts quoted here relate) proclaims: 'A novel of today with a freshness and raw fury that "makes *Room At The Top* look like a vicarage tea-party".'

[2] James Gindin implies that Sillitoe actually sees life as chaotic—'Nothing really changes Sillitoe's jungle world. A man may win or lose, depending on the wheel of chance, but he cannot control the wheel or change his position', *Postwar British Fiction— New Accents and Attitudes*, London, 1962, p. 33. Gindin nevertheless regards Sillitoe as one of the three most outstanding contemporary British writers (op. cit. p. 237).

to lead such an "unsatisfactory life". "It is the story of a man," said Mr Sillitoe, "who has his earthly bread but not his spiritual bread. He has no spiritual values because the kind of conditions he lives in do not allow him to have any." [3] Artists do not always speak perceptively about their own creations and Sillitoe himself has sometimes appeared to see his literary work mainly in terms of its socio-political implications. [4] However, his comment that *Saturday Night and Sunday Morning* is 'the story of a man who has his earthly bread but not his spiritual bread' deserves investigation.

The novel is divided into two; Part One, the first twelve chapters, is called 'Saturday Night' and Part Two, the final three chapters, is called 'Sunday Morning'; Part One ends with Arthur's beating by the two soldiers and Part Two opens with his lying in bed recovering from this attack; it is reasonable to assume that the split in the novel at this point is not fortuitous, and that, accordingly, Arthur's beating is not only the climax of the novel but also, specifically, the most significant crisis in the career of its hero. Moreover, there seems an implied connection between whatever symbolic significance is possessed by the respective titles of the two parts and whatever change is to be discerned in the character of the hero as a result of his beating.

Part One actually opens on Saturday Night—'the best and bingiest glad-time of the week, one of the fifty-two holidays in the slow-turning Big Wheel of the year, a violent preamble to a prostrate Sabbath. Piled-up passions were exploded on Saturday night, and the effect of a week's monotonous graft in the factory was swilled out of your system in a burst of goodwill' (p. 5). At the start of his novel Sillitoe thus establishes a contrast and a connection between Saturday night, with its explosive anarchic rebellion, and the rest of the week, filled as it is with 'monotonous graft'; the latter is the direct cause of the former, and the former is in turn 'a violent preamble to a prostrate Sabbath', Sunday morning being not only that part of the week spent in near-oblivion as the result of Saturday night's revolt but taking its place, too, with the rest of the week as time spent in passive acquiescence in a stifling round of imposed conformity. This inevitable relationship between 'Saturday Night' and 'Sunday Morning', between violent irresponsible rebellion and dull, grinding submission, between irrational conflict and near-extinction, is, in fact, the main theme of the

[3] *Evening Standard*, Friday, 1 September 1961, p. 8.
[4] See, for instance, his essay 'Both Sides Of The Street' in *The Writer's Dilemma*, London, 1960, pp. 68–75.

novel. 'He who makes a beast of himself', as Samuel Johnson said, 'gets rid of the pain of being a man'.

Part One opens and closes with Arthur's being drawn into participation in violent, irrational conflict and, as a result of this, sinking almost gratefully into oblivion. In the opening scene, after his drinking-match with Loudmouth, he falls down the pub stairs—'This rolling motion was so restful and soporific, in fact, that when he stopped travelling— having arrived at the bottom of the stairs—he kept his eyes closed and went to sleep. It was a pleasant and faraway feeling, and he wanted to stay in exactly the same position for the rest of his life' (p. 7). At the end of Part One Arthur, having been severely mauled by Winnie's revenge-seeking husband and his friend, falls unconscious from his injuries—'with a grin, he slipped down in a dead faint, feeling the world pressing its enormous booted foot on to his head, forcing him away from the lights, down into the dark comfort of grime, spit and sawdust on the floor' (p. 154).

Life in Part One of the novel, as typified in the career of Arthur Seaton, is a cycle of violent rebellion and imposed conformity, each breeding the other; the problem is how to break this circle. To eschew revolt and 'knuckle under', as Brenda's husband, Jack, advises (p. 165) is hardly a satisfactory solution, for Jack himself is a dull dog whose very lack of creativity, and consequent dedication to a routine of passivity—watching racing (p. 12), filling-in his pools and entering-up the union dues (p. 138)—drives his own neglected wife to revolt and to seek in her affair with Arthur some of the satisfaction she fails to get from her marriage. Moreover, as a result of his wife's reaction, Jack finds himself forced to connive at an act of violence he deplores, in revenging himself on Arthur. In fact, Jack's attempt at passivity in the hope of some kind of minimal material security is a no more successful effort at coping with life than is Arthur's refusal to surrender anything of his individuality in return for such security; both men alike remain bound to the destructive wheel of Saturday Night and Sunday Morning.

Part One, 'Saturday Night', begins and ends in Autumn, and is concerned with Arthur's attempts at rebellion, expressed mainly in terms of drinking, whoring and brawling; this rebellion stems from his prison-like confinement, for most of his life, in Army, factory and Dole-dominated domesticity. What Arthur comes to learn is that mere rebellion is no way of breaking the circle; he learns that the jungle[5] he

---

[5] Sillitoe repeatedly and overtly refers to Arthur's life in Part One as a 'jungle' existence, e.g. 'spoiling the fangs and blunting the claws of his existence' (p. 86), 'You

enters when he flouts the morality of social life has its own laws, which operate as inevitably as, and more ruthlessly than, the laws of the society he opts out of. For instance, when Arthur refuses to respect the civilized institution of marriage and brings the habits of the jungle into his sexual life, he necessarily removes himself also from the protection of the social institution of law and order and exposes himself to the jungle law of revenge—'a kind of wild justice' as Bacon called it. Sillitoe emphasizes that there is nothing 'fair' about the justice meted out to Arthur as a result of his adulterous adventures—two attack one, boots supplement fists, and blows are administered to all parts of the body; Sillitoe's imagery deliberately recalls, in its savagery and impersonality,[6] a jungle battle between wild animals—'Two shadowy figures came level . . . blood behind his eyes distilled to defiance and a hard-gutted core of self-preservation . . . there was no escape . . . except by his own outnumbered sinews . . . They were undifferentiated and without identity . . . the world had shrunk for him to a struggle being decided in the space of a few square yards' (pp. 151-4).

This grand instance of jungle justice rewarding jungle behaviour is led up to, and mirrored, by a series of similar instances—which sequence is itself evidence of Sillitoe's careful construction of his novel. Firstly, a young hooligan impales Arthur's leg with a dart and refuses to apologize, whereupon 'Arthur stood up and hit him' (pp. 91-2); secondly, a man who shatters an undertaker's window with a beer mug is ignominiously arrested by a woman in khaki, a 'fawce bogger' who has 'aligned herself with order and law' (pp. 93-5); thirdly, Arthur is knocked down by a drunken motorist who takes the initiative in ap-

---

[6] In the film of the novel, scripted by Sillitoe himself, the fight was effectively shown in terms of the enormous, grotesque shadows of the participants thrown on a blank brick wall.

might as well live in a jungle with wild animals' (p. 98), 'The jungle was safer than he thought' (p. 105), 'It was a dark life and a dark deed' (p. 136), 'caught in a game of fang-and-claw' (p. 145), 'they . . . had bested him on the common battleground of the jungle' (p. 156), 'When wounded he liked to be alone in his lair' (p. 160); Doreen, with unintended irony, tells Arthur about the film she saw on the night he was assaulted—' "Drums in the Jungle". You should have been there, Arthur.'

One of the most recurrent themes in Sillitoe's work is the dream of escape from the drab prison of urban, industrial life to the 'freedom' of some kind of exotic jungle, and how the dreamer may come to realize the identity of prison and jungle and that true freedom lies in substituting for the destructive cycle of repression and rebellion, a positive cycle of sympathetic insight and creative love; cf. Noah's Ark, The Fishing-Boat Picture, Mr Raynor the Schoolteacher (in 'The Loneliness of the Long Distance Runner'), The Magic Box (in 'The Ragman's Daughter') and the novels *The General* and *Key to the Door*—as well as, of course, the novel at present under discussion.

portioning the blame, whereupon Arthur and his brother Fred, 'locked in a revengeful act', overturn his car (pp. 99–101); fourthly, the 'malicious gossip' Mrs Bull is shot in the face by a marksman armed with an airgun; the marksman is, of course, Arthur, about whom Mrs Bull has been 'continually gossiping'; Fred says of Arthur, 'If anybody gets on the wrong side of him he can do what seem very dirty tricks indeed— if you didn't know that his motive was revenge' (pp. 101–2).

But of course, as Arthur himself is to find, other denizens of the jungle can also do very dirty tricks when their motive is revenge. Goose Fair is the particular jungle in which at one and the same time Arthur's predatory sex-life attains its high-water mark, and the predatory forces of revenge which this sex-life has set in motion, begin to hunt him down. With a married sister on each arm, and a third girl deceived, Arthur seems to have wrought his masterpiece in sexual betrayal, but at the moment of his greatest triumph an ominous note is struck. Goose Fair is a symbolic chaos—'The fair lights were a sheet of pale corruscating orange obliterating the darkness. Crowds were thick along the pavements, moving in uneven intermingling streams to and from the tents and roundabouts. Children clutched Donald Duck balloons, women and girls wore paper sailor hats saying: Kiss me quick or You've had it; others hugged train-sets and china dogs won at hoop-la and darts. The pungent air smoked brandy-snap and vinegar. They heard the thumping pistons of red-painted engines that gave power to Caterpillars and Noah's Arks, and distant screams came down at them from the tower of Helter Skelter and the topmost arc of the Big Wheel,[7] noise and lights a magnetized swamp sucking people into it for miles around. He dragged his women along . . . and as they swung in through the entrance he narrowly missed castration on the steel post invisible in the crush of people'. (pp. 138–9).

Arthur's behaviour at Goose Fair becomes increasingly outrageous —'Sanity was out of reach: they were caught up in balloons of light and pleasure that would not let them go. The four-acre fair became a whole world, with tents and caravans, stalls and roundabouts, booths and towers, swingboats and engines and big wheels, and a crowd that had lost all idea of time and place locked in the belly of its infernal noise' (p. 140); eventually, after being the Demon King on the Ghost Train

[7] The Big Wheel epitomizes the Fair Ground as the Fair Ground itself epitomizes Arthur's world of 'Saturday night' excess and 'Sunday morning' retribution, providing its riders with a recurrent cycle of exhilaration and alarm—as in Part One, Arthur and his friends are bound to 'the slow-turning Big Wheel of the year' (p. 5).

(pp. 141–2), Arthur arrives at the top of the Helter Skelter and feels himself, however precariously, the Lord of all this Misrule—'Arthur sat on his mat, waiting for the next person to come up and give him a flying push. He looked over the lights and tent tops and people bellowing out a rough voice to the sky, at the three-day-ritual bout of forty thousand voices. He felt like a king up there with so much power spreading on all sides below him, and until two hands stabbed into his back and pushed him into oblivion he was wondering how many columns of soldiers could be gathered from these crowds for use in a rebellion' (p. 143). Arthur's symbolic dethronement as Lord of Misrule immediately precedes his actual dethronement—more treacherous and violent in its execution—as King of the Wood—'He was near the earth once more, close to the chute-end, ready to slide out safely on to a pile of mats. He felt relaxed now that it was nearly over. There was nothing else to do but wait, a voice said to him. But wait for what? He turned the last bend at the height of his speed, emptied of thought, supremely purified, until he hit the pile of mats at the bottom. Winnie and Brenda stood in front of the crowd, Jack, wearing overalls, his face expressing surprise at seeing Arthur, held Winnie's arm; to the right stood the big swaddie and his friend still in their khaki, Bill's face swelling with rage and thoughts of vengeance as he leapt out of the crowd with the clear and definite intention of strangling Arthur as soon as he could get hold of him'. (p. 144).

Sillitoe reinforces his symbolic use of the Goose Fair episode with his equally symbolic use of Arthur's fifteen days Army service; as Arthur's 'Sunday morning' life of penal servitude in the factory precipitates his 'Saturday night' explosion at Goose Fair, which in turn precipitates his total immobilization by the two 'swaddies', so the 'Sunday morning' constraint of Army life promotes his nightly escape into drunkenness, which, in turn, leads to his eventual total immobilization by his fellow-soldiers, for he is tied-up in his bed after assaulting the C.O. (pp. 122–3). The thunderclap which terrifies Arthur while he is on his military service foreshadows the eventual retribution of violence with violence.

As Jack gains no lasting satisfaction from his 'Sunday morning' existence of attempted passivity, so Arthur gains no lasting satisfaction from his 'Saturday night' existence of attempted rebellion; both men find that the different kinds of self-indulgence they choose actually deprive them of real love; as Jack loses his wife's affection, Arthur loses Jack's friendship; and, while Arthur loves children and gets on well with them, the child that is the fruit of his illicit liaison with Brenda and which he would like to keep, has to be aborted.

As Saturday night's anarchistic revolt brings Sunday morning's lifeless conformity, it would seem that Arthur, the wild lover of Brenda in Part One, may, as a result of his beating, dwindle into Arthur, the hen-pecked husband of Doreen, in Part Two. Indeed, as Part One is dominated by Brenda, the securely married woman seeking sexual adventure, Part Two is dominated by Doreen, 'afraid of being "left on the shelf"' (p. 134) and apparently willing to barter her sex only for the security of marriage; moreover, the jungle of terrace houses which is Brenda's world in Part One gives way to the new, starkly ordered Broxtowe Estate, which is Doreen's world, in Part Two, and Saturday night, spent, in Part One, by Arthur in orgies with Brenda at the pub, is, in Part Two, spent by him passively, at the pictures with Doreen. But Sillitoe gives some implication in the novel of how the circle of revolt and conformity may be broken and this lies in his treatment of Arthur's character. Arthur is obviously the novel's hero; he is, of course, in many ways an objectionable young man, but he has one great quality that commends him to us, and that is his capacity for self-criticism. We feel him a sympathetic personality in so far as we realize that, however brash he often seems, he is fundamentally unsure of himself and looking for some deeper meaning in life than he has so far found; this self-awareness, however groping and intermittent, enables Arthur himself to have a sympathetic insight into the unhappiness of others and thus prevents his ever becoming a mere lout, or insensitive escapist. Early in the novel Sillitoe tells us, 'When someone said to Arthur: "I've got yo' weighed-up," his stock reply was: "Oh, 'ev yer? Then ye'r bloody clever, mate, because I ain't got meself weighed-up, I can tell yer"—which was equally effective in shutting them up, and perhaps equally truthful in that though everybody might have the ability to weigh-up others it never occurred to them to attempt a weighing-up of themselves. Arthur had stumbled on this lack from which all seemed to suffer, though as yet he had not thought of applying it with any great force to himself' (p. 35). After his beating, Arthur does begin to 'apply it with greater force to himself', for, as he lies in bed recovering from his injuries he undergoes a kind of spiritual death and resurrection—'he lay there for days on end like a dead dog. . . . He didn't much care whether he lived or died. The wheels of change that were grinding their expressive tracks through his mind did not yet show themselves off in him to advantage . . . he only vaguely noticed the combined pandemonium rolling over the black cloud of his melancholy . . . nothing could drag him out of the half sleep in which he lay buried for three days' (p. 155). Symbolically, on the third day he rises to life again, and although he does not at present appreciate it, he is a changed man—'He knew it was no use fighting against the cold weight of his nameless malady, or asking how it came about. He did not ask, believing it to be related to his defeat by the swaddies . . . He did not ask whether he was in such a knocked-out state because he had lost the rights of love over two women, or because the two swaddies represented the raw edge of fang-and-claw on which all laws were based, law and order against which he had been fighting all his life in such a thoughtless and unorganized way that he could not but lose. Such questions came later' (pp. 155–6). In so far as Arthur ever consciously asks these questions he tends to answer them in naively adolescent terms of continuing his individualistic fight against life (pp. 158, 191) but the real change in his attitude to life is brought out by Sillitoe obliquely.

At first, Arthur's slowly formulating sense of the futility of jungle life—'The plain fact was that the two swaddies had got him at last—as he had known they would—and had bested him on the common battleground of the jungle' (p. 156) is at odds with his intention of resuming the old cycle of his life—'He told himself that he would be able to go back to work soon, to the pub again in the evening. . .'; already, however, he is made aware of the essentially destructive nature of this old cycle, for he is 'plagued by crowding and inexpressible thoughts, thinking that he was going mad'. And consequently, for him, time itself, the outward manifestation of inward order, takes on the appearance of a chaos—his three days in Purgatory 'seemed like a hundred years, wheeling their brilliant Goose Fairs and Bonfire Nights and Christmases around him like branding irons in a torture chamber. When he stopped looking at the wall he lay back to sleep, and awoke after violent yet unrememberable dreams to see the grinning face of the cheap mantelpiece clock telling him that only two minutes had gone by' (p. 155).

Nevertheless, although Arthur's purgatorial experience of his past life as a chaotic and destructive cycle leads him to appreciate the futility of constant rebellion and retaliation, he still distrusts mere passivity, which seems to him at present the only possible alternative. Certainly, 'if you lived in a cave in the middle of a dark wood you weren't safe' (p. 158) but neither were you safe if you tried to float down securely through life on a parachute, for 'one day you hit the bottom without knowing it, like a bubble bursting when it touches something solid, and you were dead, out like a light in a Derbyshire gale'—'Well, that's not for me' he says (pp. 158–9). And so, caught up in 'the tumultuous lake and whirlpool in his mind', it seems to him he can only look forward to being 'free to carry life on where he had left it'.

However, he is delivered from the wheel of chaos by two women who, in helping him unstintingly in his greatest need, reveal to him the way of compassion, rather than retaliation. Firstly, his own mother, after pointing out the inevitability of retribution for his kind of rebellion—'You can't play wi' fire wi'out gettin' yer fingers burnt'—nurses him back to health without question or complaint, but because 'Ye'r my own son, aren't yer?' (p. 157). And secondly, Doreen, to whom he has first of all lied regarding the origin of his injuries, and then sought to injure by telling the truth in as brutal a way as possible, accepts him despite his faults—'I like you, Arthur, and I kept on hoping you were all right' (p. 162). Affection breeds affection and Arthur responds— 'He held her by the wrist, and they talked for another hour. "We'll go to the pictures on Monday," he said'. Doreen, thus inclining Arthur to a new, creative cycle of reciprocal love, makes time meaningful to him again—'Monday was not far off, and perhaps time would pass quickly' (p. 163).

What Arthur has learnt he immediately puts into practice; he now refrains from retaliation himself in two instances. Back at work again, he encounters Jack in a deserted corridor—'Arthur clenched his hand . . . He didn't think it was worth it: an eye for an eye, and a tooth for a tooth, but he had had more than his fair share of both' (p. 164). Jack is awe-struck by the blood on Arthur's hand and offers him a cigarette; although Arthur declines the cigarette, the ice is broken between the two men and their reconciliation, not overtly acknowledged, is nevertheless achieved (p. 165). Later, when his apology over a beer-spilling incident is not accepted, he nevertheless refrains from answering violence with violence (pp. 168–9).

Yet he remains suspicious of the way of non-retaliation, as he remains suspicious of Doreen's motives. Does non-retaliation mean always being put upon? and ought one never to stand up for one's rights? Is Doreen being tender simply to ensnare him into marriage? and will marriage inevitably mean submission? The incident at the Christmas party, when Jane cracks her husband Jim on the head for some alleged and unspecified slander, acts as a catalyst in helping

Arthur to resolve his own dilemma (pp. 175–6), for he is now convinced that rebellion may sometimes be justified and that marriage need not be mere submission. He sees that he can still be a rebel, but only in defence of human dignity against the humbugs and exploiters who seek to destroy it—'Blokes with suits and bowler hats will say: "These chaps have got their television sets, enough to live on, council houses, beer and pools—some have even got cars. We've made them happy. What's wrong? Is that a machine gun I hear …" … to live with his feet on the ground did not demand, he realized fully for the first time, that he go against his own strong grain of recklessness' (p. 177). Arthur, naturally, is not very coherent in his conscious formulation of his new-found attitude but this attitude is clear enough; and in his newly declared war against humbug and exploitation his main weapon is to be cunning (as Stephen Dedalus's was) rather than violence—'the broad-fisted exuberant cunning of a man … caught up in his isolation and those half-conscious clamped-in policies for living that cried for exit' (p. 177).

And at this time, significantly, Arthur chooses to become 'Doreen's young man'. Sillitoe very effectively conveys the creative struggle which the evolution of their kind of love-relationship involves; for instance, after the first consummation of their love, Arthur and Doreen have their first clash of wills (pp. 180–2). That Arthur is achieving maturity through his relationship with Doreen is finely brought out in his chance encounter with Winnie's husband in a pub. Now, Arthur not only abjures retaliation but shows an underlying understanding for, and compassion with, the man's position, and, in fact, seeks reconciliation with him: 'He's a brainless bastard. I can't see what Winnie sees in him, the poor sod. I'll bet he's having more trouble with her. I'll ask him to have a pint on me: "Have a pint, mate",' he said.

"No thanks," the swaddie answered.

"Come on," Arthur said in a friendly way "have one." He ordered it, and another for himself, and the jars were placed side by side on the counter. The swaddie looked at it suspiciously, as if it were a mug of poison.

Arthur lifted his glass: "Cheers. Drink up, mate. I'm getting married next week."

The swaddie came out of his bitter trance, saying: "Good luck to you then," and finished off the beer in one swallow' (pp. 182–3). Through Doreen's influence, Arthur has begun to appreciate the inter-relatedness of self-respect and compassion, and that wisdom is love.

Thus Arthur acquires wisdom gradually and half-instinctively from the events in which he is caught up, rather than from any conscious philosophizing about life, which would be alien to his nature. Most of us, indeed, if we grow wise at all, do so in the way Arthur does. Like D. H. Lawrence, Sillitoe has an insight into the emotional springs of much of our behaviour, and into the manner in which an emotional crisis is precipitated not so much by one great event as by a concatenation of individually minor and apparently unrelated events suddenly brought to focus; and again, like Lawrence's, Sillitoe's fictional method relies on the juxtaposition of incidents rather than on interpretative comment. Thus Arthur's beating is not an isolated event which suddenly changes his whole attitude to life, but is rather a particular event which helps him to elucidate his own previous experiences by stimulating that capacity for self-criticism in him already evinced earlier in the novel.

Sillitoe further emphasizes the essential continuity of Arthur's educative process by linking his new attitudes to rebellion and marriage with his old love of fishing. ' "There's nowt I like better than going out into the country on my bike and fishing near Cotgrave or Trowel and sitting for hours by myself" ' he asserts;[8] fishing has always seemed to him to provide him with an experience different in kind from the cycle of Saturday Night explosion and Sunday Morning oblivion. Like the rest of us, he has always sought some relationship with his environment that will enable him both to develop as fully as possible as an individual, and at the same time to feel himself playing a significant part in a larger whole, an 'informing purpose' at work in the world. In contrast to Saturday Night's rabid self-assertion and Sunday Morning's enforced insignificance, fishing offers a way of combining a sense of one's individuality with a sense of being in harmony with one's environment, and hence an insight into the nature of a really worthwhile mode of life. In fishing, Arthur can combine the exercise of creative skill with enjoyment of real tranquillity: 'On long summer evenings he sat on the front doorstep with a penknife and a piece of wood, carving the replica of a fish for his float, with a cigarette burning uselessly away on the step by his side while he held the half-shaped fish lightwards to gauge the proportions of head, body, and tail. . . . And sitting on the canal bank below Hemlock Stone and the Bramcote Hills he cast out his line over the narrow sleeve of still water, with elderberry leaves bending across from the opposite bank and white cloud-edges moving

[8] p. 129; cf. pp. 23, 111–12, 179–80, 188.

225

above green branches. It was a quiet and passionless place to be. . . .
There was no sign of the city' (p. 19). Naturally, Arthur never submits
his love of fishing to this kind of analysis, but his insight into the
fundamental relationship of creativity to self-respect is implicit in his
contempt for his father's addiction to the television—' "Sittin' in front
of the T.V. You stick to it like glue from six to eleven every night. It
can't be good for you" ' (p. 19) and in his awareness that although
people of his class are better off materially than they were before the
war, they need something more than earthly bread to recompense them
for their prison-like existence in the factory. It is natural therefore, that
Arthur should bring his new awareness of compassion—bound-up as
it is for him with non-retaliation and marriage—to the measuring-
stick of his old love, fishing.

Will marriage mean the end of fishing? Will the sense of freedom-in-
harmony that fishing has always brought give way to the disgruntled
selfdom of 'being hooked'? At the end of the novel, Arthur begins to
realize that marriage and fishing, in his case, shed light on each other.
True freedom goes with a sense of being involved in something that
you really care about; creativity fosters commitment as commitment
stimulates creative action: 'If you went through life refusing all the bait
dangled before you, that would be no life at all. No changes would be
made and you would have nothing to fight against' (p. 189). In marriage as in fishing, individuality and harmony can be achieved together,
for in the highest form of love for another, self-love is most complete,
for love is itself the highest form of creative activity. Fishing and
marriage to Doreen, Arthur decides, are compatible: ' "You aren't
going fishing today?" ' asks the lemonade seller when she sees him with
Doreen.

' "Not today," he answered the woman. "I'm courtin' now" . . .
"Courtin'?" the woman exclaimed. "Oh well, the fishes can rest in
peace from now on."

He paid her, and she shut the window. "There'll still be time for
fishin', I expect," he said' (p. 179).

The closing chapter begins, 'He sat by the canal fishing on a Sunday
morning in spring, at an elbow where alders dipped over the water like
old men on their last legs, pushed by young sturdy oaks from behind.
He straightened his back, his fingers freeing nylon line from a speedily
revolving wheel. . . . Sun was breaking through clouds, releasing a
smell of earth to heaven. . . . Another solitary man was fishing further
along the canal, but Arthur knew that they would leave each other in

peace, would not even call out greetings. No one bothered you . . . it was marvellous the things that came to you in the tranquillity of fishing' (pp. 188–9). This is no longer the 'prostrate Sabbath' which has so far been the inevitable successor to Saturday Night, but a time of re-birth; Sillitoe's imagery here not only vividly re-creates the experience of fishing but incorporates symbolically all the strands that compose the main theme of his novel. Arthur, the Lord of Misrule of the earlier part of the novel, has become the Fisher King. Whether Sillitoe's use of this symbolism is conscious is uncertain,[9] but the essential part played by the awakening of compassion in ending a cycle of sexual and spiritual conflict and consequent sterility, which was a feature of some of the Grail legends, is certainly evident in his novel.

The breaking of the Saturday Night–Sunday Morning circle, then, seems to depend fundamentally on creative self-expression, which attaches one instead to a new, dynamic and meaningful cycle of constant satisfaction and stimulation; the circle, we recall, as symbol, has always held this dual and contrasting significance of eternity and chaos. Creative self-expression fosters self-awareness and self-respect, which in turn promote that respect for others which is compassion; compassion thence stimulates, not passivity, but that creative self-expression which is intervention in human affairs on the side of goodness and justice. Peace, on earth at any rate, necessarily involves struggle, and accordingly, 'spiritual bread' is not so much consolation as a sense of purpose.

Sillitoe underlines his point about the difference between earthly and spiritual bread by including the delightfully ironic episode of Sam's stay with Aunt Ada. Sam, a quiet, self-possessed, intelligent, neat and courteous negro, is obviously highly 'civilized' in the only sense that matters, but because he comes from Africa, he is treated as a savage by Aunt Ada's 'tribe', who for once pride themselves on the 'civilization' of their Nottingham jungle—'He thinks all telegrams are sent by tom-tom. . . . Could he read and write? Who taught him, then? Did he believe in God? . . . Will you get married at church?' (pp. 166–7). The 'civilized' Dave and Bert 'lounge in armchairs by the parlour fire, smoking, listening to people walking by outside whose feet punctuated the empty weekend hours between football matches and opening time'.

Alan Sillitoe is the first writer of any importance to have emerged from the English urbanized and industrialized working-class. This vast,

[9] For Sillitoe's acquaintance with T. S. Eliot's poem 'The Waste Land' see 'The Rats and other poems', London, 1960, p. 44.

important, underprivileged and exploited section of our society has always lacked a spokesman in the sphere of art and Sillitoe is unique in having rendered it imaginatively articulate. In this respect he is essentially different from D. H. Lawrence, whose background he is sometimes supposed to share. Lawrence was a countryman, highly educated and half middle-class, whereas Sillitoe's strength lies in his completely unsnobbish acceptance of his origins in working-class Nottingham. In fact, Sillitoe is at his best when re-creating the actuality of working-class experience in this particular modern industrial city, e.g. his description of Jack's parlour—'a small dark area of isolation, long familiar with another man's collection of worldly goods: old-fashioned chairs and a settee, fireplace, clock ticking on the mantelpiece, a smell of brown paper, soil from a plant-pot, ordinary aged dust, soot in the chimney left over from last winter's fires and the mustiness of rugs laid down under the table and by the fireplace' (p. 13) and of Doreen's mother's kitchen—'smelling of stale gas and washed clothes. . . . A line of dry washing hung diagonally across the room, and both dresser and shelf were crowded with old recumbent Christmas cards, snapshots standing against hairbrushes, clocks with no hands and cigarette packets. A twenty-year-old wireless crackling from a dresser was switched off by Doreen's mother as they came in. The table was set for supper: teapot and cups, sugar, a tin of milk, bread, cheese and some knives and forks' (p. 183); his re-creation of the city atmosphere at different times and seasons—'The Castle was invisible, hiding behind a night-screen of mist, smoke and darkness. A wind ascended from low-lying marshalling yards, from swampy canal banks and minnow streams, causing Bert to swear at the rawness of it' (p. 68–9), 'July, August, and summer skies lay over the city, above rows of houses in the western suburbs, backyards burned by the sun with running tar-sores whose antiseptic smell blended with that of dustbins overdue for emptying, drying paint even drier on front doors, rusting knockers and letterboxes, and withering flowers on windowsills, a summer blue sky up to which smoke from the factory chimneys coiled blackly' (p. 110), 'The sun came through the window, carrying street noises on its beams, a Sunday morning clash of bottles from milkmen on their rounds, newspaper boys shouting to each other as they clattered along the pavement and pushed folded newspapers into letterboxes, each bearing crossword puzzles, sports news and forecasts, and interesting scandal that would be struggled through with a curious and salacious indolence over plates of bacon and tomatoes and mugs of strong sweet tea' (p. 14), and his swift evocation of local features—'He heard the conductor's bell and, like a lighted greenhouse growing people, the [trolley] bus trundled away up the hill' (p. 151), 'They crossed Slab Square and, fresh from a pint in the Plumtree, rolled to the Red Dragon and from there pushed into the Skittling Alley and the Coach Tavern and finally elbowed through the squash of people packing the Trip to Jerusalem, a limpet of lights and noise fastened on to the carcass of the Castle Rock' (p. 169), 'A dull heavy jangle of trucks, like the manacled advance of some giant Marley over Trent valley, came from the nearby railway line' (p. 171) and 'Generators whined all night, and during the day giant milling-machines working away on cranks and pedals in the turnery gave to the terrace a sensation of living within breathing distance of some monstrous being that suffered from a disease of the stomach. Disinfectant-suds, grease, and newly-cut steel permeated the air over the suburb of four-roomed houses built around the factory' (p. 20).

D. H. Lawrence's sensitivity was refined and reinforced by his countryman's link with the natural world and by his educated awareness of a cultural tradition. To a large extent, Sillitoe has been denied these advantages and his sensitivity can only base itself on his determination to explore as accurately and unflinchingly as he can his own personal experience of the city. The result is that sometimes Sillitoe's indignation becomes mere anarchic spleen, and his creative zest dissipates itself in a sort of slapdash violence that is unintentionally comic; violence of all kinds is, of course, concomitant with modern urban life but sometimes Sillitoe's images verge on the grotesque—'The evening dug a slit-trench in his brain' (p. 80) 'Digital chimneys like pigs' tits. . . . Stars hid like snipers taking aim now and then when clouds gave them a loop-hole' (p. 144). The poem 'The Rats' shows Sillitoe at his slapdash and splenetic worst, e.g.

> I smoke my pipe
> And play the sniper,
> Prop my gun
> On a windscreen wiper;
> Push in the bolt
> Of my word-filled rifle—
> To give the Rats
> A final eye-full . . .[10]

Nevertheless, all Sillitoe's best work so far has been based on his own

[10] Op. cit., p. 55.

life and in the main on his formative years in Nottingham. His novel 'The General' represents his sole departure from his personal experience and is lifeless. Out of his determined imaginative re-creation of his own experience has emerged his perception that a society that has merely added the circuses of T.V. to the bread of the Dole for the majority of its members, and has done nothing to provide them with spiritual bread, is binding them, and so ultimately itself, to a destructive cycle of explosion and repression; along with this, Sillitoe has perceived something of the nature of the spiritual bread needed-self-respect born of a sense of having a worthwhile contribution to make to society. Like all artists, Sillitoe anticipates the findings of psychologists and sociologists; the explanation of teenage malaise expressed in riots at Clacton, Margate and Hastings is contained in the pages of *Saturday Night and Sunday Morning* and so is the clue to its cure.[11] Sillitoe has presumably saved himself from his environment through his creative writing; Arthur Seaton, his hero, is saved through fishing and marriage —but only after having his head broken; the rest of us, through the kathartic effect of art, can profit vicariously, if we will, from Arthur's experiences. It is because of Sillitoe's capacity to re-vivify the greatest of the great commonplaces—man's need of love—through his vivid imaginative re-creation of the contemporary scene, that he deserves his place in our literary tradition.

Furzedown College, London

[11] The point has not, of course, been missed by all educationists. There is a quotation from Sillitoe in the recent Newsom Report 'Half Our Future' (p. 27). It is pertinent in this context to recall the comment of F. R. Leavis and Denys Thompson first made in 1933: 'The modern labourer, the modern clerk, the modern factory-hand live only for their leisure, and the result is that they are unable to live in their leisure when they get it. Their work is meaningless to them, merely something they have to do in order to earn a livelihood, and consequently when their leisure comes it is meaningless, and all the uses they can put it to come almost wholly under the head of . . . 'decreation'. . . . Men are now incapacitated by their work, which makes leisure necessary as it was not before, from using their leisure for *humane* recreation, that is, in pursuits that make them feel self-fulfilled and make life significant, dignified and satisfying.' *Culture and Environment*, London, 1933, 9th imp., 1962.

INDEX